CHAUVET CAVE

Dedicated to our departed friends
Philippe Morel and François Rouzaud

First published in North America by The University of Utah Press, Salt Lake City, 2003

Translation by Paul G. Bahn ©2003, Thames & Hudson Ltd.,
and The University of Utah Press. All rights reserved

First published by Éditions du Seuil, Paris under the title:
La Grotte Chauvet, l'art des origins ©2001 Éditions du Seuil

ISBN 0-87480-758-1
Library of Congress Control Number 2002116011

 The Defiance House Man colophon is a registered trademark of
The University of Utah Press. It is based upon a four-foot-tall,
Ancient Puebloan pictograph(late PIII) near Glen Canyon.

Printed and bound in France

CHAUVET CAVE
THE ART OF EARLIEST TIMES

Directed by
JEAN CLOTTES

Translated by
PAUL G. BAHN

Maurice Arnold
Norbert Aujoulat
Dominique Baffier
Jean Clottes
Évelyne Debard
Jean-Jacques Delannoy
Jacques Évin
Valérie Feruglio
Philippe Fosse
Catherine Ferrier

Carole Fritz
Michel-Alain Garcia
Bernard Gély
Jean-Michel Geneste
Michel Girard
Claude Guérin
Bertrand Kervazo
Yanik Le Guillou
Frédéric Maksud
† Philippe Morel

Christine Oberlin
Craig Packer
Yves Perrette
Michel Philippe
Joëlle Robert-Lamblin
† François Rouzaud
Jean-Louis Schefer
Nadine Tisnérat
Gilles Tosello
Hélène Valladas

The University of Utah Press
Salt Lake City

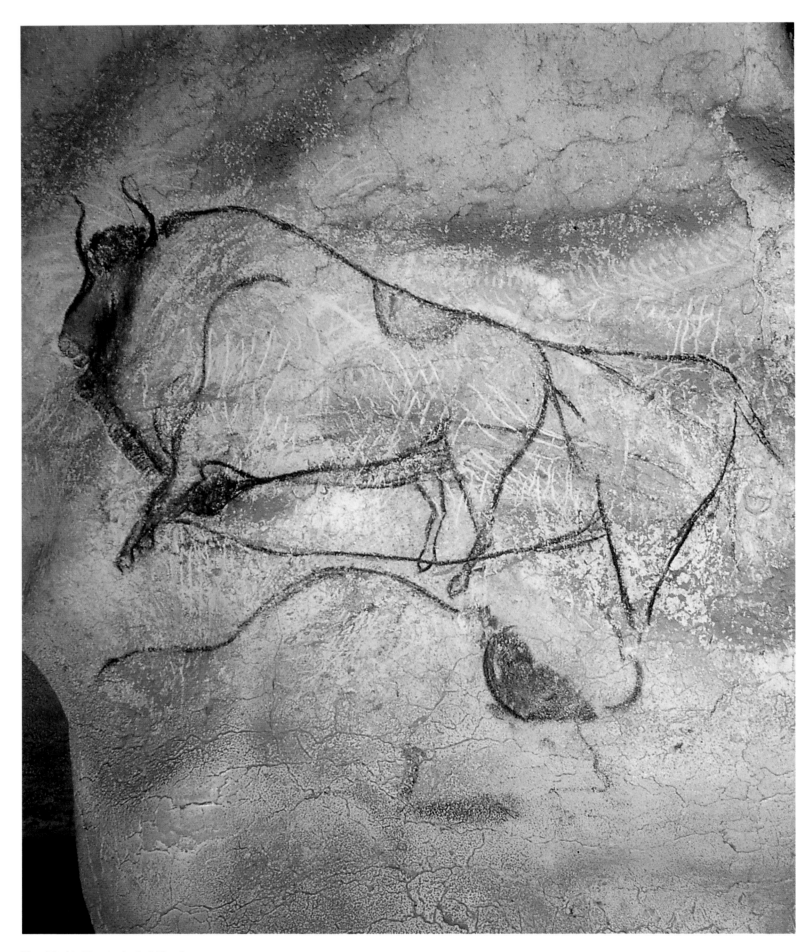

Ill. 1. The big bison in the End Chamber.

CONTENTS

1

Ill. 2. The Pont d'Arc (Bridge of Arc),
a natural curiosity that must have played
a major role in the myths of the
valley's prehistoric inhabitants.
The cave is just half a mile away,
at the foot of the cliff in the
background on the right.

HOW TO STUDY THE CAVE?

At the end of 1995, the Ministry of Culture asked for tenders for the scientific study of Chauvet Cave. Having begun work on this cave as soon as it was discovered, I decided to respond and put together a multidisciplinary team.[1] We drew up a programme of joint research. Our project was presented to a nine-member jury (including two foreign specialists, a German and a Spaniard), firstly, in the form of a five-volume dossier, and then, secondly, in a presentation on 31 May 1996. The jury listened to us, as well as our competitors, then deliberated and voted unanimously, in a secret ballot, in favour of our project.

1

HOW TO STUDY THE CAVE?

Ill. 3. Gilles Tosello at work in front of the Panel of the Horses.

Our Initial Project,
In Response To the Call for Tenders

'The exhaustive study of this cave (but can a study be exhaustive?) will take many years.[2] [Sixty] years after the discovery of Lascaux, research work still continues there. Moreover, methods, techniques and the theoretical basis of research are constantly evolving. It is certain that, twenty or thirty years from now, our successors will be examining sites in relation to points, and with means, that we cannot imagine today.

One absolute requirement is to make sure that the cave, its walls, climate and floors are preserved. We must leave our successors an intact cave in which all kinds of research are still possible. This requirement has various consequences regarding the study of floors and walls and monitoring the climatic conditions.

In addition, we need to avoid any risk of accidental damage in these particularly fragile surroundings where a blunder can have catastrophic consequences. That is why, in putting together the basic team, the first condition was that [the participants] must have plenty of experience of working in an environment deep underground, and, especially, must have carried out cave research during the past few years.

The goals set for our study of Chauvet Cave are those that have been defined by

modern research into decorated caves in the last few years. Listing, recording, studying and reproducing all the parietal art is the first stage. Equally indispensable aspects include establishing and dating the various (possible) phases of the art and of human visits, analysing the components of the paintings, studying the techniques used by the artists, seeing the works in the context of the appearance and nature of the walls and of the cave's topography, and verifying their spatial relationships. The archaeological context, whether internal (relating to the activities of humans and animals inside the cave) or external (relating to the dwellings and other decorated caves of the region) also needs to be studied carefully. The aim is not to carry out an exhaustive study of this part of the Ardèche, but, eventually, to shed light on human activities in Chauvet Cave and their relationships with other sites.

In order to attain these objectives, we [wanted to] set up a programme of intersecting research, calling on specialists from various disciplines – a wide range of them – but always with specific aims in mind. This research requires close, multidisciplinary collaboration, whether it be palaeo-environmental analysis, study of tracks, or even problems of interpretation and aesthetics, for which we have brought in artists who are already sensitive to prehistoric art, ethnologists and art historians.

The problem of preserving the paintings requires the cave's climate to be studied and monitored. As was the case at Niaux, it will be possible to follow the changes in climate from day to day in all its aspects, including – but not only – during the scientific work, and consequently to lessen the disturbances caused.

The conservation of the floors is another major aspect of the cave's preservation. Before being able to have access to certain walls, particularly in the deep areas, but also in certain parts of the entrance zones (the Panel of Hand Prints, for example), it will be necessary to install a fixed passageway, already planned along the exact route followed and marked out by the discoverers, and then light raised (or suspended) means of access to get as near as possible to the floors and walls to be studied. These installations govern the studies to come, but they must also allow all sorts of observation, both to avoid damage and to gather as much information as possible.

[With regard to the tracks and remains on the floors,] the questions being asked at present are as follows:

• Visiting the cave: were there adults and children, as in all the decorated caves with prints?

• Is it possible to detect several visits (by analysing fires, studying tracks)?

• What activities took place in the cave (fires for illumination, or others)? – the evidence of the prints and bones stuck into the floor?

• The abandoned objects: about ten flints have been observed on the surface. Without undertaking excavations, at least at first, can other remains of human activities be found? After being photographed in situ, recorded and described, some of these objects will be removed and studied in the laboratory for DNA and microwear studies, before being returned to their original location; the bear

skull that was moved and placed on a big stone will have to be studied to try to detect whether it has been handled by humans; it will be necessary to do the same to the animal bones that might bear traces of human activities.

• There are numerous traces and tracks of bears: they will be studied with the aim of establishing their relationship (or lack of it) with human visits. On the one hand, the bear remains may have been (and, in one case, certainly were) moved by humans or even by water. Are the accumulations of bones all over the cave of human origin (and if so, why, according to which criteria?) or are they the result of natural phenomena? The answer will require the collaboration of geologists, archaeologists and faunal specialists. On the other hand, the bears came into the cave before and after humans: we already know this fact because their clawmarks are superimposed on the engravings and paintings and vice versa. The study of their tracks and remains, and the dating carried out on their bones, should make it possible to obtain clear information about the various incursions by humans and bears: because, in order to understand the artists' motifs, it would be useful to know if the bears visited these galleries at more or less the same periods as they did, or if the human visits were separated by millennia from those of the bears.

• Human tracks are rare on the soft floors of Chauvet Cave. The study will have to establish the reasons for the lack of tracks. At present, one may suppose that, after the visits by people, water covered some floors and obliterated their tracks, and that the bears returned afterwards. But all of this will require confirmation.

[Regarding the decorated walls,] it is important to stress the need for real tracings, that is to say, of the images, their techniques, their superimpositions, through the eyes, the critical mind and the hand of the specialist. Direct analysis of photographs is indispensable, but the results are always very inferior to those obtained through tracings, which provide the most useful information about the works and the wall.

Ill. 4. Form used as the inventory for each graphic entity.

CHAUVET CAVE	Inventory of graphic entities	

No. entity	Date	Name

Location		○ Entrance ○ Middle ○ End ○ Other

Sector code		Site	
Panel name		Distance/site	cm

Wall	○ Right ○ Roof ○ Pendant	Width	cm
	○ Left ○ Ground	Height/floor	cm

Theme	○ Animal ○ Sign ○ Trace ○ Human ○ Composite ○ Undetermined

○ Horse ○ Megaloceros	Sign	
○ Bison ○ Feline	Hypothesis	
○ Aurochs ○ Bear	Composite	
○ Ibex ○ Mammoth	Trace	
○ Red deer ○ Rhinoceros	Other	
○ Reindeer ○ Undetermined		
○ Hand stencil ○ Hand print	Anatomy ○ Complete ○ Partial ○ Segm.	

Support	□ Hardened □ Soft □ Powdery	Floor	
□ Rock □ Clay □ Utilized relief		□ Rock □ Clay	
□ Calcite □ Mondmilch □ Other....		□ Calcite □ Other.....	

Technology	Nearest figure	Deterioration
□ Painting		□ Calcite film
□ Drawing		□ Superimposition
□ Stumping		□ Obliterated
□ Engraving		□ Eroded
□ Scraping		□ Corroded
□ Finger tracing		□ Other

Situation/Panel	Colour □ Black □ Red □ Yellow □ Brown □ Other		
○ Left section	Profile □ Left □ Full face □ Right		
○ Central section	Orientation High Low Hor. Oblique Vertical		
○ Right section	Iconometry		
	H = cm L = cm Manual reach = cm		
○ Upper register			
○ Middle register	Recorder	Film / view	
○ Lower register			

This study, which will be very detailed, will aim to extract as much information as possible from the drawings on the walls. It will also examine the preparation of the walls and the animal tracks, which will be studied jointly with archaeo-zoologists, as it is known that, in certain caves, the presence of such traces was a determining factor in the choice of panels and even influenced certain drawings.

The study must not cause any damage. The tracings are planned so that there will be no direct contact with the wall, in order

methods. Numerous macrophotographs will be used for the study of techniques. Three-dimensional recordings will be produced under the control of the specialized team. The digital images will be studied with the help of computers (reduced to the same scale, reversals, superimpositions to make all sorts of comparisons).

The problems that we shall make particular efforts to solve, through the tracings and the various photographic methods, are as follows:

• Studying the wall (possibly with the help of geologists): morphology, natural irregularities, preparation of the surfaces by scraping (tools used), animal tracks.

• Establishing the phases of panel production by studying superimpositions and spatial localizations in the panel, as well as the figures in relation to each other.

• Studying the techniques used: engravings with flint, by finger, etc; use of crayon or brush; stump drawing methods; outlining.

• Studying various 'hands': repetition of certain little details either in the animals' morphology or in techniques.

• Comparing subjects between the different panels; associations.

The variety of animal species and the natural way in which they are depicted require identifications that are much more finely tuned than those normally attained by researchers in parietal art, whose experience of animals could never come close to that of specialized ethologists. For this reason we plan to study the animal figures in collaboration with ethologists.

We will then turn to comparisons, firstly, with the Palaeolithic art of the Ardèche caves, and, secondly, with the Palaeolithic art of other regions.'

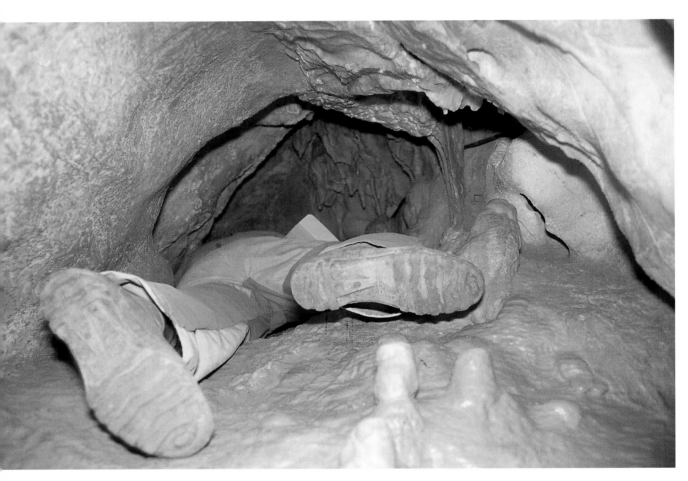

Above
Ill. 5. The narrow passage that leads to the cave, through which the team had to crawl during the first period of the study.

Opposite top
Ill. 6. Valérie Feruglio descends into the cave.

Opposite bottom
Ill. 7. Carole Fritz takes notes in front of the Panel of the Horses.

to avoid any damage and any risk of pollution, which might hamper later studies. We thus envisage proceeding by using tracings from photographs and digital recordings with image processing. The members of the team who have been designated for this work have previous experience in these modern and innovative

The Research Team

The team, put together in accordance with the aims indicated, began its fieldwork in the spring of 1998. This beginning was unanimously considered a success, despite the obvious difficulties in an enterprise involving the collaboration of experienced researchers from different spheres. Since then, some, including the discoverers, have voluntarily left us for personal reasons. Two of our original companions (François Rouzaud and Philippe Morel) have died. Other specialists have come to join us, as the need arose.

The team, as it was conceived and as it exists now, led by Jean Clottes, assisted by Jean-Michel Geneste, comprises three 'circles', which are brought in at different levels:

• The first is the permanent team, those who take full part in all the spring and autumn field campaigns. At present it comprises fourteen people for archaeological topography, Palaeolithic art and the human and animal remains and tracks on the floors. Each of them, naturally, has his or her speciality(ies).

• The second circle is made up of scientists from disciplines other than archaeology. It comprises about forty people, for the following specialities: geology, karstology, palynology, anthracology, ethnology, plastic arts, art history, algology, ethology, DNA, palaeo-parasitology, studies of subterranean climate, of the state of the walls, of the pigments, of the microwear traces on flints, dating of charcoal, of bone and of concretions.[3] The Rhône-Alpes regional office of cultural affairs arranged for the exact topographical recording of the cave, and the plans were placed at our disposal. Some of these specialists occasionally come to work in the cave, either during the two usual campaigns of the year, or at other times (to avoid having too many people in the cave at the same time).

• Finally, the third circle, the International Committee of Scientific Advisers, was created to make the advice of the most experienced specialists available and to ensure that information about our work is spread rapidly. At present it comprises twenty-six specialists in parietal or rock art from ten countries: Australia, England, France, Germany, Italy, Portugal, Russia, South Africa, Spain, USA. Every year they are kept informed of the study's progress, and their advice is sought when needed. More than half of them have visited the cave when spending time in France during our field campaigns.

The Work Carried Out and Its Problems

During the first three years of the project, we have worked in the cave regularly for two weeks in May and October (including weekends and holidays), rather than devote a whole month at a stretch to the research, after climatological studies showed that the cave's atmosphere was more sensitive to disturbance during the summer. Moreover, two well-spaced campaigns diminish the inevitable impact of our visits, and avoid the fatigue that can lead to clumsiness. Sporadic campaigns of less than a week each (geologists, topographers) take place between the main campaigns.

In order to avoid having too many people in the cave at one time, part of the team goes there for the day, while the rest remains at the base camp, at Salavas, using the computers to process images, plans and tracings, or to produce finished versions.[4]

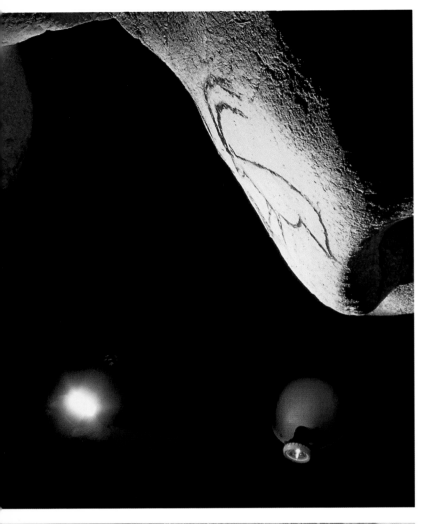

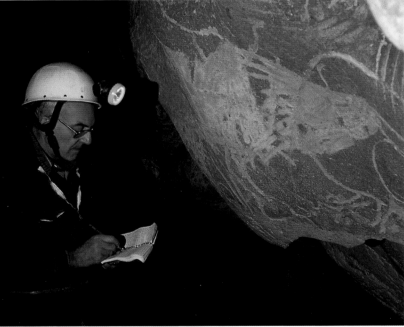

Top
Ill. 8. Photographic work underway
in the Megaloceros Gallery.

Above
Ill. 9. Jean Clottes at work in front of
a panel of engravings in the Hillaire
Chamber.

The principal themes of our work are those defined in the initial project. It was necessary to come to know all the parietal works as soon as possible, and leave until later the details that would be impossible to obtain before the works were traced. So we drew up a form so that each figure could be recorded (ill. 4). These hundreds of forms were subsequently systematically checked. Henceforth they serve as a statistical base.

Whether it be tracings or the study of the floors, the work was carried out according to which walls, remains and tracks were accessible, without taking the slightest risk regarding the integrity of the untouched floors. When the locations (End Chamber; Brunel Chamber) required heavy protection with the installation of walkways before any study could be carried out, they were set aside until these installations were in place. This means that our research on the walls and floors has concentrated on, without putting conservation to risk, the accessible locations and not on those where we might sometimes have wished to work. We have constantly had to adapt to circumstances. For example, Yanik Le Guillou developed an original method for photographing in places that could not be reached or seen, using a digital camera fixed on the end of a telescopic pole.

Numerous samples have been taken for analysis, once again in accordance with what was possible, and without posing the slightest risk to the drawings or remains. This analysis will add greatly to both our knowledge of human activities in the cave and to their context.

This is the first time in the world that such a complete multidisciplinary team, made up of professionals, has been brought together to study a major rock art site, and has adequate means at its disposal thanks to the decision and the financing of the Ministry of Culture, and the help of the Ardèche département. There are several requirements:

• The first is the diversity of approaches. The aims that have been declared are those of any research in a decorated cave, but the methods used in these studies must not be standardized. From the very beginning of this project, the broadest possible spread has been advocated, whether it be in the participation of specialists from very different domains, or in the methods and techniques used by the team.

• The second requirement is teamwork. The diversity of approaches should not lead to a multiplicity of ill-assorted research projects, each disconnected from the rest. The practical organization of our work took care to ensure the necessary contacts, the sharing of knowledge, and the bringing together of research, with team meetings, during which each member presented the work accomplished, the methods used and the results obtained.

• The third requirement, which was the motivation behind this collective book, is to communicate our results to our colleagues and the general public.[5] We are more aware than anyone that it will be years before the painstaking recording of the walls and floors will be finished. We are only at the start of what will be a very long piece of research. Nevertheless, these three years of hard work have enabled us to make considerable progress in the approach and study of one of the most beautiful and most important decorated caves ever discovered. It is this knowledge that we wanted to share without delay.[6]

Jean Clottes

Location of the main decorated panels

1 Corridor

2 Around the Sorcerer Panel

3 Lion Panel

4 Niche of Dots

5 Panel of the Rhinoceroses

6 Panel of the Big Lions

7 Right panel

8 End Chamber

9 Pubic triangles

10 Entrance Chamber

11 End Panel

12 Panel of the Scraped Mammoths

13 Reindeer on rock pendants

14 Big Blocks

15 Panel of the Horses

16 Alcove of the Lions

17 Reindeer Panel

18 Black drawings

19 Scraped animals

20 Owl on rock pendants

21 Panel of the Engraved Horse

22 Intermediate panels

23 Rhinoceros pendants

24 Panel of the Little Bear

25 Panel of Hand Stencils

26 Panel of Hand Prints

27 Panel of the Signs

28 Panther Panel

29 Panel of the Red Bear

30 Panel of the Dominoes

31 Alcove of the Yellow Horses

32 Panel of the Dotted Animal

33 Recess of the Bears

34 Engraved Stoup

35 Sacred Heart Panel

Right

Ill. 10. General plan of Chauvet Cave,
with the names of the main chambers and galleries.[7]

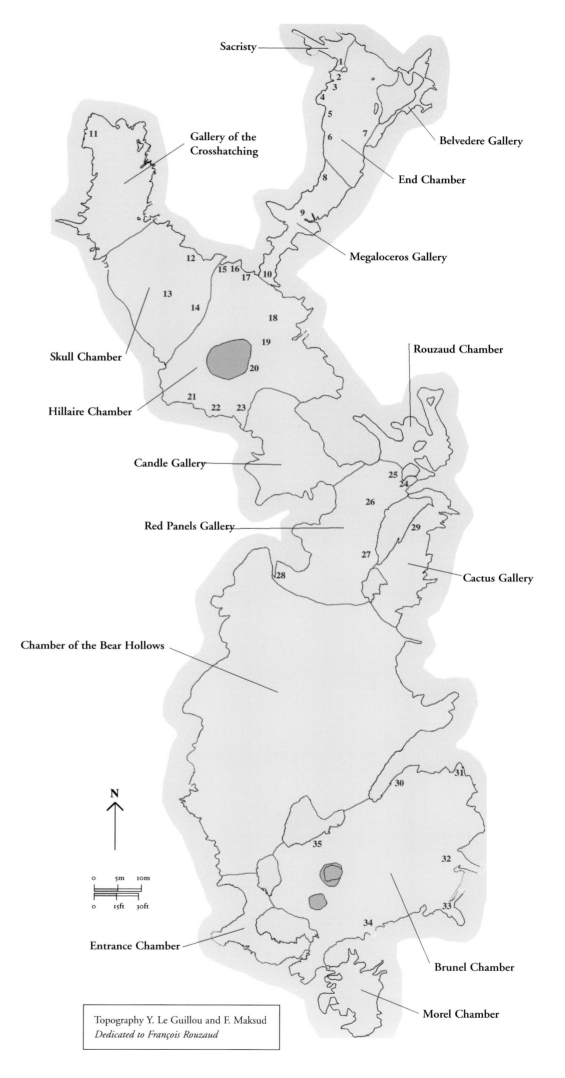

Sacristy

Gallery of the
Crosshatching

Belvedere Gallery

End Chamber

Megaloceros Gallery

Rouzaud Chamber

Skull Chamber

Hillaire Chamber

Candle Gallery

Red Panels Gallery

Cactus Gallery

Chamber of the Bear Hollows

Entrance Chamber

Brunel Chamber

Morel Chamber

N

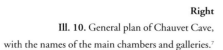

Topography Y. Le Guillou and F. Maksud
Dedicated to François Rouzaud

2

Ill. 11. From the valley, a long walk along the cliff leads to the cave. The flat surface in the foreground corresponds to the ancient course of the Ardèche River (a re-cut meander).

THE CAVE IN ITS SETTING

A decorated cave, whatever its importance, is not a gallery of paintings. It can only be understood in its particular setting and context. It is located in a landscape whose characteristics influenced the ways of life and the beliefs of Palaeolithic people. Its works of art originate in their myths and their practices. What do we know locally of these ancient cultures? Do other decorated caves in the region bear witness to comparable activities?

As for the cave itself, its morphology is something to which its ancient visitors had to adapt. Each cave is unique, because of the nature of the rock, the processes involved in its being hollowed out, and the vicissitudes of its long life before the Aurignacians entered it for the first time and left their remains, their traces and their works. After them, the cave continued to evolve – slowly, certainly, on a human scale, but in more than thirty thousand years it underwent collapses and depressions, drainings and erosion, runoff and calcite formations. All these phenomena influence our perception and our knowledge of the prehistoric human activities in the cave.

2

THE CAVE IN ITS SETTING

Chauvet Cave is located in a region with exceptional landscapes where nature, more than elsewhere, was able to play with contrasts. The horizontal plateaux of the Bas-Vivarais contrast with the vertical gorges cut by the Ardèche to rejoin the Rhône Valley. The vertical lines of the escarpments are echoed by the broad meanderings of the gorges. The whiteness of the limestone cliffs stands out against the dark mantle of evergreen oaks that cover the slopes and edges of the plateaux. The aridity of the limestone plateaux contrasts with the everlasting waters of the Ardèche that flow from the crystalline 'mountain'. This pattern of natural contrasts makes the Ardèche gorges a site of great heritage value, which was classified in 1980 as a 'Nature Reserve'.

The Pont d'Arc and its Surroundings

The entrance of the Ardèche gorges is dominated by the Pont d'Arc. This geological phenomenon is unique in the world, and comprises a natural arch under which a permanent river flows (ill. 2). This arch was created by the waters, which, after meandering through the limestone mass (the Cirque d'Estre), cut through its rocky stem underground.

The actions of the subterranean waters, particularly visible in the Pont d'Arc, are found throughout the whole gorges, and have created hundreds of caves, including Chauvet Cave, which are located in the limestone escarpments. A number of them contain archaeological remains. This high value in terms of the cultural heritage has also contributed to the Ardèche gorges and the site of Pont d'Arc being listed.

Chauvet Cave is located in the cliffs of the Cirque d'Estre, which dominate the ancient meander and the Pont d'Arc (ill. 12). The question immediately arises of whether prehistoric people saw this same natural spectacle.

The study of the alluvia deposited by the Ardèche during the Quaternary and the slope deposits make it possible to propose that the natural contours existing at the time of the human occupations of Chauvet Cave had essentially the same features as today. According to this research, the profile along the Ardèche, as we see it today, is not very different from that of around 400,000 years ago. Since then, the gorges have undergone phases of infill and incision linked to the climatic variations that punctuated the recent Quaternary. During the last great cold phase

Opposite

Ill. 12. Chauvet Cave and the Pont d'Arc. The entrance of Chauvet Cave is located at the foot of the Urgonian (Lower Cretaceous) cliffs of the Cirque d'Estre. These cliffs rise up from the regular slopes that take their shape from the former meander of the Ardèche. The riverbank is covered with scree caused by frost action during the cold episodes of the Quaternary. The last cold phase began around 100,000 years ago, and ended around 15,000 years ago. It was interrupted by short episodes of warming, known as interstadials; the period when the cave was visited by humans corresponds to one of these interstadials. Part of the scree on the slopes also comes from the collapse of sections of limestone cliffs; these phenomena produce a huge mass of debris that can block cave entrances.

(Würm glaciation), the alluvial fill reached a maximum level of + 15 m to + 20 m in relation to the present-day bed of the Ardèche. The composition of these terraces shows that they were deposits linked to high floods. The +15 m level corresponds to that of the abandoned meander, which means that this ancient meander, already slightly elevated by the middle of the last cold phase, must have been regularly invaded by the Ardèche in flood. The height of these inundations was emphasized here by the bottleneck effect produced by the Pont d'Arc, which, being incapable of absorbing all of the high waters, brought about a rise in the level of the Ardèche, which in turn overflowed into its former bed. This scenario must have been common in those times, but is exceptional today and has not been observed since the great floods of 1827 and 1890.

This reconstruction makes it possible to state that the Pont d'Arc already existed in the Upper Palaeolithic, and that people must regularly have seen the meander of the Cirque d'Estre invaded by the Ardèche floods.

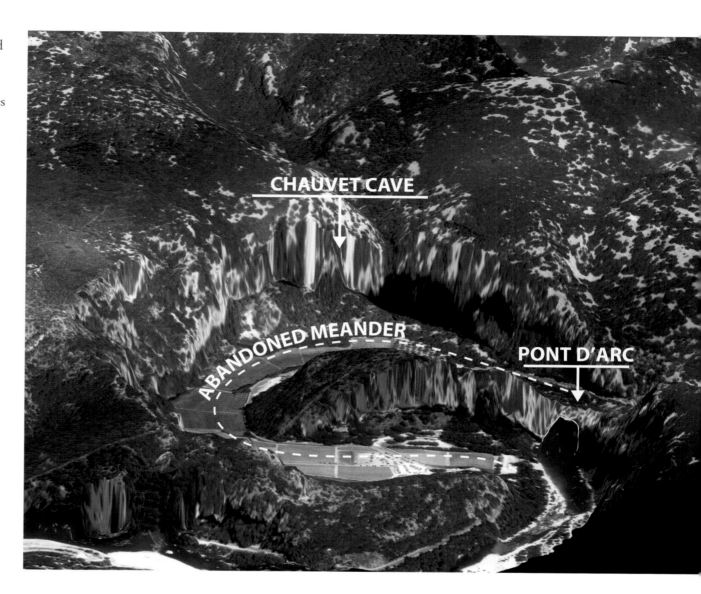

Chauvet Cave and its Geological Life

The present-day entrance into the cave is not the one that was known to prehistoric people, because their entrance is now blocked by scree. The modern entrance is via a side passage cut through by the retreat of the cliff. This passage, which was widened by the discoverers, leads into the real cave through a ten-metre (about 30-foot) shaft.

Once one is in the gallery, the first thing to strike one is its size. The Brunel Chamber, in which one emerges (ill. 13), is more than 40 m (130 feet) wide and almost 30 m (100 feet) high. Apart from its scale, it is characterized by a chaotic landscape that is very perceptible in the stalagmitic structures. Numerous columns, detached from the ceiling, have tipped over. Some have stabilized, others have collapsed. The destabilization of these ancient stalagmitic structures was caused for two reasons: firstly, the clay layer subsided and continued to do so, thus causing depressions, and, secondly, the mechanical expansion linked to the proximity of the hillside. This proximity brings about a decompression of the rocky mass, which is the cause of the fallen blocks and the rubble that lie strewn over the floor of the Morel Chamber and the original entrance area. The question arises of whether the Aurignacians saw this chaotic landscape of the Brunel Chamber. In this

Double page overleaf
Ill. 13. The Brunel Chamber.
A vast chamber whose ceilings, walls and floors are covered with concretions. These concretions are very old, as is shown by the tilting, and even collapse, of the stalagmitic structures (to the left and below the man). This destabilization can be explained by subsidence of the thick clay deposit on which the stalagmitic floors and the stalagmites were formed. At some points, this subsidence continued as depressions that formed deep holes in the gallery's floor.

Above
Ill. 14. The Chamber of the Bear Hollows. The horizontal floor here can be attributed to the presence of an ancient underground lake.

Below
Ill. 15. Detail of the ceiling in the Cactus Gallery. This limestone pendant contrasts strongly with the ancient reddish stalagmitic floor.

particular instance the answer is in the affirmative because several panels of red dots are located at the base of collapsed stalagmitic structures (ill. 60).

When one leaves the Brunel Chamber and goes deeper into the hill, the underground landscape changes completely. From the chaos of the entrance chambers, one passes into a vast gallery about 50 metres (164 feet) wide, with a perfectly flat floor: the Chamber of the Bear Hollows (ill. 14). Its ceiling is sculptured by deep solution pockets, the signs of ancient phreatic activity. They contrast with the flatness of part of the ceiling, which resulted from the collapse of a section of it that broke on the floor into imposing blocks. Paradoxically, the presence of these enormous blocks does not give an impression of chaos; the extremely horizontal floor does away with that feeling. In this case as well, it is certain that prehistoric people and animals saw this subterranean landscape, as is shown by the bear hollows dug into the clay floor, and the polish on the blocks left by these plantigrades passing by and rubbing against them. The only features that do not seem to have been known by our ancestors are the few stalagmites and clusters of white, thin stalactites that decorate this chamber.

The Chamber of the Bear Hollows passes northwards into two parallel galleries: the Cactus Gallery and the Red Panels Gallery, both of which have spectacular patterns of colour combining red and white. The whiteness of the walls, the limestone pendants and stalagmitic structures contrast with the red of two generations of stalagmitic floor. The first, pinned to the ceiling, provides evidence for an ancient episode when these galleries were filled (ill. 15). The second is fed by the recent waterflows that took on their colour by passing through red clays. These same clays were used by prehistoric people (Panel of the Red Bear, Panel of Hand Prints and Panel of Hand Stencils). The natural contrast is echoed here by the contrast in paintings. Whereas the Cactus Gallery and Rouzaud Chamber come up against stalagmitic fills (tiered gours), the Red Panels Gallery provides access to the rest of the cave.

A low passage, linked to the ancient stalagmitic fill, leads to the Candle Gallery, where there are old eroded concretions and potholes that provide evidence for ancient, turbulent underground flows (ill. 18). More recent concretions mould these ancient forms of erosion. Dating them has shown that this passage, at the time of our ancestors' visits, had the same characteristics as today. The Candle Gallery, located slightly lower down, is similar to the Red Panels Gallery and the Cactus Gallery.

There are abundant concretions here, growing out from the eastern wall, where there is a mixture of old and present-day stalagmitic structures. The crust progressively reaches the western part of the chamber, where the clay floor reveals much palaeontological evidence: bear and wolf prints, and bear hollows. The base of a ceiling pendant in this chamber was broken to turn the clay ramp leading to the Hillaire Chamber into a stepping stone (ill. 39).

The Hillaire and Skull Chambers belong to the same gallery, separated by a curtain of old stalagmites (the Big Blocks; ill. 16). It is on the wall opposite these concretions that the Panel of the Horses is located. The position of these two chambers, lower than the Candle and Megaloceros Galleries and the Gallery of the Crosshatching, is the result of a generalized subsidence of the clay floor. It is known that this subsidence is ancient because of the adjustments made to its edges by people. This subsidence occurred with different intensity in the two chambers. The end of the Skull Chamber was only slightly depressed, though sufficiently to collect the waterflows that produced a reddish calcitic crust; this has fossilized numerous bear bones and bear and wolf prints, which indicate that the clay floor was then extremely humid. In the Hillaire Chamber, the continuation of the subsidence was responsible for a depression ten metres (over 32 feet) in diameter that forms a deep hole in the floor. It is at least partly later than the human visits, as the engraved rock pendants, which today are located above the hole (ill. 16), reveal.

The Gallery of the Crosshatching is on the same axis as the Candle Gallery, Hillaire Chamber and Skull Chamber. It is different from the rest of the cave because of its low height – 1.5 to 3 m (nearly 5 to 10 feet) – caused by the presence of a major fill of clay. The surface of this fill bears the only human prints known in the cave at present, as well as abundant traces of animal occupations (prints, hollows, deteriorated bear skeletons). At its northern extremity, the gallery comes up against a fill that is a mixture of old stalagmitic floors and recent, or even present-day, concretions.

The Megaloceros Gallery has one feature in common with the previous gallery: it developed on the ceiling of an ancient gallery that is largely filled in. The Megaloceros Gallery begins with a succession of solution pockets in the ceiling aligned on a fracture that dominates a clay fill in which discreet prints of plants can be seen. Several steps give some variety to the gallery's floor. They represent ancient stalagmitic cascades, behind which gours developed. These gours were then filled by

Above

Ill. 16. The Hillaire Chamber. The deep depression, in the foreground, is one of the outstanding features of the Hillaire Chamber. It partly postdates the human occupations of the cave, as is shown by the engravings on the rock pendants that today are located above the void (above the person on the right). This subsidence had already partly happened. The bank of earth that can be seen on the left, and towards the back of the photograph, is a sign that the floor had begun to sink for the first time; the traces of prehistoric people and of animals on this bank indicate that this subsidence predates them. At the back of the chamber it is possible to see the beginning of the Megaloceros Gallery, which leads to the End Chamber and the lowest point of the cave. Behind the curtain of stalagmitic columns, located to the left of the Megaloceros Gallery, is the Skull Chamber. This chamber, which, like the Hillaire Chamber, underwent a first phase of subsidence, collects the underground running water that temporarily inundates the floor. The Skull Chamber leads to the Gallery of the Crosshatching.

clay deposits bearing ancient hearths, tools (flints, spearpoint) and bones. The descent towards the End Chamber comprises vast tiered gours filled with clay and modified by the bears (hollows).

The End Chamber is exceptional, not only because of its natural forms (deep solution pockets in the ceiling) but also because of its frescoes (Panel of the Big Lions, Panel of the Rhinoceroses, Lion and Bison Panels; ills. 1 and 126). Like a balcony, it dominates the lowest point of the cave – going down 23 m (75 feet), covered with clay bearing the prints of bears and

ibex. This evidence of their visits, as well as that located in the Megaloceros Gallery and the Gallery of the Crosshatching, indicates once again that prehistoric animals and people moved around in a cave that had already acquired its present-day traits.

From this rapid description, it is clear that only the cave's entrance area has undergone profound modifications since the human and animal occupations. The reconstruction of the cave's history makes it possible to understand the process of its closure.

From Geological Times to the Era of Humankind

Chauvet Cave is like a big, almost horizontal gallery containing several generations of concretions and a few depressions. These elements of the subterranean relief are not the result of chance, but correspond to the different phases that can be understood because of the memories stored in the gallery's shapes and the deposits. They make it possible to go back several million years and to reconstruct the underground landscape that was known by prehistoric people.

The cave's characteristic forms are the solution pockets present in the ceiling and the walls (ill. 18). These forms, as well as the cave's subhorizontal development and its semicircular vault, bear witness to the gallery having been hollowed out in the phreatic zone. The fact that, in a certain period, the cave was completely filled with water means that it was then below the level of the Ardèche (ill. 19). The cave's drowned operations thus make it possible to identify an ancient, poorly embanked bed of the Ardèche and to indicate that the gorges were cut later. The formation of the gorges is the cause of the cave's lofty position and its being emptied of water, after which the first stalagmitic structures were deposited in the cave. They stand on reddish clays (contemporary with the drowned phase) in the form of stalagmites

several metres in diameter, or thick stalagmitic floors.

In some sectors (Brunel Chamber, Cactus Gallery), these concretions had totally blocked the gallery. They were then subjected to a powerful erosion brought about by turbulent waterflows, as shown by the solution pockets hollowed into them (ill. 15), the remains of floors hanging from the ceiling, and the potholes in the stalagmite flows. These features of erosion make it possible to establish that the waters of the Ardèche penetrated the massif and that the cave then served as a swallow hole. This scenario supposes that the Ardèche's bed underwent a rise of sufficient magnitude to attain the level of Chauvet Cave once again (ill. 19). In the region's geological history it is possible to link the Ardèche's formation (responsible for the cave being emptied of water) with the Messinian crisis that was marked, 5.7 million years ago, by a quasi-drying of the Mediterranean. So the alluvial rise in the Ardèche's bed is probably tied to the Pliocene transgression (5.3 to 4.5 million years ago), which was reflected in the Mediterranean's rising into the Rhône Valley. This example shows how memories of the past are contained in the subterranean landscape and help us to transport ourselves several million years into the past, long before modern human beings appeared on Earth.

Afterwards, the cave was no longer traversed by major waterflows. This lack of water can be linked to the Ardèche gorges being cut by the upthrust of the Ardèche plateaux. Chauvet Cave was thus left perched high above the Ardèche and its subterranean circulation, a situation marked by a draining and a first phase of subsidence of the clay floor (ill. 19). This subsidence was responsible for the destabilization of the stalagmitic structures, especially visible in the Brunel Chamber (ill. 13).

Infiltrating waters fed the modest flows which, in the low areas, contributed to the formation of two subterranean lakes separated by a sill located between the Red Panels Gallery and the Candle Gallery. The first extended into the Brunel Chamber and the Chamber of the Bear Hollows, and the second developed in the Candle Gallery, Hillaire Chamber and Skull Chamber, the Megaloceros Gallery and the Gallery of the Crosshatching. The flatness of their floor is the result of this lacustrine episode.

Following this episode, new subsidences marked the clay floor; the most important was that which lowered the Hillaire Chamber and Skull Chamber. This subsidence predated the cave's occupations, as is shown by the impact of humans on its edges, and the traces of bear slides.

So, apart from the entrance area, prehistoric people experienced an underground landscape that was similar to that of today: the stalagmitic chaos of the Brunel Chamber, the flatness of the floor in the Chamber of the Bear Hollows and the Gallery of the Crosshatching, the subsidence of the Hillaire Chamber and Skull Chamber, and the concretions in the Cactus Gallery and Candle Gallery.

The entrance at that time was relatively huge, and led directly to the Brunel Chamber and the Chamber of the Bear Hollows, as is shown by the scree that descends into them. Several clues suggest that the natural entrance was closed abruptly. Had the entrance closed gradually, through falling blocks caused by frost action and gravity, there would be numerous traces of small mammals in the cave, but there are

not. Moreover, the appearance of the scree that blocks the cave entrance supports the hypothesis that part of the cliff collapsed. This hypothesis tallies with the feeling that the cave is exactly as it was left by the last occupants.

Another consequence of the cave's closure was that it brought about climatic conditions that favoured the conservation of the paintings and the development of the concretions, which, by fossilizing the bones on the floor, the traces of passage and the evidence of occupation by humans (wood charcoal), guaranteed that they would last for some time.

Through this reading of the underground landscapes it has been possible to reconstruct the history of the cave before, during and after its visits by prehistoric people.

**Jean-Jacques Delannoy,
Evelyne Debard, Catherine Ferrier,
Bertrand Kervazo and Yves Perrette**

Above

Ill. 17. Several generations of stalagmitic structures are visible in this picture. The most recent, the white stalagmites, grow on the gallery's wall and floor. This wall, like the floor, corresponds to ancient concretions that were greatly eroded after being deposited. The potholes that can be seen on this ancient stalagmitic floor show the power of the waterflows that passed through the cave.

Double page overleaf

Ill. 18. The ceiling of the End Chamber has deep solution pockets and long limestone pendants. These forms are characteristic of the hollowing out caused by a phreatic zone. When the gallery is totally filled with water, chemical erosion by the water can do its work on both the floor and the ceiling of the passage. This erosion occurs at the level of the weak points, such as fissures and bedding planes. The photograph shows that the gallery follows a fissure (alignment of cupolas above the man) and that it widens at the bottom at the level of a joint between two strata.

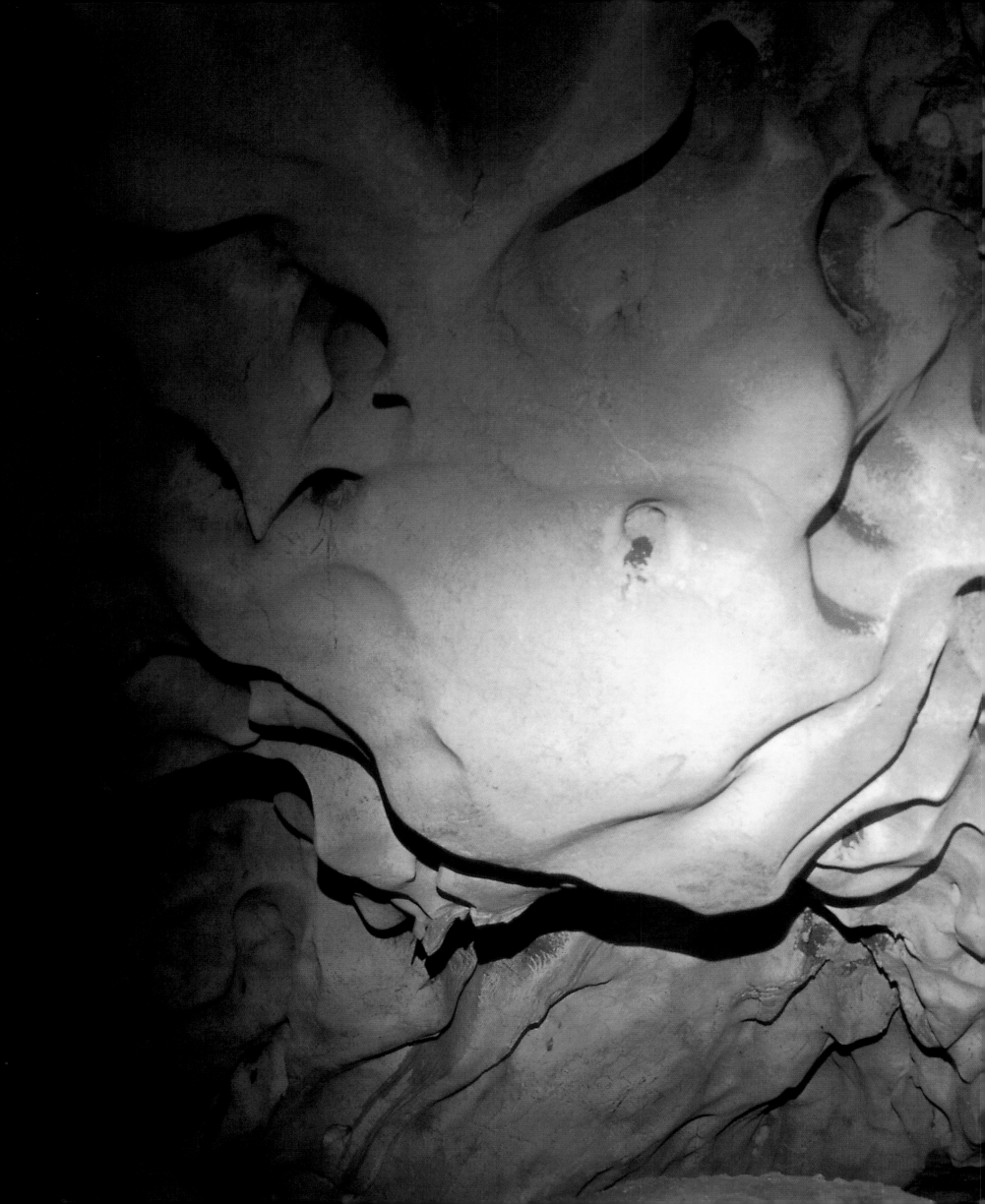

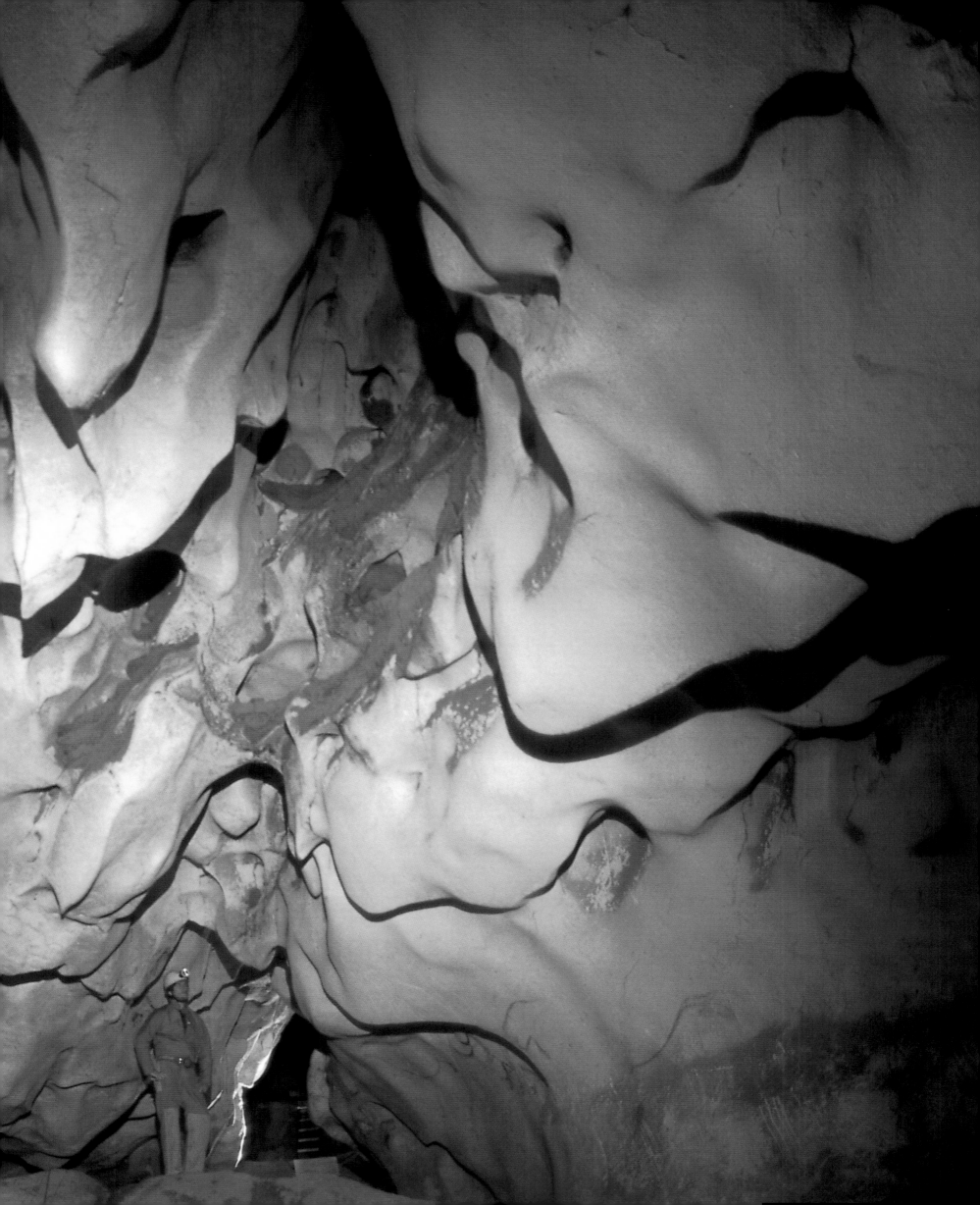

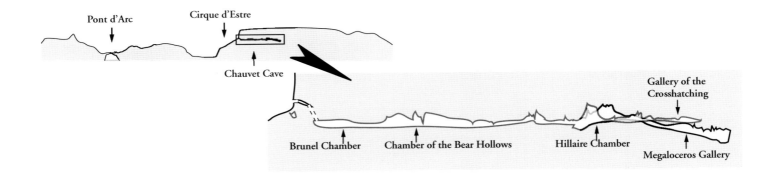

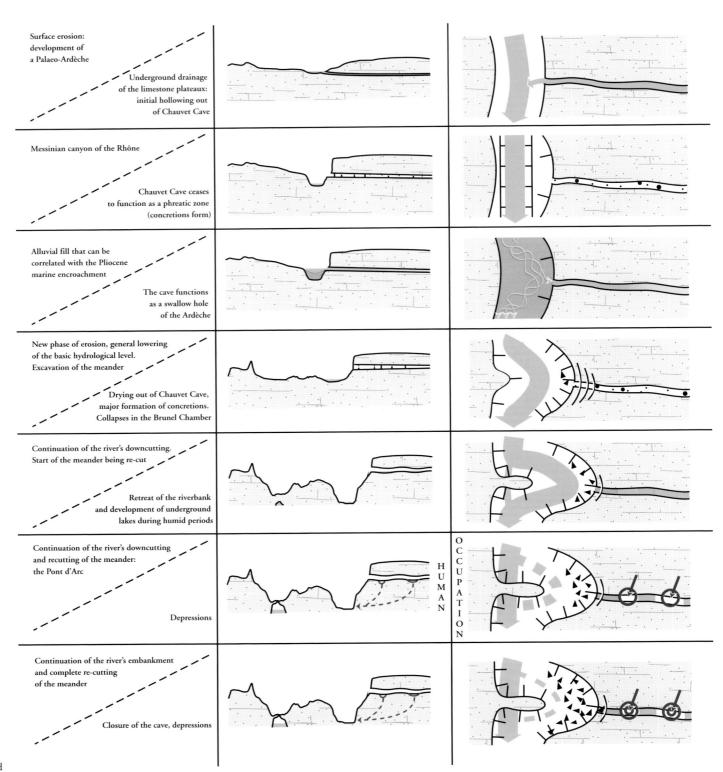

Ill. 19. The evolution of the cave and
its environment.

The Climate

Like all living species, human beings are dependent on the changes that occur in their environment and so, if their history is to be reconstructed, it is necessary to determine the nature of the environments in which they evolved. Thus, since they began their research, prehistorians have examined the sediments and the faunal remains associated with prehistoric tools to obtain information about the climate. The nature of the plant landscape remained inaccessible to them for a long time, and was only recognized around the 1950s because of analyses of the spores and pollen grains preserved in Palaeolithic layers.

Produced by Cryptogams (non-flowering plants) and Phanerogams (flowering plants), these microscopic elements have specific morphologies that lead to the identification of the plants from which they come, as well as a practically unalterable chemical structure that enables them to survive in most sedimentary environments (ill. 21). Moreover, they are emitted in very great numbers, which provides an image of the original vegetation that needs to be decoded. Hence these properties make it possible to know the composition of vanished landscapes from the collection of ancient pollen and to determine the corresponding climate.

The methods by which spores and pollen arrive differ according to the type of site in which they are found: in the open air, they arrive essentially through wind dispersal, whereas, in an underground environment, they depend on carriers of variable intensity (air currents, waterflows, visits by living beings). At Chauvet, a deep cave, the presence of pollen certainly owes much to human activities, and to being visited by animals. On the one hand, the multiple prints of plants that can be observed in places on the floor (ills. 35 and 36) indicate that prehistoric people introduced

numerous plants, and consequently pollen, into the cave. On the other hand, the existence of bear hollows and the presence of cave bear bones show that the cave was often used as a shelter by these animals. Bears play an important role as carriers, because on their fur and in their droppings they bring the pollen from the plants in their territory underground.

The first analyses carried out on the floors bearing marks of incursions have shown that the environment of the Aurignacians was a cold and relatively dry steppe, with gramineae, artemisia, goosefoot, bedstraw and helianthemums. This landscape (ill. 20), however, contained a certain number of trees that were adapted to the rigours of the climate, such as the juniper, birch and Scots pine, which must have been confined to protected spots located close to the cave.

Michel Girard

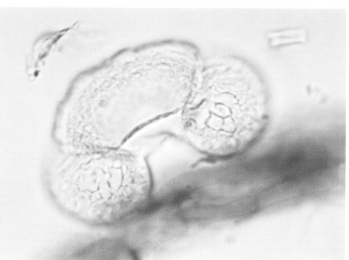

Top
Ill. 20. Example of the landscape with Scots pine.

Above
Ill. 21. Scots pine pollen.

Humans in the Ardèche in the Ice Age

The Vivarais region has a wide diversity of reliefs and landscapes. In the Rhône Valley, that unchanging thoroughfare for wild herds and people, major deposits of loess sealed open-air camps. The caves in the small steepsided valleys of the Languedoc Causses were inhabited in all periods. The limestone foothills of the crystalline Cévennes, from which the Ardèche's main tributaries come, contain a few Palaeolithic cave sites. On the edges of the Massif Central, the volcanoes of the region of Vals-les-Bains and Aubenas were dormant until the end of the Upper Palaeolithic, around 13,500 BP (before the present).

The great succession of cultures in France between 37,000 and 12,000 BP are represented in the Ardèche in an intermittent way. As for the list of decorated caves, it has grown constantly since Léopold Chiron mentioned the engravings in Chabot Cave (Aiguèze, Gard) in 1878.[1] Today, about twenty caves are known in the Ardèche gorges and the surrounding area (ill. 22). This collection, in which the Gardon Valley should be included, was considered of secondary importance until the discovery of Chauvet Cave. Finally, the engravings of several caves, including some of the most important (Ebbou, Figuier, Huchard, first chamber of Oulen) are not precisely dated.

Where the **Aurignacian** is concerned, between 37,000 and 27,000 BP, there is little evidence, whereas there is plenty further south, in the Languedoc (La Salpêtrière, at Remoulins, Gard). There are some old mentions (the Figuier cave at Saint-Martin-d'Ardèche).[2] The only convincing evidence is probably the split-base bone spear point from floor F9 (dated to $26,760 \pm 1000$ BP) in the Abri des Pêcheurs at Berrias-et-Casteljau in the Chassezac Valley.[3] Although several decorated caves, including La Baume Latrone (Russan-Sainte-Anastasie, Gard), have been attributed to the Aurignacian, its parietal art was poorly known before Chauvet. The drawings in the Grotte aux Points (Aiguèze, Gard) and La Bergerie de Charmasson (Vallon-Pont-d'Arc) could belong to this period.

Gravettian sites are more numerous: the above-mentioned Abri des Pêcheurs, five caves in the Ardèche gorges, the better-preserved levels of the cave of Oulen (Labastide-de-Virac/Le Garn). In the loess sediments of the Escoutay Valley, the open-air site of Bouzil (Saint-Thomé) has yielded several stratified occupations that are rich in dwelling structures, heaps of flint debitage, hearths and discard-areas. Also in the Rhône Valley, mammoth remains, sometimes accompanied by a poorly worked lithic industry, have been unearthed between Châteaubourg and Saint-Péray, especially in the loess sediments of the Toulaud Valley at Soyons. These finds represent either the scavenging of carcasses or the presence of real kill sites. On the whole, the industries, which are often small, have been attributed to the late Gravettian (Noailles burins facies),[4] and only the dates obtained in Chauvet Cave refer back to an earlier phase, around 27,000–26,000 BP.

The **Solutrean** develops between 23,000 and 18,000 BP,[5] a time of particularly severe climatic conditions. The early phase, rich in unifacial points, is well represented in the Ardèche gorges: the ten sites known constitute a possible centre for the emergence of this culture, which is also known in the Chassezac (Pêcheurs) and as far as the Rhône Valley, where the cave of Granouly (Le Pouzin) is its northernmost point. By contrast, more recent sites are rare (level 9 at Oulen). Several caves with paintings and engravings have been dated or attributed to the Solutrean: La Tête du Lion,[6] Chabot, Les Deux-Ouvertures, the second chamber of Oulen and the Grotte Sombre.

Opposite

Ill. 22. Map showing Upper Palaeolithic sites in the Ardèche:

1 Chabot (Aiguèze)
2 Sombre (Saint-Martin-d'Ardèche)
3 Le Figuier (Saint-Martin-d'Ardèche)
4 Huchard (Saint-Martin-d'Ardèche)
5 Les Deux-Ouvertures (Saint-Martin-d'Ardèche)
6 La Tête-du-Lion (Bidon)
7 Les Points (Aiguèze)
8 Oulen (Labastide-de-Virac/Le Garn)
9 Potiers (Saint-Remèze)
10 Colombier I and II (Vallon-Pont-d'Arc)
11 Bouchon (Vallon-Pont-d'Arc)
12 Ebbou (Vallon-Pont-d'Arc)
13 Chauvet and Planchard (Vallon-Pont-d'Arc)
14 Charmasson (Vallon-Pont-d'Arc)
15 Mézelet (Vallon-Pont-d'Arc)
16 Déroc (Vallon-Pont-d'Arc)
17 Curé (Saint-Montan)
18 Trois A (Gras)
19 Pêcheurs (Berrias-et-Casteljau)

At the end of the second pleniglacial period, small groups of humans visited the Ardèche gorges, but the filiation and evolution of these industries are poorly understood for the moment: the open-air site of La Rouvière at Vallon-Pont-d'Arc (**Salpetrian**), level 10 of La Baume d'Oulen, open-air sites between Bourg-Saint-Andéol and Saint-Marcel d'Ardèche.

Finally, the period between 17,000 and 10,500 BP saw the **Magdalenian** expansion and the first Azilian groups in the region, about thirty sites covering the limestone country of the Ardèche. The variety of flint industry, which changes very rapidly, reflects a large diversification of tasks. The bone industry (unilaterally and bilaterally barbed harpoons at Oulen and the Grotte du Colombier at Vallon) and portable art (cervid ribs, engraved and painted with ochre, from the cave of Les Deux-Avens at Vallon) are fairly rare, like everywhere in eastern France.[7] Some affinities with the Pyrenees have been noted. Finally, at Vallon once again, caves were decorated around 15,000 BP: a detailed engraving of a bison at Ebbou, the engraved ibex and aurochs of Colombier I and II, and the female outline of Gönnersdorf type that is painted in red in the Grotte du Planchard, 50 or so metres (over 160 feet) from Chauvet Cave.[8]

Bernard Gély

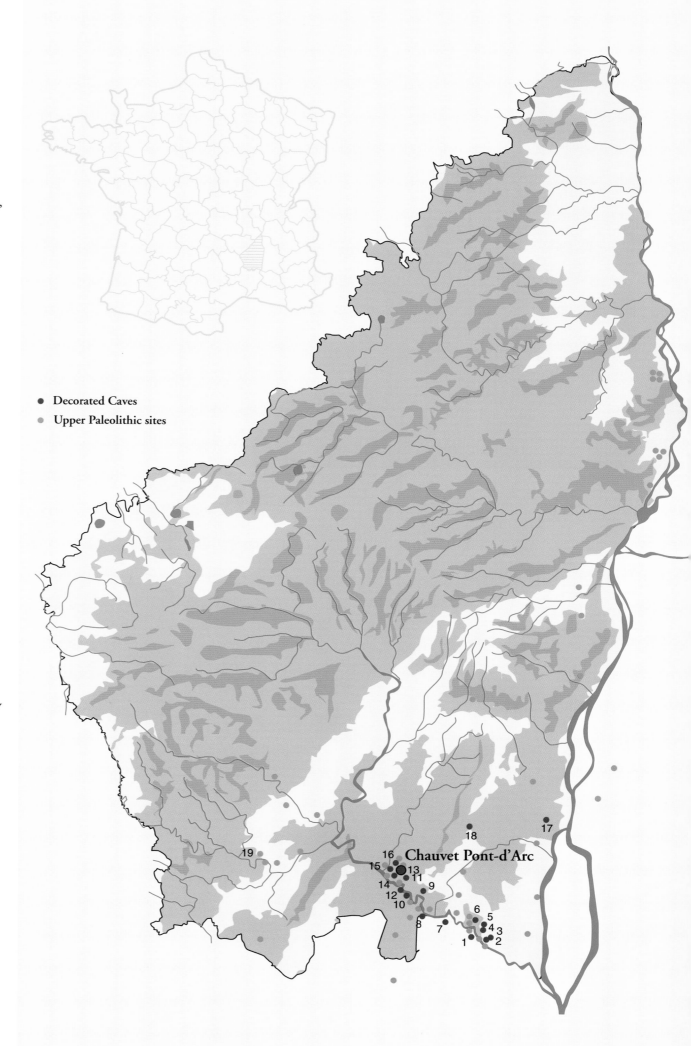

● Decorated Caves
● Upper Paleolithic sites

3

Above

Ill. 23. The loggia of little slabs. At the entrance to the Cactus Gallery,
2 m (6½ feet) above ground, on a rocky shelf, some plaques of concretion
and small slabs were arranged to form a kind of paving. A flint object
was also found there.

Opposite

Ill. 24. The central part of the Skull Chamber where,
on the floor, it is possible to see prints and bones and, on the
wall, clawmarks, engravings, paintings, hand prints and torch wipes.

- DATES OF THE INCURSIONS INTO THE CAVE

- THE PRINTS AND TRACES OF HUMANS AND ANIMALS

- VISITING THE CAVE AND HUMAN ACTIVITIES

- THE ANIMAL BONES ON THE CAVE FLOOR

THE FLOORS AND INCURSIONS INTO THE CAVE BY ANIMALS AND PEOPLE

From the start of our research in 1995, thanks to direct observations and the first radiocarbon dates, we were able to establish that the cave was visited by humans in two main periods. Since then, we have carried out further analyses, both of the black charcoal drawings and of the remains on the floor. The prints left by people and animals on the soft clay have begun to be studied systematically. The floors, which on the whole are extremely well preserved, have retained numerous traces, but it is also possible to see on them the remains of human activities – fires, charcoal, a few flints. Before and after the visits by Palaeolithic people, animals lived in the cave and died there, leaving the traces of their claws on the walls, the hollows where they lay, their numerous bones. These activities bear witness to the life of the cave and of its fleeting visitors.

3

THE FLOORS AND INCURSIONS INTO THE CAVE BY ANIMALS AND PEOPLE

Dates of the Incursions into the Cave

So far, about thirty samples have been dated by the Carbon 14 method. Most of the analysed fragments of wood charcoal (or of bone) come from the area beyond the Candle Gallery. They comprise parietal samples taken directly from six drawings and two torch wipes, as well as twenty fragments collected from the floor (see table opposite). Dating was carried out in well-controlled experimental conditions.[1] In certain cases, it was possible to test the reliability of the analyses by making two independent measurements of the same sample.

Most of the dates obtained fall into two periods a few millennia apart. The older period, represented by twenty-two dates, is located between 32,000–30,000 years ago, and comprises the studied pictorial depictions: two rhinoceroses that seem to be fighting and a running cow from the Panel of the Horses, a megaloceros (from the Megaloceros Gallery) and a big bison from the End Chamber. Contrary to expectations, as far as the horse head from the Panel of the Horses was concerned, the charcoal fraction gave a younger age (20,790 ± 340 BP) than the associated humic fraction, the age of which (29,670 ± 950 BP) is compatible with the date for the other paintings; the reason for this is that the analysed charcoal probably became contaminated by recent carbon. The contamination was not eliminated by the chemical treatment: the most probable age for the horse head is thus about 30,000 years. Most of the samples (fifteen) collected from the floor of the Hillaire Chamber, the Skull Chamber and in the hearth areas of the Megaloceros Gallery also belong to this early period.

The second period of occupation, represented by seven dates, is located between 27,000–26,000 years ago. Apart from four samples collected from hearths or nearby (Candle Gallery, Hillaire Chamber and Megaloceros Gallery), it comprises the two torch wipes, one of which was made on a calcite film deposited on one of the paintings of the Panel of the Horses. Its date confirms the antiquity of the pictorial depictions underneath. At present, no painting has been dated to this second period.

In addition to these two great phases when the cave was visited, it is possible to contemplate the existence of a third, more recent phase, represented by a date of 22,800 ± 400 BP, but this figure requires confirmation.

The Carbon 14 dates already available are coherent and bear witness to the very great antiquity of the pictorial representations. At the present time, Chauvet Cave is the rock art site that has been subject to the most dating.

Hélène Valladas, Nadine Tisnérat, Maurice Arnold, Jacques Evin and Christine Oberlin

Below

The twenty-eight Gifa dates were obtained using the technique of accelerator mass spectrometry at the Laboratoire des sciences du climat et de l'environnement (Gif-sur-Yvette, France); the two Ly dates came from using the classic technique at the Centre de datation par le radiocarbone de Lyon (Lyons, France). Finally, the Ly-118/Oxa measurement was carried out at the Research Laboratory for Archaeology and the History of Art in Oxford after the sample was prepared at Lyons. These results, expressed in years before the present (BP), are uncalibrated and so do not correspond to calendar ages. The associated standard deviation is at one sigma, that is 67% chance of being in the correct timespan.

ZONE	LAB REFERENCE	AGE	ERROR	NATURE
Candle Gallery	Gifa 99081	26,230	280	hearth
	Gifa 95127	26,120	400	torch wipe
Hillaire Chamber				Panel of the Horses
	Gifa 95126	30,940	610	confronted rhinoceroses, left
	Gifa 95132	32,410	720	confronted rhinoceroses, right
	Gifa 95133	30,790	600	confronted rhinoceroses, right
	Gifa 96065	30,230	530	running cow
	Gifa 98157	20,790	340	horse 'charcoal fraction'
	Gifa 98160	29,670	950	horse 'humic fraction'
	Gifa 95130	26,980	420	torch wipe on calcite deposit
	Gifa 95129	26,980	410	covering painting
	Lyons-118/Oxa	24,770	780	ground below painting
Skull Chamber	Gifa 99809	32,360	490	beneath bear skull
	Gifa 99810	31,390	420	beneath bear skull
	Gifa 99811	32,600	490	beneath bear skull
Megaloceros Gallery	Gifa 96063	31,350	620	Megaloceros (gallery entrance)
	Gifa 99237	25,440	250	entrance on carbonate crust
	Gifa 99238	31430	420	entrance
	Gifa 99239	29,740	390	entrance
	Gifa 99768	31,910	390	zone 1
	Gifa 99769	31,520	360	zone 2
	Gifa 99770	31,860	380	zone 3
	Gifa 99771	32,220	400	zone 4
	Gifa 99773	31,020	350	zone 7, burnt bone
	Gifa 99774	32,500	400	zone 8
	Gifa 99775	32,080	430	zone 6
	Gifa 99776	32,900	490	zone 10
	Gifa 99777	26,590	300	charcoal zone, lower level
	Gifa 99778	31,020	370	beneath Big Block
	Ly-6878	29,000	400	below horse with double mane
End Chamber	Ly-6879	22,800	400	
	Gifa 95128	30,340	570	big bison

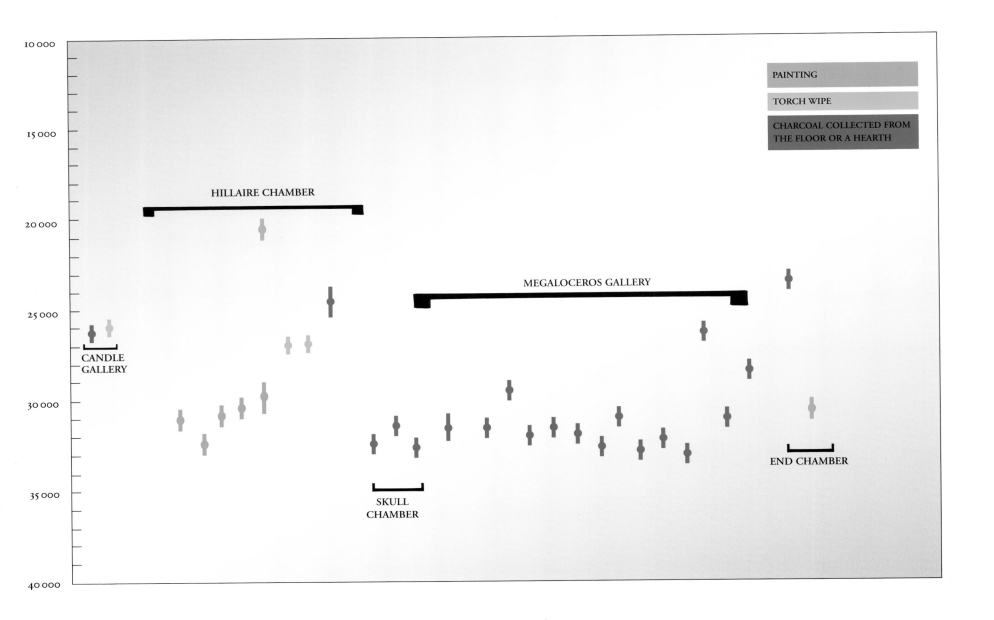

LEGEND:
- PAINTING
- TORCH WIPE
- CHARCOAL COLLECTED FROM THE FLOOR OR A HEARTH

HILLAIRE CHAMBER

MEGALOCEROS GALLERY

CANDLE GALLERY

SKULL CHAMBER

END CHAMBER

The Prints and Traces of Humans and Animals

Above

Ill. 25. The radiocarbon dates from Chauvet Cave, expressed with two sigma.

Opposite

Ill. 26. Plan showing the trail of prints and animal remains.

Since the start of the scientific study, the meticulous examination of the floors and undecorated walls has only been possible in the areas accessible from the path used by the discoverers.

The Human Prints

In the study of the traces on the floor surface the most striking fact is without any doubt the authentication of human footprints in the Gallery of the Crosshatching (ills. 28 and 29). It has been possible to get close to these remains thanks to the installation of supplementary protective elements on the discoverers' path in this rarely visited area of the cave.

However, a very large part of this sector remains unknown because of its distance from the protected section.

Our investigation is focused on about twenty traces of human feet that constitute the beginning and end of a track about 70 metres (nearly 230 feet) long, leading from the heavily calcited part at the end of the Gallery of the Crosshatching to the Skull Chamber. They can be fitted exactly one on top of the other, so it is possible to assert that this was one single individual, although the middle part of the track remains inaccessible for the moment.

In the final part of the Gallery of the Crosshatching, the permanent presence

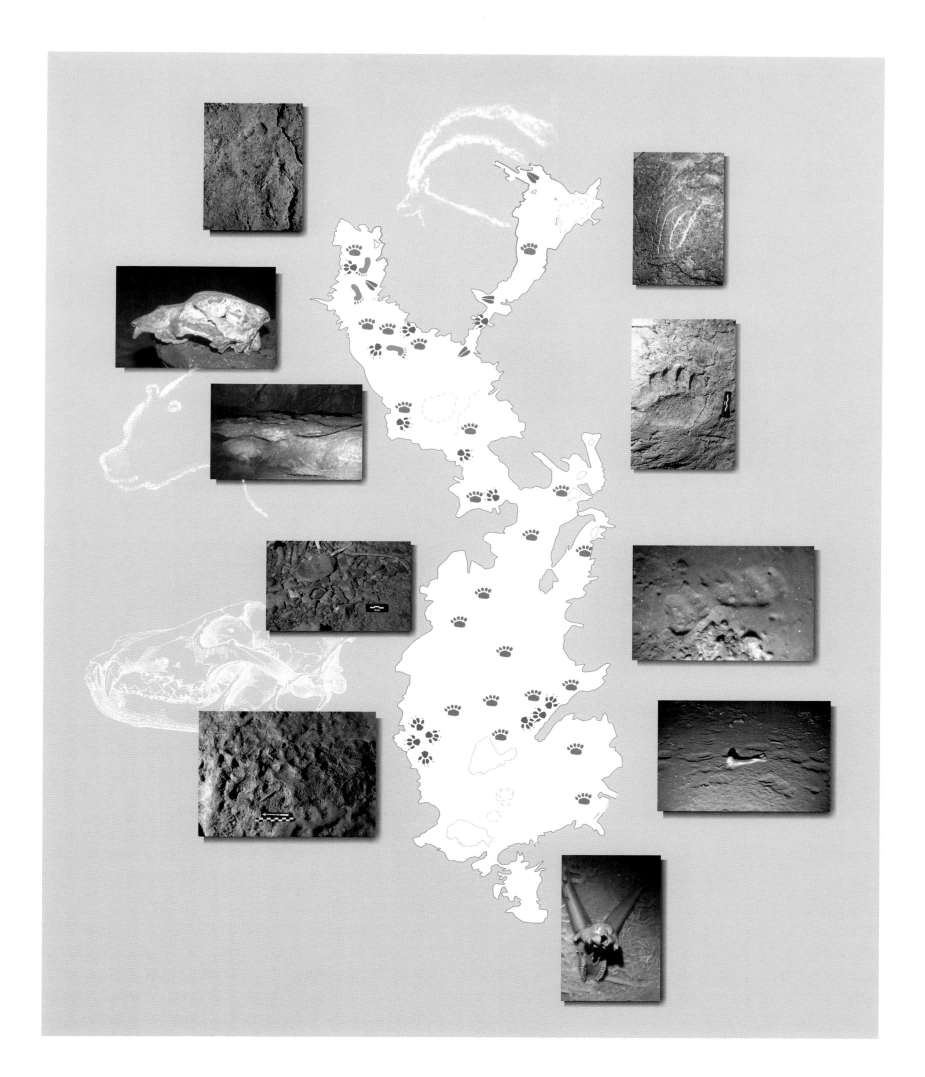

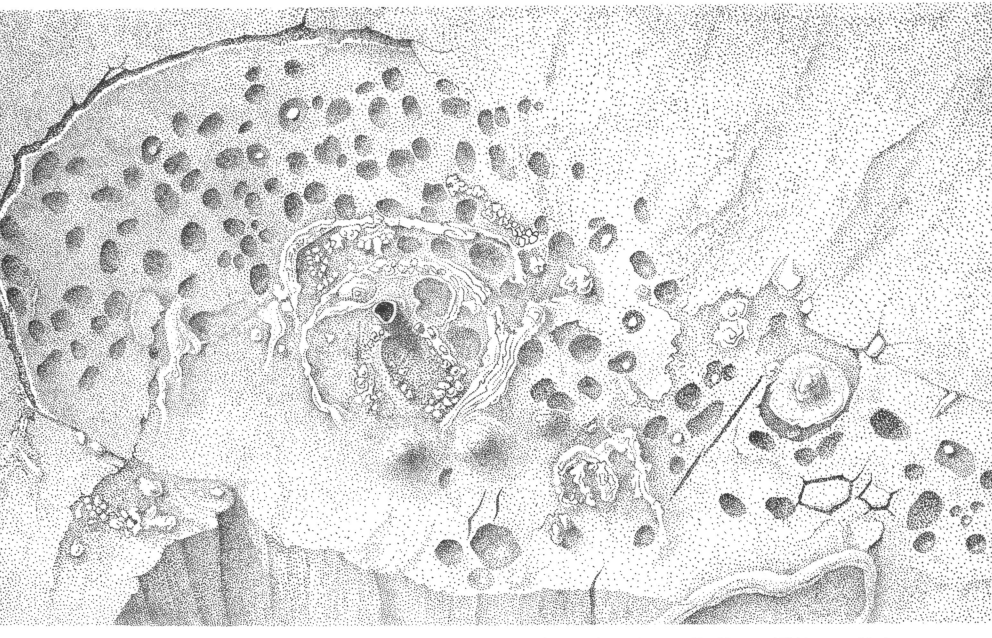

Above

Ill. 27. The Niche of Dots. Located to the left of the entrance to the Cactus Gallery, in the Chamber of the Bear Hollows, 1.7 m (5½ feet) above the present floor, this roughly hemispherical cavity measures 1.1 m (3½ feet) at its broadest. The back, originally covered with plastic clay, is currently hardened because of dripping from a thin stalactite at its centre. Four rings of finger dots seem to emphasize the central stalagmite. These initial, well-aligned dots were completed with others that fill the whole space available; 120 dots have been counted, all made with fingertips.

of percolating water has caused intensive stalagmitic activity that makes it impossible to carry out any pertinent observations at the start of the track. At the track's end, the prints stop at the abrupt edge of the scree that marks the boundary for the accumulation of clay around the basin of the Skull Chamber, giving the impression that this formed an obstacle to progress. For the moment, it is impossible to reach the right-hand sector, to which the child was probably heading (only a few prints can be detected through binoculars).

The Age of the Track Maker
We have referred arbitrarily to series of anatomical measurements of the feet of present-day Europeans that are known to be roughly equivalent to those of the Cro-Magnons.[2] If this prerequisite is accepted, then the prints must be those of a pre-adolescent about 1.3 m (4½ feet) tall. The low length/width ratio of 21.4 cm (8½ in.)/9.2 cm(3¾ in.) rather suggests a boy.[3] The foot's instep, whose axis of maximum length passes between the first two toes, displays the classic appearance of the 'European' foot.

The Age of the Prints
Only external arguments and/or elements can help us to date the prints.

The trail of human prints was compelled to follow a route where the vault rises appreciably. The child regularly wiped his torch on it above his path. These charcoal marks, dated to 26,000 years ago, seem to have been placed contrary to the direction

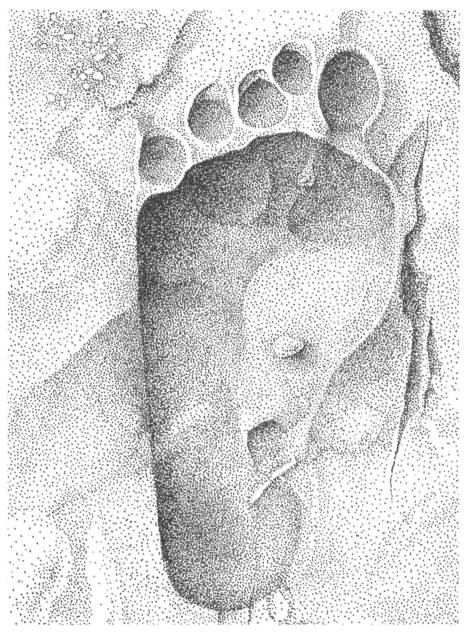

Above left

Ill. 28. Print No. 1. Reading the cast makes it possible to eliminate the aberrant images provided by direct vision alone. The child's foot was completely imprinted as it moved, which shows it was walking slowly and carefully on a homogeneous and soft floor.

Above right

Ill. 29. Print No. 1 and its cast. Casting prints with elastomer silicone produces absolutely faithful results that make it possible to carry out an anatomical reading, as on a living person. But this can only be done after prior consolidation, and numerous tests on an identical support.

Ill. 30. Fissiped prints. The bear and canid prints form part of a large collection of trampled marks at the entrance of the Candle Gallery. The animals trod on broad clay mounds, and their prints, protected from erosion by flowing water, have been perfectly preserved here. One can recognize distinctly the prints of canid front and back autopodia (feet) as well as part of a print from a bear's front paw. This drawing was made in part from direct observation and in part from a reading of an elastomer silicone cast.

of progress on purpose, as if to mark the way back.

Identical marks can be found, on the one hand, along the left wall of the Hillaire Chamber (including on the Panel of the Horses and at the entrance of the Megaloceros Gallery) and, on the other, in the Candle Gallery. It is thus possible to reconstruct the child's progress thanks to both this correlated evidence and the presence of two places where a child's clay-stained right hand was placed against

a few square metres in front of the entrance of the Megaloceros Gallery, in order to know whether any prints survived there. A hard blackish crust certainly looks like a floor shaped by frequent comings and goings. During this operation, two pieces of charcoal were brought to light; one adhered to the upper part of the crust, the other was contained within it, 10 cm (3⅞ in.) away. The two pieces of charcoal were dated to 25,440 ± 250 BP and 31,430 ± 420 BP. These samples, taken with the utmost care

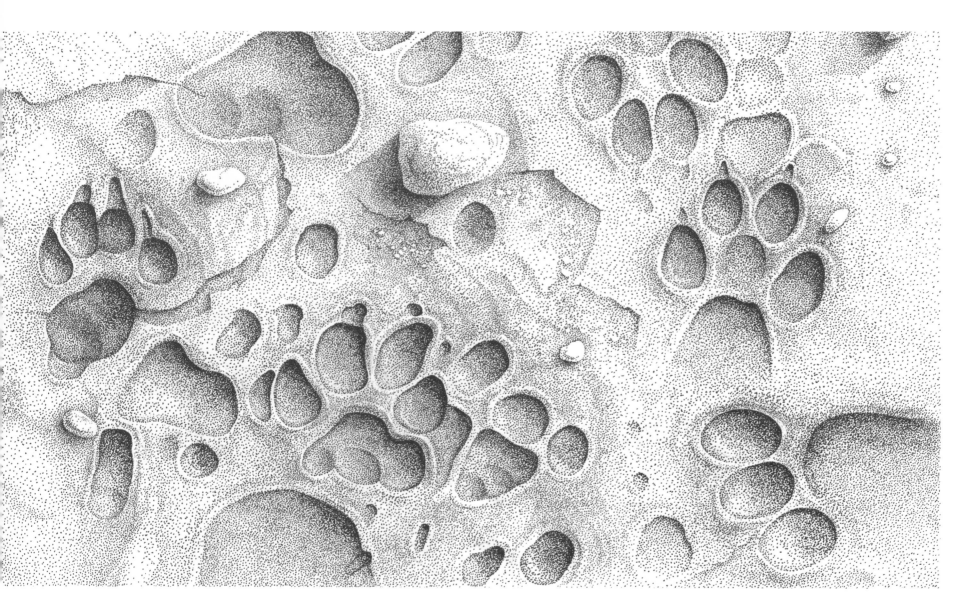

the lower right part of the Panel of the Scraped Mammoths. The size of these hand prints corresponds to the size of the feet in the trail (ills. 28 and 29).

Related Dates
We brushed away the loose sediment that had recently fallen from the ceiling on to

and analysed by an identical method at Gif-sur-Yvette by Hélène Valladas (see above), guarantee great accuracy in measuring their age. The more recent date corresponds, in our opinion, to the child's visit. It tallies with a fleeting intrusion that occurred long after the events linked to the art and the cave's main frequentation.

The Animal Prints

Our first observations suggested that all of the carnivore traces other than the cave bear were those of a single wolf that had moved around the Skull Chamber. It had left by the Gallery of the Crosshatching, close to the start of the child's trail.

Because of its ease of access, the clay bank located along the wall of the Panel of the Scraped Mammoths seemed to us to be the most suited to the study of the animal tracks noticed at the very start of the work,

The Canid

The examination of all the canid trails, although still incomplete, confirms the first observations and allows us to reconstruct the route followed by this animal (ills. 30 and 31) in the part of the cave between the Gallery of the Crosshatching and the chaotic narrowing between the Red Panels Gallery and the Candle Gallery (see plan, ill. 10).

Two distinct trails branch off from a common trunk (Crosshatching–Skull Chamber). One of them goes along the right

because the prints here are distinct and clearly individualized. This is an area trampled by fissipeds.[4] One very broad print was made by the pressure of the palm-pad of a young bear. The other prints belong to a large canid.

wall of the Hillaire Chamber and enters the Megaloceros Gallery, while the other follows the Panel of the Scraped Mammoths, and then crosses the Skull Chamber and heads towards the end of the Candle Gallery.[5]

As we wished, our analysis was carried out on perfectly identifiable and measurable prints in clay supports of variable plasticity.

Above

Ill. 31. Prints of a canid and a twig at the foot of the Panel of the Scraped Mammoths.

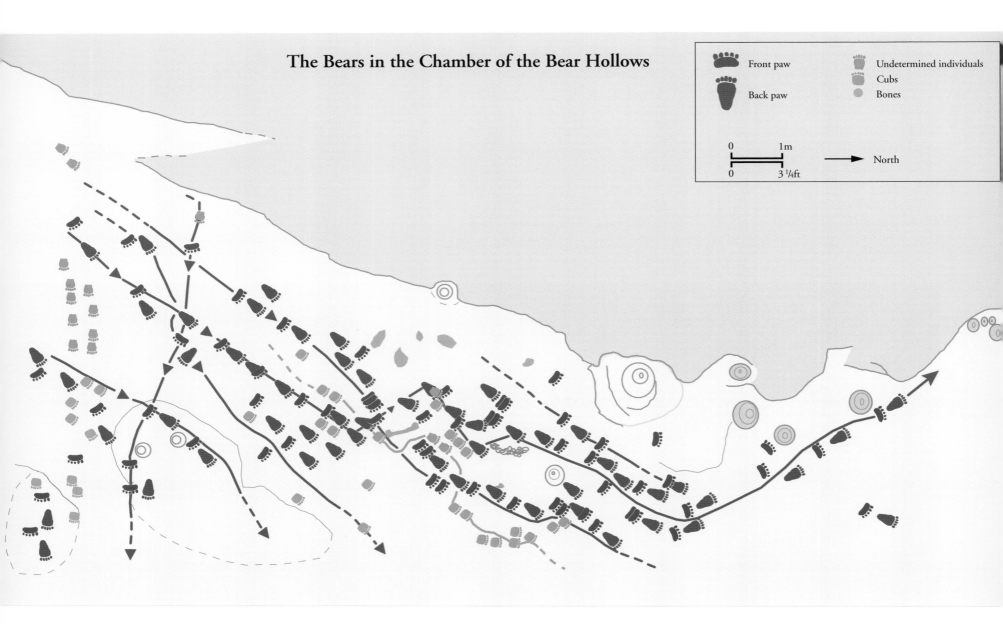

The Bears in the Chamber of the Bear Hollows

Front paw — Undetermined individuals
Back paw — Cubs — Bones

0   1m
0   3 ¼ft   → North

Above

Ill. 32. The bear tracks in the Chamber of the Bear Hollows. Thanks to specially adapted equipment, we plotted, and identified, with François Rouzaud, the topographic location of three main tracks of adults and one of a cub. The animals head towards the porch, moving along the wall. They are medium-sized individuals, accompanied by an infant cub romping about in the same direction. A few obstacles, such as a big bear humerus and concretions, forced them to alter their route. As bears do not have good nocturnal vision and, in order to move around and find their way in the dark, they have to rely almost exclusively on their sense of touch.

One observation is particularly significant: the morphology of the autopodia[6] differs from the wolf's in that the relative length of the middle digits is reduced. This can be seen in the geometry of its image in the hollow of the print (or in relief in the cast): the digital pads of the second and third digits are clearly positioned between the laterals, which is the rule for dogs, including the largest specimens (ills. 30 and 31).

Can this characteristic, as displayed by a single canid, be used to ask whether the wolf was different in these ancient times? It should be remembered that evidence for the existence of the first dog is not available until 14,000 BP at Oberkassel.[7] Nevertheless, this strange characteristic should be emphasized, at a time when genetic studies are putting forward a serious argument for the wolf transforming into the dog around 100,000 years ago.[8] In this

regard, the study of the canid bones in the cave will be of the greatest importance, even if it will be very difficult to link them to the study of the prints.

We have still not come across any child's prints and canid's prints on top of each other, and thus no proof that they existed at the same time. Nevertheless, this line of research should not be neglected, as their paths are so identical.

For the most part, their route avoids the depression formed by the Skull Chamber, which leads to the conclusion that it was filled with water when they passed. This was not the case for the bears, whose prints are scattered all over the bottom of the 'lake'.

By the right wall, at the top of the scree at the edge of the Skull Chamber, and along the canid's trail, there is a collection of spheroid and oblong coprolites, of about 2.5 cm (nearly 1 in.)

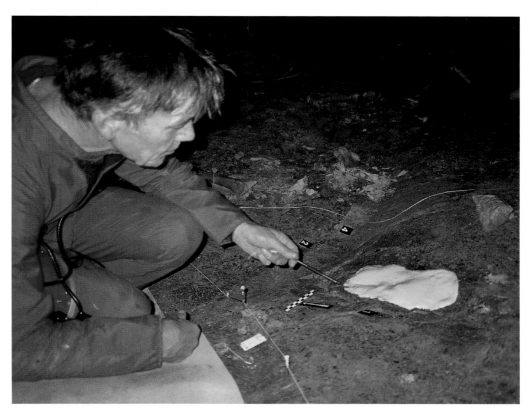

Left
Ill. 33. Michel-Alain Garcia making a cast, after consolidating the floor.

Below
Ill. 34. A canid coprolite.

in diameter. Another perfectly preserved specimen is located at the end of the Candle Gallery, close to a large concentration of prints. In both cases, they are fossilized canid droppings (ill. 34).

The Canid Prints of the Brunel Chamber and the Chamber of the Bear Hollows
Close to the entrance scree, in a vast 'conch' in the left wall of the Brunel Chamber, we discovered areas of about 30 square metres (320 square feet) that had been moulded by the passing of numerous fissipeds. The bear trails are always superimposed on them. A few rare isolated specimens show that the whole collection resulted from canids of various sizes trampling on the ground. These same cupulas, caused by the canid trampling, are found to the right of the Brunel Chamber's entrance. At the time of our first study of the bear trails, we thought

that they were micro-reliefs caused by circulating water.

The Ibex
An ibex jumped from the talweg of the End Chamber on to the clay scree that forms the floor of the Sacristy. It slid, deeply scoring the rock with its sharp hooves. It then headed for the end of this side passage. The ungues, clearly spread apart, show the animal's fright at finding itself in a dead end. It retraced its steps and stopped, standing firmly opposite the entrance. The prints of its four autopodia are very clear and help to assess its size: probably a big adult male. We pick up its trail again, without being able to say whether it was coming or going, in the middle and at the entrance of the Megaloceros Gallery, as well as on the scree giving access to the Gallery of the Crosshatching.

The Cave Bear
Brunel Chamber and Chamber of the Bear Hollows

In this part of the cave, the bear prints form trails that can be followed in their entirety. The chambers have a flat floor, with a regular covering of clay. The animals moved through here calmly, leaving clear imprints of their autopodia. A few stalagmitic layers sometimes seal them in, although it is still possible to make a morphological reading. One sector, the Chamber of the Bear Hollows, was subjected to a detailed study (ill. 32). These trails are certainly among the longest known in any cave. They were made by a small number of individuals, compared with the enormous quantity of bones scattered throughout the whole cave.

Hillaire Chamber, Skull Chamber and Gallery of the Crosshatching

It is not really possible to speak of trails, as the tracks in these chambers are all mixed up, especially in the mud at the bottom of the lake in the Skull Chamber or on the great accumulation of silty clay in the Hillaire Chamber. The readable prints in the Hillaire Chamber, where the finest bear hollows of the cave can be seen, are located at the edge of the areas where the numerous comings and goings make any decipherment impossible. This is also the case in general on the clay shelves. By contrast, the prints at the bottom of the lake will be easy to analyse.

Phantom Objects

At the time we were examining and cleaning the floors at the entrance of the Megaloceros Gallery we were puzzled by the presence of elongated perforations in the surface crust. They were scarcely more than 2 cm (¾ in.) wide and 20 cm (7⅞ in) long, and reminded us of twigs or sticks trapped in the floor, of which only hollow phantoms survived. This interpretation was validated by the study of the bank of prints beneath the Panel of the Scraped Mammoths, where these same kinds of remains occur. They are obviously made of wood, and sometimes a small carbonized part even prolongs the print of the twig.

Subsequently we found such imprints on overturning broken calcite plaques in the Hillaire Chamber (ills. 35 and 36). These twigs were clearly brought in by people. The way they were dispersed could be linked to not only human activities, but also circulating water.

Conclusion

Chauvet Cave is remarkably rich in ichnological evidence.[9] Taking account of the surfaces that have been explored, a wealth of documentary evidence has been discovered. We are aware that this first glance presents a distorted image

absolutely the idea that there was no communication between the Red Panels Gallery and the Candle Gallery, nor the idea that an entrance existed through the end of the present cave around 25,000 years ago, knowing full well that our geological colleagues think the opposite.

Taking into account only the results of the study of the prints and traces, it is possible to picture the following scenario: around the 30th millennium, or earlier, the Aurignacians were very active artistically in the cave. They brought in quantities of wood and this carbonized wood was used for lighting and for drawing. Then the site

of what the final study will show, when the whole of the cave's space has been understood. Some parts may seem to have exaggerated importance today, like the Crosshatching–Hillaire area, where there are many more prints than in the other sectors. It is already possible to observe a clear dichotomy between, on the one hand, tamped or trampled floors and, on the other, well-individualized trails. Leaving aside those of the bears, the three isolated trails that have been recognized so far are all located in the second part of the cave. They are also the most recent. For these reasons, we cannot reject

was abandoned and henceforth was only visited by bears. Five or six millennia later, it was still possible for animals as well as humans to enter the cave, and one human has left clear evidence of his visit. This version agrees with the first hypotheses put forward about the incursions into the final part of the cave, and tallies with the cave having a single period of decoration.[10]

Michel-Alain Garcia

Opposite and above

Ills. 35 and 36. Natural casts of plant materials (stalks, pieces of wood) from the Hillaire Chamber.

Visiting the Cave and Human Activities

The exceptional state of preservation of the walls and floors is in large part due to the cave's hydrological conditions over time. In particular, it is the prolonged absence of waterflows that helped to preserve the traces and objects resulting from human activities on not only the walls but also the surface of the floors.[11] Hence, the galleries located in the deep parts of the cave – the Gallery of the Crosshatching, the Megaloceros Gallery, the End Chamber and the higher areas of the Hillaire Chamber and Candle Gallery – all contain well-preserved remains. Conversely, in the areas close to the entrance, whether in the Brunel Chamber and Chamber of the Bear Hollows or in the Cactus Gallery, the presence of temporary waterflows caused concretions to grow in a particular area, walls to be washed and new sediments to be deposited, all factors that have affected or totally altered the morphology of the floors and, consequently, the traces and remains that might be located there. Moreover, prolonged visits by bears to the cave, after and between the human incursions, may have disturbed the way the archaeological remains were originally placed or may have obliterated more discreet or ephemeral traces by trampling.

The tens of thousands of years that have passed since the cave was visited in prehistory have resulted in a far higher number of factors that have affected the way the floors (rather than the walls) have deteriorated and altered, so that today the archaeologist is confronted by palimpsests of floors that are very complicated to interpret.

Despite the numerous phenomena that have become confused, following one another in an order that is still vague at present, it is nevertheless still possible

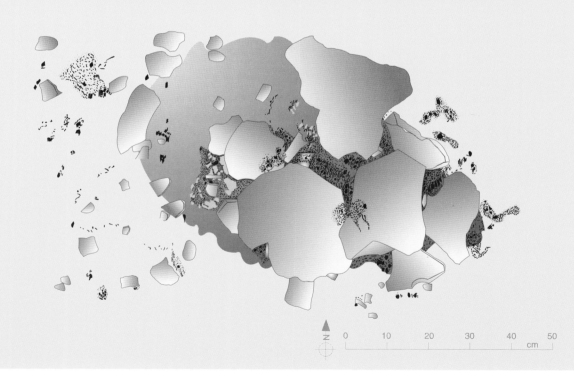

Above

Ill. 37. The hearth in the Candle Gallery is the only installation made by humans that survives in this well-trodden area (top: photograph; above: map of the fire). Its late age of 26,230 ± 280 years ago certainly explains why it is so well preserved and contains so little charcoal, unlike the hearths in the Megaloceros Gallery (ill. 38; opposite) that were fed copiously to produce quantities of charcoal.

to identify a series of archaeological facts that, although disjointed in time and scattered through space, provide evidence about human visits to this subterranean environment.

**Hearths Set up to Produce
a Colouring Material: Wood Charcoal**

Some hearths were preserved in the final part of the cave, starting in the Candle Gallery, where the first one occurs (ill. 37), a small combustion structure 50 cm (19⅝ in.) in diameter, constructed by means of several plaques of limestone. Water action probably dispersed the wood charcoal, which is sparse in its centre, unless the hearth was used for a very short time or it was only fed with a fuel other than wood. It is 26,230 ± 280 years old. [12]

In the Gallery of the Crosshatching, two small bear hollows seem to have been used as hearths, judging by the accumulation of charcoal residues linked with slabs of concretion at their base, as well as the intense and localized reddening of the ceiling above them, which is not very high in this part of the gallery. A flint flake is present in one of the depressions and a trail of human prints passes close to it. [13]

The clearest hearths, which did not escape the notice of the discoverers, [14] are those of the lower and final part of the Megaloceros Gallery. They are scattered along the left wall, along the axis of the passage, the only place where the ceiling is high enough to allow anyone to stand upright. In contrast to the combustion structures of the other sectors, these hearths are characterized by an abundance of wood charcoal produced by burning branches of fairly large Scots pine. [15]

It thus appears that, quite apart from their function as illumination, already mentioned elsewhere, [16] the hearths were certainly intended to produce wood charcoal as a raw material for colouring. This spot seems to have been chosen in order to meet two requirements: to provide a large quantity of charcoal and to make sure of its size and quality. Part of the charcoal produced here was used to make

Ill. 38. The hearths in the final part of the
Megaloceros Gallery were set up so as to avoid
the total combustion of the Scots pine branches,
which would have produced ash, but rather to
obtain wood charcoal of good enough quality
to be usable as a colouring material. In this
view of the left wall, a black horse with a double
mane, drawn with charcoal, is visible, as well
as numerous pieces of charcoal accumulated
on the floor directly beneath the figure.

Above

Ill. 39. At the entrance of the Candle
Gallery, in the Hillaire Chamber, a step
was deliberately made.

the black drawings on the walls of the
Megaloceros Gallery, which are adjacent
to the hearths. Hence, at the level of the
double-maned black horse on the left wall,[17]
an elongated but very dense concentration
of charcoal is present at the foot of the wall,
2 m (6½ feet) from the original
combustion area (ill. 38). The charcoal
elements are very fragmented here and
partly reduced to powder; they come
from the pieces used for drawing the horse
immediately above crumbling away.
Other charcoal, concentrated in small
depressions on the edges of the hearths,
fits with secondary, natural accumulations.
Natural factors, whether climatic
(air currents), geological or biological
(bears, humans), may independently
or jointly have played a role in displacing
these charcoal pieces, which are particularly
light and easy to move.

The absence of hearths for producing
charcoal in the Hillaire, End and Skull
Chambers, where they could easily have
survived, implies that the material used
for the paintings and drawings on these
walls also came from the hearths in the
Megaloceros Gallery. A small heap of wood
charcoal visible in a depression in the floor,
at the foot of the great central panel of
the End Chamber, is certainly from
those hearths.[18]

Analyses carried out on charcoal samples
taken from the heart of these fireplaces
and from the peripheral areas have all
yielded ages between 32,500 and 31,500
years ago.[19] Burnt bone from inside one of
the hearths and from a black figure in the
Megaloceros Gallery both gave dates from
the same period. These very close dates,
as well as the exclusive use of Scots pine
determined by S. Thiébault, indicate that
the hearths and a large part of the cave
art in this area are contemporaneous.[20]

In the upper level of the Megaloceros
Gallery, there is another hearth installed
on an incline that is partly filled with
limestone flakes fallen from the walls.
Its position on the edge of the escarpment
that overhangs the two lower levels of
this gallery, as well as the small amount
of charcoal discovered, can perhaps be
explained by the fact that it was used

for illumination. Although its exact age
is not known, a piece of charcoal that
probably comes from it, which was picked
up in the area around it, indicated by its
age that this hearth, so different from
the others, was the result of a more recent
visit by humans than that in the low part
of the gallery.

From the Installations to the Area around the Decorated Zones

Broken stalactites and accumulations of
limestone blocks or, more often, pieces
of broken-up stalagmite floor have been
observed in several locations: to the left
of the entrance of the Cactus Gallery,
in front of the Panel of the Hand Prints,
and in two places in the Hillaire Chamber.
Only a detailed study of these structures,
which cannot be explained by any natural
cause, will enable us to understand
their significance.

At the level of the 70 cm (27⅝ in.) step
that separates the Candle Gallery from the
Hillaire Chamber, along an ancient path
marked by the compression of the floor,
progress was made easier by moving a bulky
block that functions as a stepping stone
(ill. 39). Not far from there, close to the
left wall of the Hillaire Chamber, at the
foot of the panels of engravings and
finger tracings,[21] eight large fragments of
limestone concretions are accumulated in a
surface of 1 square metre (10¾ square feet).
These pieces cannot come from the ceiling
at this spot; they originate from ancient
stalagmitic floors about 10 metres (32 feet)
away, in the Candle Gallery, and so they
provide evidence that they were
accumulated and transported on purpose.

To the left and in front of the Panel of
Hand Prints,[22] another mound of blocks
was set up (ill. 51), some of which are
upright and wedged in place by smaller
blocks around them. Their position could
perhaps facilitate access to the upper part of
the little ledge that overhangs the panel's
upper area, although in this spot it is
undecorated. So these installations cannot
be directly related to the task of drawing or
the function of the decorated walls.

The carbonated plaques and slabs that
are usually the pieces concerned may also

have been used as props for other technical or ritual activities.

Flint Implements as Evidence for Repeated Visits

Almost twenty worked flints have been found. Most of the time they have been observed in the cave from a distance. The small number of flints confirms that humans only visited the cave for a short time and that the flints were abandoned, or sometimes intentionally left, after brief, but perhaps repeated, use. Although the results of a microwear study of ten of these objects, entrusted to Hugues Plisson at the end of 1999, are not yet fully known, their condition suggests they were implements that were not used too often.

Three are retouched: a simple dihedral burin, a fragment of a retouched backed piece, and a blade with continuous retouch. The rest is made up of raw knapping debris (flakes and blades). As these pieces are isolated from those products usually associated with them, they were clearly knapped and shaped outside the cave. Conversely, in the Megaloceros Gallery, the discovery around the big charcoal hearths of small flakes of beige flint that are identical to those produced when a flint tool is reworked (burin, scraper, retouched backed piece) can be related to the making and maintenance of tools.

The flints are all distributed in the deep part of the cave (ill. 40), starting at the entrance to the Cactus Gallery. Most of these objects, with the exception of a flake and a few scales placed inside a drapery of concretions in the Brunel Chamber, and a blade hidden in a cavity in the stalagmitic floor in the Cactus Gallery, were found scattered on the ground. The concentration of flints around the hearths in the Megaloceros Gallery, where flint implements, bone objects and combustion waste from the fireplaces were abandoned, corresponds to a more intensively visited and naturally cramped thoroughfare. This is a sector where, logically, it would be advisable to carry out further research and analyses, in order to link more accurately the fairly rich archaeology of the floors with that of the decorated walls.

Below

Ill. 40. The flint implements come from the deepest parts of the cave, where the floors are the best preserved. Made from flint nodules identical to those found naturally around Chauvet Cave, they were worked outside the cave and brought into it. Only sporadic incidents of reworking tools took place in the Megaloceros Gallery. No trace of any flint implements has yet been observed on the bones of the bear carcasses that litter the floor.

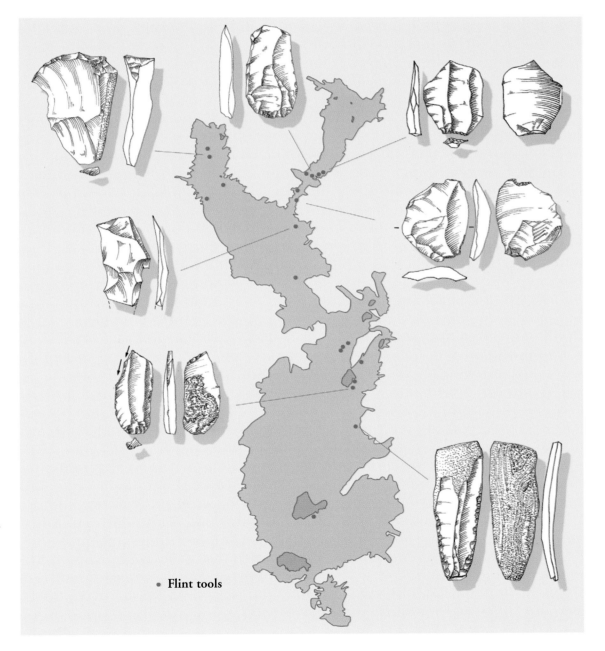

• **Flint tools**

A Projectile Point of Mammoth Ivory

It was in the sector close to the hearths that
an ivory object was found under a thin
film of sediment that had accumulated since
the prehistoric occupation. This mammoth
ivory point, biconical in form, has a
damaged end (ill. 43). It must have
measured almost 30 cm (11¾ in.) in
length, which is exceptional, and its
oval cross-section is 2 cm (¾ in.) wide.
The shaft appears to be smooth, with no
ornamentation or decorative grooves,
while its base has an ancient fracture
that was certainly caused by use.

Objects of this type, which were fitted to
hunting projectiles, are known throughout
the Upper Palaeolithic. However, points as
massive as this one, made of ivory (and not
of reindeer antler, as is almost always the
case), are well known at the start of the
Aurignacian in Germany and in Central
Europe.[23] In the light of studies carried
out on these objects and the most recent
radiocarbon dates, it appears that this type
of weapon is widespread during the
Aurignacian, where it also co-exists with

different types of reindeer-antler points.[24]
Although the Chauvet object cannot be used
in isolation to characterize a particular phase
of the Aurignacian, it nevertheless has much
in common with Aurignacian projectile
points made from reindeer antler, bone
or ivory.

At the level of cultural material, it tends to
confirm that the various dates obtained from
the hearths (wood charcoal and burnt bones)
and directly from the black paintings in the
final parts of the cave do correspond to the
growth phase of the Aurignacian in Europe.

The Use of Bear Bones by Humans

A cave bear skull was moved and placed
on purpose on a rock in the Skull Chamber.
Another was marked with black lines
(ill. 202). Many others were probably
collected together in the same chamber.
Not far from the entrance, two humeri
(already mentioned) may perhaps have been
stuck into the floor (ills. 41 and 42).
Sometimes there are many reasons for an
object being disturbed. For example, an
animal rib apparently stuck into a fissure,

at a person's height, on the left of the Cactus Gallery, close to the Niche of Dots (ill. 44), may have been caused by geological phenomena.[25]

Imprints of Plants and Fossilized Wood under the Calcite
In the centre of the Hillaire Chamber, in the Large Collapse area, the grey and sooty clay floor dates from the same ancient period as the cave art preserved on the ceiling (owl and horse drawn by finger and an implement on the soft wall, a bison and other animals drawn in black). On lifting the fragments of calcite that covered the floor close to the path where they had been moved, numerous imprints of plants appeared, moulded by the calcite or preserved as a hollow in the clay floor (ills. 35 and 36).

The size and nature of the plant residues preserved in this way vary from twigs to fragments of branches that are 6–7 cm (2⅜– 2¾ in.) in diameter. Such residues abound in the first centimetres of clay sediments beneath the archaeological surface marked with charcoal traces. These observations match those made in 1998 in the chambers of this sector and, especially, in the Candle Gallery, Gallery of the Crosshatching and the Megaloceros Gallery. At that time, rod-shaped imprints that are in quite good condition on the surface of the preserved zones had led M.-A. Garcia, P. Morel and myself to evoke the presence of twigs and branches, of which only the imprints had survived to the present day. The stratigraphic position of these remains at the level of, and below, an archaeological occupation surface confirms their antiquity.

The abundance and diversity of these residues represent an exceptional source of information to broaden our knowledge of the climate and vegetation of this period at the start of the Upper Palaeolithic. Without going beyond descriptive and photographic observation and recording of the data, we immediately implemented a study programme with the anthracologists S. Thiébault and I. Thiéry and the palynologist M. Girard.

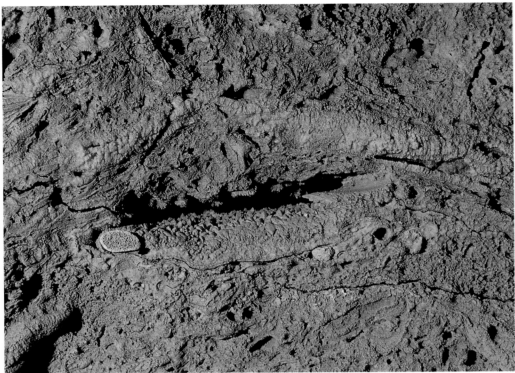

Above left
Ill. 43. Ivory point in the Megaloceros Gallery.

Above right
Ill. 44. Fragment of a bear rib in a fissure in the wall of the Chamber of the Bear Hollows, 1 m (over 3 feet) from the Niche of Dots. This may be a natural geological deposit.

Human Incursions into Chauvet Cave: A Giant Jigsaw of Information to be Put Together

The diversity and relative abundance of the traces and remains of all kinds that are today gathered together close to the exceptional decorated walls of the cave may give the illusion of a fairly dense network of information that would be easy to bring together by making chronological links and suggesting a possible scenario. However, this is not the case, because other phenomena indicate that major periods of time may separate these different elements from each other, and that this complex palimpsest will only be deciphered gradually.

We shall have to take numerous precautions to cross-reference systematically all the assorted scraps of information in order to put the events recorded on the walls, the floors, in the stalagmites or in the sediments in chronological order, so that we can construct a plausible history of human visits to the cave.

At present it is only possible to be sure that traces of human visits to Chauvet Cave have been recorded at two different times. The first period, between about 32,000 and 30,000 years ago, corresponds to the creation of the black paintings and the hearths that produced the colouring material. The second period is later, around 27,000 or 26,000 years ago, with more transient traces. Before, in-between and after these periods, it seems that the cave was always visited by bears who have considerably diminished our sense of human visits.

Jean-Michel Geneste

The Animal Bones on the Cave Floor

Although Chauvet Cave's reputation is closely linked to its parietal depictions, the abundance of bones, primarily of bears, and the other evidence for animal activities (prints, hollows, clawmarks) have also aroused admiration and contributed to the arrangements made for, firstly, its preservation and, secondly, its study (palaeontological identifications and photographic recording from a distance).

On the one hand, this 'horizontal' research, aimed at limiting movement inside the cave and preserving the floors (without excavating), presents us with the great privilege of making a direct, instantaneous reading of human and animal archaeological remains on the floors and walls – are sometimes difficult to understand.

Chauvet Cave shows an exceptional combination of human and animal activities on the floor (human and animal prints, hearths, hollows, flint tools, bones) and on the walls (paintings, engravings, clawmarks) and has resurrected the sensitive and complex subject of human/bear relations in the Palaeolithic. All our hopes were concentrated on the remarkable Skull Chamber, even before it was studied. No matter how obvious and necessary it is, investigating the palaeontological, geological and (ethno)archaeological

activities in the cave. On the other hand, it hampers the dynamic reading of a global chronology (no stratigraphy). In addition, the relationships between the piles of bones – both in the various chambers and between them or between the different categories of data concerning the role of the bear in the symbolic thought of Palaeolithic people has proved to be a difficult undertaking, with very real scientific and ideological constraints. It will only be possible to undertake this research after we have

Above

Ill. 45. A wolf skull, probably belonging to a female, in the Brunel Chamber.

Above

Ill. 46. Into the light sediments of the cave the bears dug hollows, which are particularly well preserved in the Hillaire Chamber and the End Chamber.

more details relating to the bears' occupation of the cave.

General Presentation of the Fauna

The bone remains belong to carnivores (bears, wolves, foxes, martens or stone martens), ungulates (ibex, roe deer, horses), birds, rodents, bats and reptiles. The bear was not the only animal to visit the cave: all the species identified, apart from horses, could have entered it actively in the Pleistocene (bears, wolves, ibex, birds?) or the Holocene (martens/stone martens, roe deer, birds, bats); some wolf and ibex prints have been recorded, as already mentioned.

The wolf (*Canis lupus*) is identified by two complete skulls. The first is small

(female?), and comes from the Brunel Chamber, opposite the Panel of the Dominoes (ill. 45); the second is much more robust, and was found in a clay plug at the end of the Belvedere Gallery. Between these sectors, which constitute the cave's entrance and end, some teeth and other bones of the skeleton have been recorded, mostly in the first chambers: long bones and a half-mandible at the foot of the entrance scree, metatarsal in the Brunel Chamber, a first phalange and two atlases (first cervical vertebrae), curiously found side by side among a heap of bear bones, at the level of the Panel of Hand Prints.

It is tempting to compare these bones and the prints. Some wolf coprolites have been collected from the Candle Gallery, Hillaire Chamber and Skull Chamber (see above). It is probable that these two wolves entered the cave in search of carrion.

In and around one of the hearths of the Megaloceros Gallery, an almost complete skeleton of red fox (*Vulpes vulpes*) was found, scattered over an area of about one square metre (over ten square feet). None of the bones displays any sign of having been burnt, although the patina is different from that found on bear bones in the same sector. Are these species contemporaneous?

Finally, carnivores are also represented by several skeletons of mustelids (martens or stone martens): three young individuals in the Morel Chamber, two adults at the top of the entrance scree. These animals probably come from the Holocene.

The ibex (*Capra ibex*) is represented, above all, by a magnificent skull bearing the remarkably well-preserved horn cores of a male. The systematic palaeontological inventory has enabled us to identify numerous skeletal elements distributed in the Morel Chamber, the entrance scree, the upper part of the Chamber of the Bear Hollows (skull of a young individual, several mandibles, metapodials) and in the Brunel Chamber, not far from the Recess of the Bears (all the pieces of a forelimb). Curiously, the presence of the ibex in the deep parts of the cave (Candle Gallery, Hillaire Chamber and Skull Chamber, Gallery of the Crosshatching and Megaloceros Gallery) is limited to prints. The extremely wide area over which ibex remains are spread is probably the result of transportation (and dislocation) by predators (bears, wolves?).

A few non-fossilized bones of roe deer (*Capreolus capreolus*) were found at the cave's entrance and the loggia of the Morel Chamber. They probably come from the Holocene.

As far as horses are concerned, there is an upper molar from the Chamber of the Bear Hollows, close to the Cactus Gallery, and a distal extremity of a metapodial at the foot of the entrance scree. These remains may come from carcasses brought into the cave by vultures.

In the Morel and Brunel Chambers, a few bird bones from the Alpine chough (*Pyrrhocorax graculus*) and the Eurasian dipper (*Cinclus cinclus*) were mixed with the remains of bears. In the entrance scree, several parts from a skeleton of a big bird of prey (probably a golden eagle), coated with calcite, are found on the outer area of the expanse of bones.

Other animals (rodents) entered the cave by slipping through the blocks in the scree that blocks the natural entrance or by infiltrating the little fissures that lead to the deep galleries. There are only a few garden dormice (*Elyomis quercinus*), long-tailed fieldmice (*Apodemus sylvaticus*) and snow voles (*Microtus nivalis*), and their skeletons are more or less complete. These rodents are scattered throughout the network: entrance scree cone, Cactus Gallery, Red Panels Gallery, Hillaire Chamber, Megaloceros Gallery and End Chamber.

Bats did not visit the cave very much. A few isolated bones of a large species, probably the horseshoe bat (*Rhinolophus ferrumequinum*), have been identified in the Hillaire Chamber and at the entrance to the Megaloceros Gallery; a humerus of a big mouse-eared bat (*Myotis myotis*) has been noticed in the End Chamber. Finally, in the Brunel Chamber, downhill from the Sacred Heart Panel, several sections of a snake skeleton (grass snake?), partially caught in the calcite, have been found.

Although this fauna is varied in terms of species, it represents under one per cent of the palaeontological material; the bulk of the bone remains come from the cave bear.

The Cave Bear (*Ursus Spelaeus*): An Omnipresent Animal

In all the chambers, bear skulls (more than 170) and bones (2500) lie strewn over the floor, often in heaps, and sometimes isolated. In the Skull Chamber, at the foot of the great block of stone, a skull without a stop could be attributed to the brown bear (*Ursus arctos*).

Despite the large number of skulls, it is difficult to extract much morphological and morphometric information from them. Estimates of the age (sutures, tooth abrasion) and sex (development of the

Above
Ill. 47. A bear placed its clay-covered paw on the wall (under the panther's stomach).

sagittal crest, biometry of canines) often remain conjectural because of marked physico-chemical alterations (clay sediments in the Chamber of the Bear Hollows, Panel of Hand Prints, Megaloceros Gallery) or calcite (stalagmitic floors in the Hillaire and Skull Chambers). Nevertheless, adult females seem to dominate, whereas there are relatively few cubs and adult males. The cave can be considered a place where the bears spent the winter.

Cave bears visited the cave for millennia, before, during and after the visit(s) by humans. In numerous places (Hillaire Chamber: intermediate panels and Panel of the Engraved Horse) bear clawmarks were scraped before engravings were made (ill. 179). The first radiocarbon dates carried out on bear bones show that the cave was visited by bears and prehistoric people at the same time, as already mentioned. Finally, bears continued to go there for the winter, after the last visits by humans, as in certain places (Hillaire Chamber and other deep parts of the cave) a few clawmarks cut through the engravings or paintings (ill. 125). However, the cave was frequented for the most part by bears before the era of Palaeolithic humans.

More than 130 heaps of bear bones have been listed, from the entrance (Morel and Brunel Chambers, entrance scree) to the final parts (Gallery of the Crosshatching, Belvedere Gallery and Sacristy). Major thoroughfares (Chamber of the Bear Hollows, Hillaire and Skull Chambers) or secondary galleries (Recess of the Bears, Cactus Gallery, Rouzaud Chamber) contain large quantities of them (ill. 48).

The lower parts of the first chambers (base of the entrance scree, Chamber of the Bear Hollows) are truly carpeted with bones, resulting from parts of carcasses (fresh bones) or of skeletons (dry bones) being transported by the waters. Two humeri, which seem to have been stuck vertically into the clay floor, close to some skulls (ills. 41 and 42), may have floated in and then been redeposited by the flowing waters. In the Red Panels Gallery, one hundred bones spread about are the result of water or mud flows (from the Rouzaud Chamber?). In the Hillaire Chamber,

Above
Ill. 48. A heap of bear skulls and bones that are not covered with concretions, near the Large Collapse of the Hillaire Chamber.

Opposite
Ill. 49. In the Hillaire Chamber, a bear skull has been completely covered by concretions, and a large stalagmite even grew on top of it.

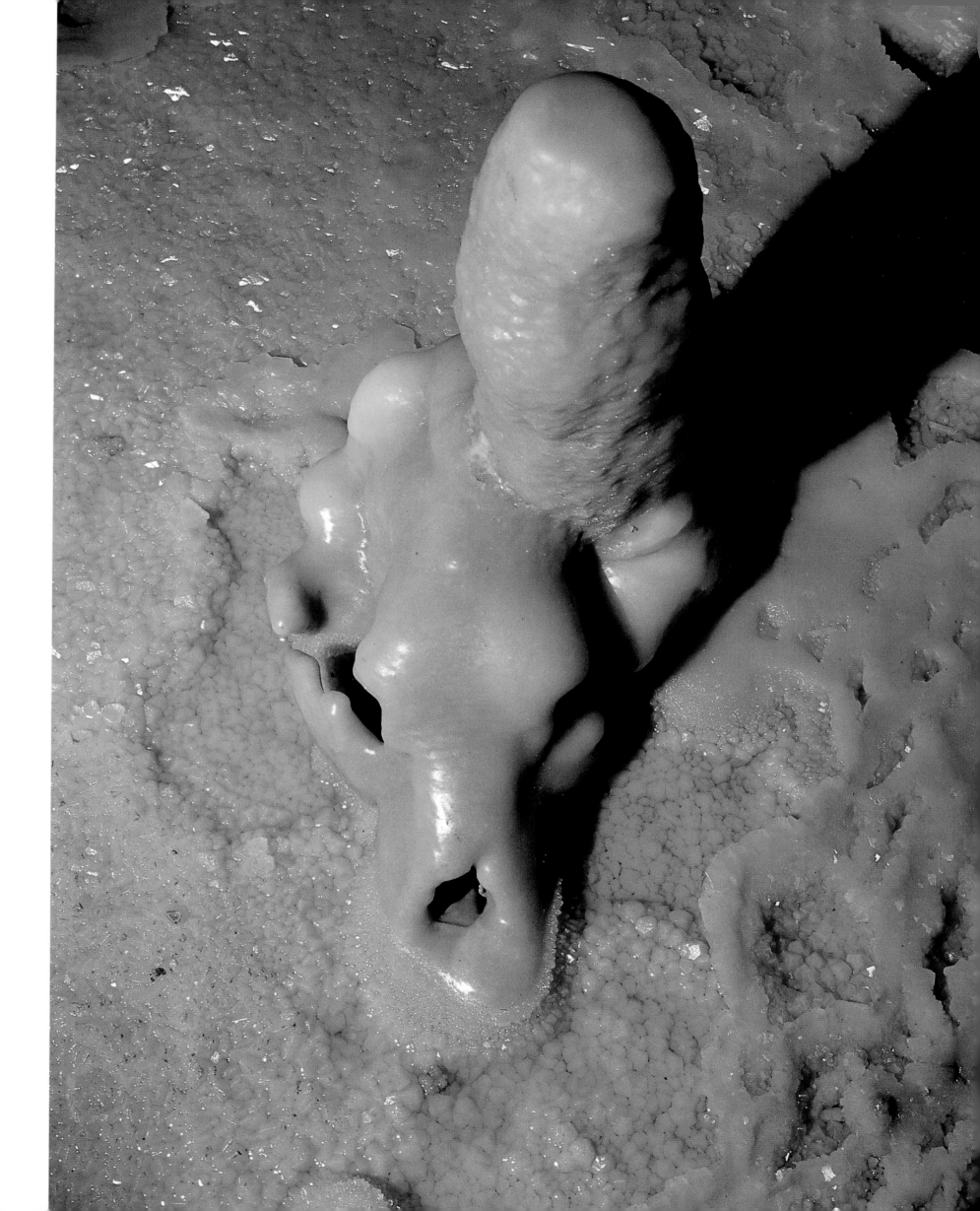

some heaps containing several bear skeletons (skulls, sections of backbones still anatomically connected, ribcages and dislocated limb bones) occur around the edge of the Large Collapse. This vast area reflects the natural modifications to which collections of bones are subjected in a karstic context (bear activities, carriage, depressions).

These bones can be compared with the prints found on the floor, either isolated or forming real tracks (ill. 32), the 'collective' sleeping areas, and, on the walls, polished areas and clawmarks.

The bear hollows, depressions averaging 1 m (over 3 feet) in diameter and about 10 cm (nearly 4 in.) in depth (ill. 46), were dug in places spared from waterflows or high humidity, the highest parts of the chambers: the central area of the Chamber of the Bear Hollows, and the right part of the Hillaire Chamber, as well as its imposing clay bank.

The bases of walls and crevices are heavily worn by animals repeatedly passing by. These animals moved in the dark primarily by means of touch ('topographical' memorizing of the chambers) and smell (marking of territory, decomposing carcasses of their fellows?). The clawmarks are mostly found at an average height of 1.5 to 2.5 m (5 to 8 feet), sometimes covering large surfaces (the left part of the Hillaire and Skull Chambers; the End Chamber; the Panel of the Big Lions), and sometimes slashing the wall from top to bottom (the Cactus and Belvedere Galleries).

An often thick layer of calcite covers the floor in numerous parts of the cave (the Panther Panel; Red Panels Gallery; Hillaire and Skull Chambers; Gallery of the Crosshatching). Out of these imposing concretions, only the upper parts of the biggest bones stick out today (sagittal crests and parietal bones of skulls). It is certain that other skeletal elements have been coated by the calcite deposits. In the Skull Chamber, at least 45 mostly complete skulls have been noted, including more than 30 in a perimeter of about 7 m (23 feet) around the big block; numerous other bones barely emerge from the stalagmitic floor. In the Hillaire Chamber, which is an extension of the preceding sector, 35 skulls, likewise covered with a thick layer of calcite, have been counted. In these chambers, the positioning of the numerous bones poses a problem that will only be solved after very detailed studies have been carried out: to what extent is the accumulation of skulls and other bones caused by humans, bears or water?

The bear skull was placed on the big block by humans (ills. 95, 204, 205), for reasons that are still unknown. Other anomalies in the way in which the bone remains were distributed have also been noticed: in the Brunel Chamber, close to the Sacred Heart Panel, a bear femur was put on a calcite bank and two cheek teeth were placed into two small hollows made by erosion in an enormous calcite block. It is difficult to interpret an isolated vertebra placed against the left wall of the Red Panels Gallery. However, it could be as a result of a person having moved it there.

Chauvet Cave is a remarkable example of a cave in which the cave bear hibernated. Apart from its other points of interest (speleological, karstological, prehistoric), with more than 170 bear skulls recorded so far in all of the accessible parts of the cave and, of course, with the other parts of skeletons and the other species, it constitutes a remarkable palaeontological site.

The combined actions of humans, animals and natural agencies (waterflows, depressions, calcite formation) explain the present layout of bones in the cave. Future studies will aim to determine the specific role of each of these agents.

Michel Philippe and Philippe Fosse

Above
Ill. 50. Cave-bear jaw and bones in the Hillaire Chamber.

Opposite
Ill. 51. Blocks gathered on purpose in front of the Panel of Hand Prints.

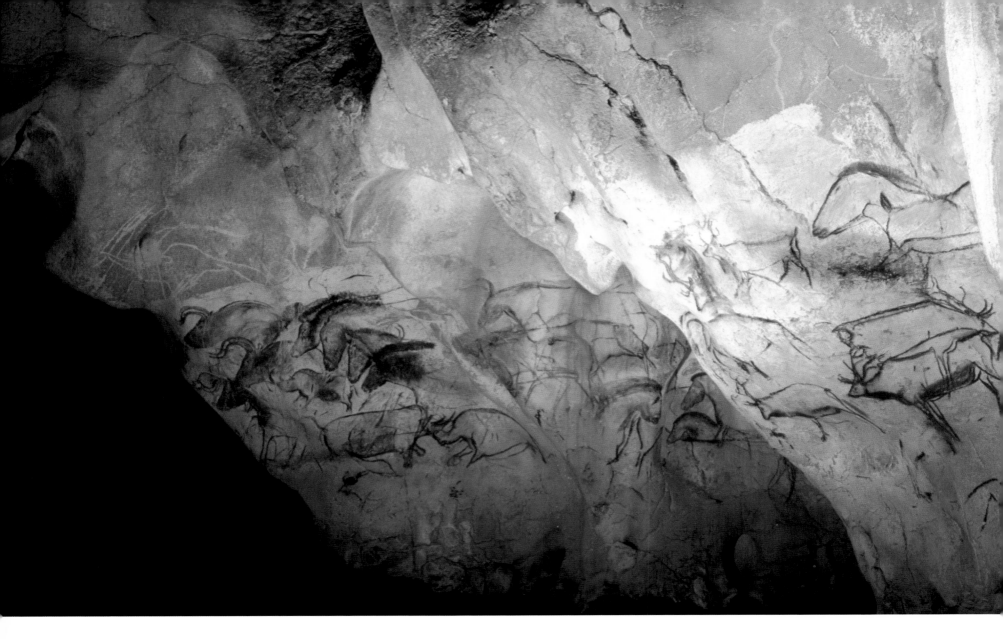

4

Ill. 52.
The Horse Sector.

DRAWING IN THE CAVE

So far we have only a mixed and partial view of the parietal works. Deepening our knowledge of them will depend on the possibilities of recording them. At present, certain accessible panels (Recess of the Bears, Brunel Chamber, Panel of the Signs, Panel of the Little Bear, part of the Panel of the Horses, entrance to the Megaloceros Gallery) have been studied as thoroughly as modern techniques allow, by a detailed examination of the walls and photographs with multiple oblique lights, before taking manual readings. Other panels (Panther Panel, Panel of Hand Prints) have had to be studied from afar, using photographic methods. Finally, it

has not yet been possible to do more than describe others, the majority, sometimes from a great distance (End Chamber). Continuing this important work will without a doubt bring new discoveries, further information and changes in thinking. Despite these reservations, we are aware that we already have a good overall view of this exceptional art, its distribution in space and the chosen themes or techniques employed. The broad lines of our observations will remain valid. The descriptions and analyses presented below follow the normal itinerary through the cave, from the entrance to the end, chamber after chamber.

DRAWING IN THE CAVE

The Entrance Chamber, the Chamber of the Bear Hollows

The Entrance Chamber is considered to have been the access to the cave in prehistoric times. The present morphology of the floor and the extent of the chamber bear no resemblance to how they were in prehistory. A scree of small blocks that have come in from outside litters the floor today.

Three openings lead from this chamber to the next part of the cave. The first, to the east, joins the end of the Brunel Chamber via a passage at the top of the scree that is too narrow to be negotiable. The situation must have been the same during the prehistoric occupations; even if it was possible to pass by this route, it would have been difficult. The second is an opening that comes out directly into the Brunel Chamber at the foot of the scree. It has easy access and must have been at least as easy in prehistory. The third, the biggest, opens into the Chamber of the Bear Hollows. The scree dies out in this chamber whose left wall constitutes the natural extension of the Entrance Chamber. Only the morphology of the floor differentiates them, because of the stones that form the scree.

The Chamber of the Bear Hollows is an immense horizontal chamber of about 2500 square metres (26,900 square feet). Its ceiling is sometimes very high (ill. 14) and it was possible to stand upright everywhere. There are a large number of tracks and traces on the floor, but so far it has not been possible to attribute anything to human activity. They postdate the main use of the cave by humans. The bears left numerous hollows and several tracks (ill. 32). Wolf prints are scattered over the floor in even greater numbers.[1] Their presence suggests the existence of a veritable lair, which seems incompatible with an area of total darkness.

The only cave art in this chamber is located at its far end. At 1.5 m (nearly 5 feet) from the ground, a big red dot is the first trace of pigment present on the left wall of the cave, more than 80 m (over 260 feet) from the entrance. On the right wall, just next to the Cactus Gallery, a red rhinoceros head (ill. 67) seems to mark the access to it.[2] The largest chamber in the cave contains no other decoration, although there are numerous suitable walls, including on the right-hand stalagmitic masses, which are only decorated on the southern face that looks on to the Brunel Chamber.

The morphology of the Entrance Chamber and of its junction with the Chamber of the Bear Hollows and the data

concerning animal occupations, as well as the absence of decoration, all lead to the Chamber of the Bear Hollows being seen in a very special light. It was probably an area of semi-darkness, in a setting where people chose to save parietal decoration for the areas of darkness. The distribution of the cave's chambers and the parietal layout in the first half of the cave is centred on the Chamber of the Bear Hollows, which functions as a hall, around which the decorated spaces are joined together: on one side, the Red Panels Gallery, on another, the Cactus Gallery, and, finally, the Brunel Chamber, a peripheral entity.[3]

Yanik Le Guillou

The Morel Chamber

Currently, access to the Morel Chamber[4] is close to the ground and involves an uncomfortable crawl through a narrow passage. Palaeolithic people made adjustments to this passage, and broke a stalactite that was blocking it. Once one has crossed this narrow passage, one emerges into a loggia of about 5 square metres (53 square feet), made of gours, some of which are deep, and niches that are difficult to reach. This small area, 2 m (6½ feet) up, dominates a flat chamber of almost 100 square metres (1076 square feet). The height of the ceiling in the first half of the chamber means it is possible to stand upright. The floor is covered with a thin layer of calcite. The low ceiling of the second half makes it necessary to crouch or move on one's knees, on an uneven floor that is cluttered with collapsed pieces of ceiling. Numerous roots, some of which are still alive, are present on the floors. On the right wall, a narrow gallery, through which it is necessary to crawl, leads to a small chamber with no traces of human activity.

The inventory of the bones that are present on the surface reveals Palaeolithic faunas (cave bear and ibex) and an odd series of more recent traces, some of them modern. The ancient faunas have been displaced by small waterflows and are now regrouped in a sort of channel. The bears left signs that they had passed by in the form of clawmarks.

The only traces of human activity are on the walls. Two small groups of black traces, the remains of dots or torch marks, are visible, one of them covered with calcite, on the right wall at the end of the chamber, the other on a column at the edge of the loggia. Three groups of fine engraved lines are superimposed on bear clawmarks. One of them could, if these last marks are included, make the shape of a mammoth. It is interesting to note the systematic connection of animal clawmarks and engravings, as if the former had attracted the latter. The most striking thing – something that could not fail to be noticed – is a series of five big red dots, located on the vertical part of the ceiling that separates the chamber into two. By virtue of their size, they have much in common with the numerous dots in the Brunel Chamber, although their poor state of preservation makes it impossible to identify hand prints. They were not made by projection of pigment. One of these dots has a narrow cluster of engraved lines superimposed on it.

The Morel Chamber holds a special place in Chauvet Cave, as it has neither the beauty, nor the colours, nor the brilliance of the rest of the cave. Access to it is difficult and unpleasant. It is off-centre at the entrance of the network, and is the decorated sector that is closest to the exterior. Its parietal depictions are difficult to compare with those in the rest of the cave. Bears did not enter it through the present narrow passage: they certainly had a direct opening to the outside at their disposal. Studies currently underway will make it possible to clarify the situation for human beings, that is, whether they entered solely through the opening they modified and in which direction they passed between this chamber and the main network. It is even possible that there were, in fact, two caves, two adjacent porches, one of them leading to Chauvet Cave and the other giving access to the Morel Chamber.

Yanik Le Guillou

Above
Ill. 55. The Morel Chamber (in pink).

Opposite
Ill. 56. A red sign resembling a claviform in the Brunel Chamber.

The Brunel Chamber

The cave's modern entrance leads to the Brunel Chamber, to the right and in front of the Chamber of the Bear Hollows. The metal ladder (ill. 6) that descends from the ceiling runs past several metres of imposing stalagmitic masses before giving access to a vast space, about 40 metres (130 feet) long and 30 (nearly 100 feet) wide, with a high, light ceiling. The dark-red floor is partially occupied by a gigantic chaos of fallen blocks and concretions that partition this chamber – evidence of natural events that occurred long before people came here. The present path skirts this chaos, around which there are a few decorated panels. This artificial way makes the panels more individual and does not take into account that they are all, in fact, within calling distance of each other. A promontory, formed by a big stalagmitic cascade, dominates the chamber. This advantageous observation post is marked by several red dots placed on one of the rock pendants of the ceiling. The light held by a visitor standing in front of the chamber's main panels is visible from this spot and restores the impression of the overall space. These panels are not located at random. Some can be seen from a distance, while others are in inaccessible crannies (Megaloceros loggia, Recess of the Bears and engravings of the Stoup). Yet what they all have in common is that they make use of the particular topography of the place, which was perfectly understood by prehistoric people, and which dramatizes the place where they have been positioned.

The collection of paintings in the Brunel Chamber will be evoked logically by following the path that is necessary today. Apart from the Sacred Heart Panel, on a big rock pillar that marks the separation with the Chamber of the Bear Hollows, which can be seen on arrival, the rest of the cave art is located in the right-hand part of the chamber.

The Sacred Heart Panel

This panel, 6 m (19½ feet) long and more than 3 m (9¾ feet) high (ills. 58 and 61), is located close to the prehistoric entrance that is today plugged by a scree. A large spread of red dots occupies the roughly vertical wall and continues up on to the ceiling. These big dots, made by applying the palm of a hand coated with ochre, are weathered (by waterflows or draughts) or have become blurred through diffusion. The collection is covered by a tracery of very fine engravings, from which it will certainly be possible to extract some animal figures. To the right of this set of dots, some red marks form a sheaf of lines surmounted by a cross-like sign (ill. 58). To the left of this sign, some faded coloured areas resemble a bison head.

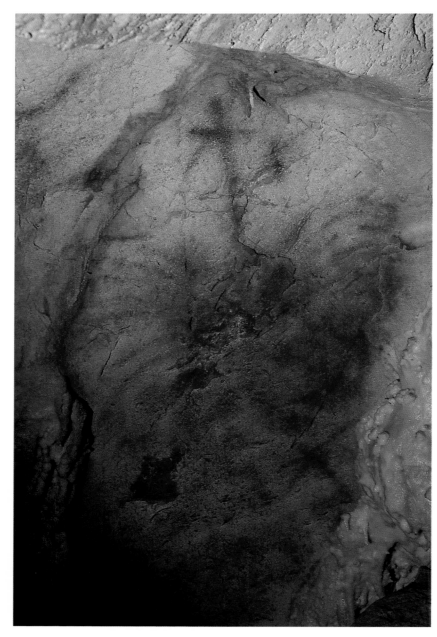

Above

Ill. 57. The Brunel Chamber (in pink).

Right

Ill. 58. Cross-shaped sign on the so-called Sacred Heart Panel.

Opposite

Ill. 59. Large Panel of Red Dots made with the palm of a hand in the entrance to the Alcove of the Yellow Horses.

Ill. 60. The Panel of the Dotted Animal, in the background, behind stalagmitic masses.

If that is the case, then this head would display the same characteristics as the black bison heads in the second part of the cave and would confirm the contemporaneity of the red and black decorated areas.

All over this big panel and on the rock pendants, red areas are too spread out for any figure to be made out on them.

draw conclusions about the different chronological phases when the cave was visited.

The Mammoth at the Entrance
The present access to the Brunel Chamber is bordered on the right by a broad stalagmitic mass that is partially active, notably in

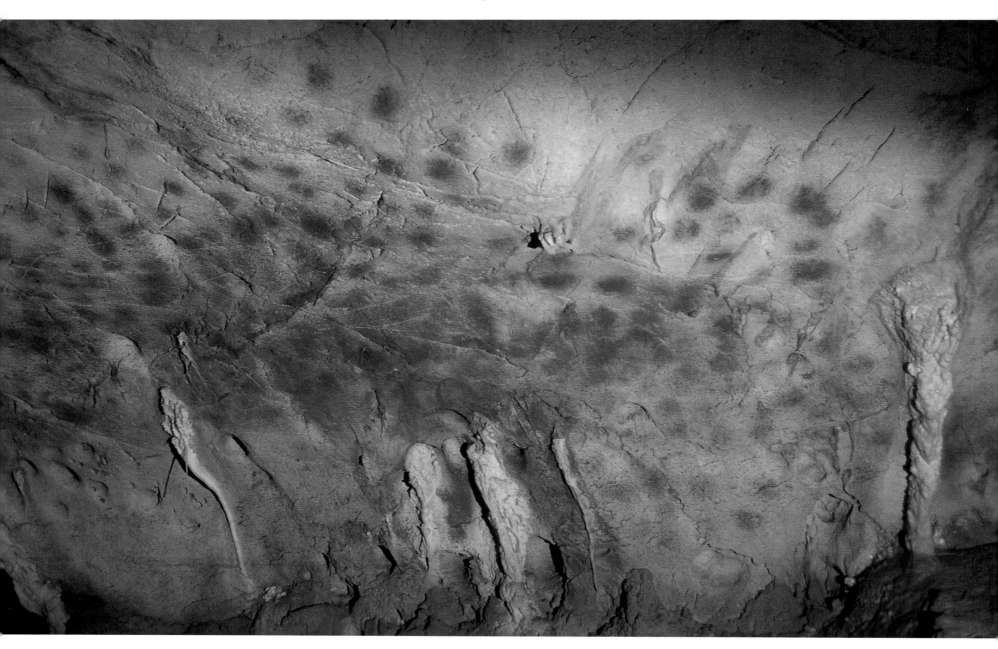

Above
Ill. 61. Big panel of hand dots called the Sacred Heart Panel, not far from the natural entrance.

Continuing on the left towards the access to the Chamber of the Bear Hollows, there is only a small red sign resembling a claviform, a typical Magdalenian sign comprising a vertical line with a slight outgrowth on one side of its upper part (ill. 56). The different forms for such a simple motif, especially of this size, about 5 cm (2 in.) high, make it impossible to assert that this figure is strictly identical to these well-known signs or to

humid periods, during which a real waterfall is produced on one of its sides. The organ-like pattern of concretions at the front of the mass forms natural outlines of mammoths – a fact that did not escape the attention of the Palaeolithic visitors: for they emphasized one of these shapes with a red line that draws the front of a mammoth facing right; its back end is obliterated by a calcite formation that is still active. The drawing is extremely restrained. The animal has no tusks, its trunk is hanging down and the interior of its body does not have any detail (ill. 54).

The Panel of the Dominoes

After moving round the masses and the blocks in the chamber's centre, the path follows the northern wall (ill. 201). The first visible figure is a feline head, the only black drawing in this chamber. It is blurred by a film of calcite, and the distance from which it can be observed prevents any close analysis. A few centimetres to its right, a barbed red sign is sketched by a series of juxtaposed little dots that may have been done with a finger. Further on, there is a collection of dots that gave the panel its name, because their layout looks like a series of dominoes. These thirteen dots, in unequal groups, were also produced with ochre smeared on the palm of the hand. Some curved lines, short or long, and a multitude of disorganized light-red traces reveal the presence of artists who manipulated ochre and spotted the wall with it. The decoration ends with the back end of an undetermined animal with a short tail, probably a cervid facing left; the front of its body either was not depicted or was spoiled by a flow of water. Above this collection, and above an ancient concretion, the painters placed a group of ten dots on the ceiling. In order to produce these dots with their palms, they had to climb up on to the concretion. Indeed, its clay covering has been crushed. It is easy to imagine that assistants helped the creator of the dots maintain balance while perched on the narrow and slippery extremity of the stalagmite.

It is interesting to observe that the decoration only occupies a small area in relation to the vast space available. Although easily visible from a distance, this panel contains no particular composition, no spectacular work, and it seems that in this place it is the individual elements and their location that have symbolic value.

The Alcove of the Yellow Horses

A few metres from this panel, the wall forms an alcove, at the entrance of which a rocky lobe is completely covered with juxtaposed

red dots (ill. 59). It was this panel that made it possible to determine the technique used to execute these expanses of dots.[5] Among these dots is the print of a complete right hand with joined fingers (ill. 146), in contrast to most of the hand prints from the European Upper Palaeolithic. It gives us the key to the neighbouring dots, which all have a shape identical to that of the palm of this indisputable hand. They are the same size, and they all display the same dislocation of the thumb. Moreover, a little dot above the big one often corresponds to accidental pollution by ochre on the first phalange of

Above
Ill. 62. Little yellow horse heads next to red signs.

the second finger. It thus becomes possible to see which way each print was facing, and to re-create the creators' gestures, although it is not possible to establish the order in which they were made, in the absence of anything being superimposed on them (ill. 156). Close by, two very short lines and a dot made with a brush can be distinguished through their purple-violet colour, which differs from the colour of the palm prints.

A complex panel occupies the opposite wall. The painted elements are small: grouped or aligned series of dots, short lines, indeterminate marks, and three horse heads, two of them yellow (ill. 62). Some yellow

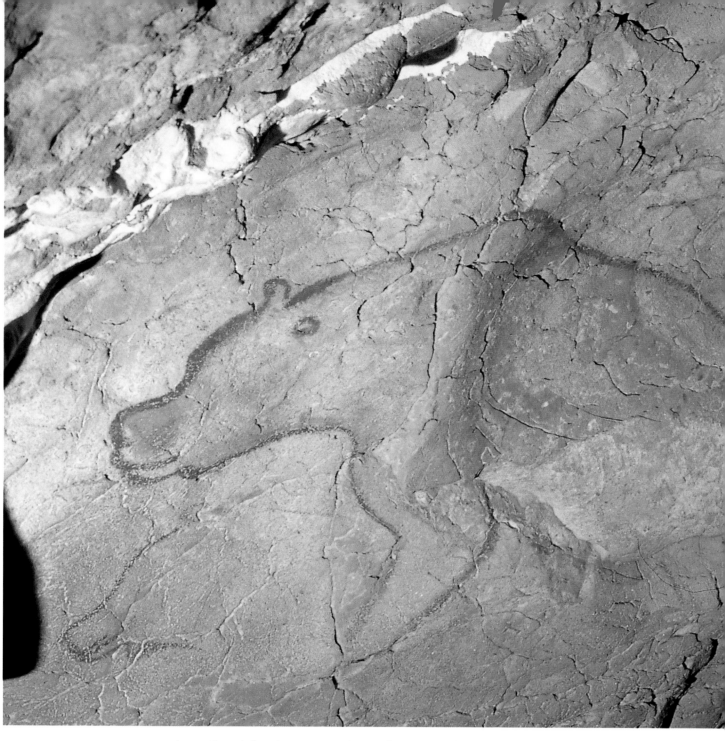

Above
Ill. 63. Three bears painted at the back
of the Recess of the Bears (the first two
are very distorted by the photograph).

marks are found elsewhere on certain panels
of the cave, but these two tiny heads are the
only figurative depictions in this colour.
They seem to have been executed before
the red ochre paintings, as it is possible
to see red marks on the mane of one of
the yellow horses.

The accumulation of simple signs and
the abbreviation and miniaturization
of the figurative depictions make this panel
unique. In general, the artistic expression
is much fuller, even in this red sector.
Moreover, these paintings seem to have
been done quickly with no great care,
using an extremely fluid red paint that
ran in some places.

The Panel of the Dotted Animal

Opposite this alcove, behind a low mass of
concretions, there is another large panel

covered in dots, whose layout evokes the
silhouette of an undetermined animal
(ill. 60). The technique used to apply this
paint is identical to that of the dotted Sacred
Heart Panel, the Panel of the Dominoes or
the Alcove of the Yellow Horses. However,
the creator is not the same, because these
prints, all of them made with the right palm,
are larger than those in the Alcove of the
Yellow Horses, which seem to belong to a
woman or an adolescent. In this instance it is
probably a big man who made the dots. The
hollow of the palm is more pronounced, and
the long, fine fingers, stained with ochre, are
sometimes visible, especially at the top and
front of the panel (ill. 157).

A bear head in right profile, using a
natural fissure, can be made out in the
middle of the dots. To the right, in front of
the dotted animal shape, some fine curved

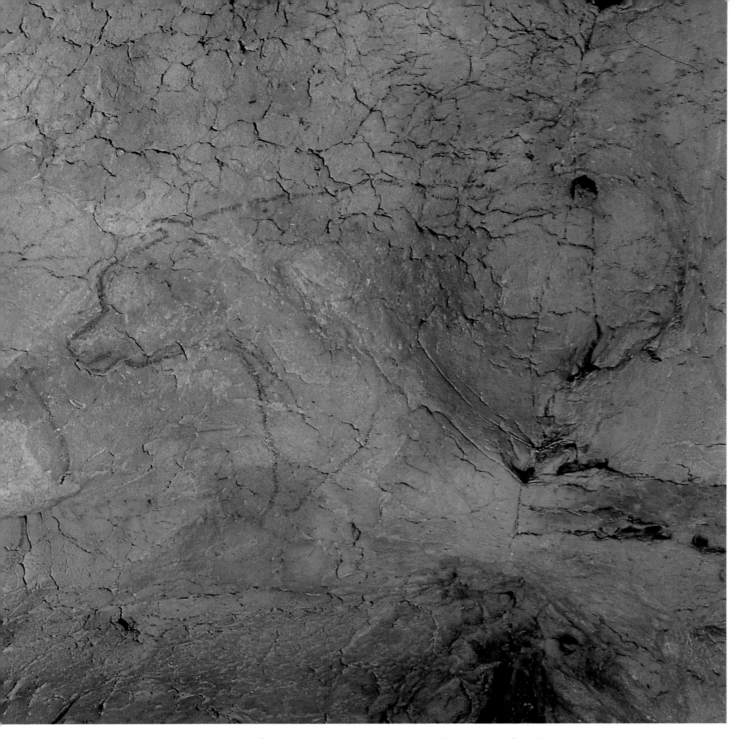

lines may depict the hindquarters of an animal or the front of a mammoth.

It is directly above this panel that the following two collections are found, but, in order to reach them, it is necessary to turn back and move round the central chaos.

The Loggia of the Red Deer

After the chaos, the layout of the wall's concretions forms a kind of small chamber. A large, incomplete cervid is painted here, and at this spot the wall has some calcite flows that are integrated with the animal figure. Only its forequarters are painted.

The head is small and has quite a few details, such as the nostrils, eyes and the mouth. A slight relief provides the shape of the chin and the jaw. Its antlers are short and palmated, and the withers form a slight hump, which bears some

resemblance, albeit slight, to that found on the megaloceros.

The Recess of the Bears

The Loggia of the Red Deer is the route that has to be taken in order to reach the Recess of the Bears, which opens more than 2 m (6½ feet) further down. The entrance corridor, low and of modest proportions, broadens out after a few metres to form a small rotunda. All the figures, which are red, are located here.

Two big bears, as well as the head of a smaller one, follow each other on the wall in a semicircle at the back (ill. 63). The first is complete. The highly developed stop on the forehead identifies it as a cave bear. The wall's contours have been skilfully used to give volume to the front leg and the abdomen. The second is incomplete, as only its forequarters are painted. Here again, the integration of the support with the figure is clear. A hollow in the wall takes the place of the hindquarters and provides a paradoxically complete view of the animal. In front of the chest of the first bear, a small bear head has been sketched. The pigment used for the small head appears 'drier' and is purple-violet, a raw material that is also found in certain parts of the second bear's body. On the right wall, two male ibex, partially painted in red, follow each other; their horns and part of their back line use natural fissures (ills. 64 and 65).

The composition and the theatricality of the layout for these figures seem obvious. This hidden place reveals its decoration

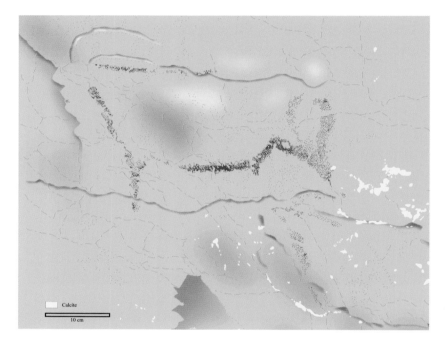

Above
Ill. 64. Tracing of the ibex figures in the Recess of the Bears.

gradually. It only appears in its entirety after one has crossed, in a crouching position, the several metres of the entrance corridor. From the entrance only the front of the first bear can be seen, and it is just gradually, as one approaches, that the second one emerges, apparently from the darkness. As for the ibex, they are only visible when one stands at the back, in the centre of the rotunda.

The Engraved Stoup
After climbing back up to the level of the cervid and following the left-hand wall, one can return to the area of the present-day entrance. It is here, in a somewhat secluded recess, that there is an ancient concretion in

the form of a stoup, on the base of which are engraved two horses (ill. 144). This collection is one of the cave's rare examples of fine-line engravings. To the left of the horses are a few indeterminate engraved marks and a circular sign.

The first horse is limited to the depiction of the head, chest, the start of the front leg, the neck and the back, which is drawn as far as the rump. It is an animal with a large head, a fine long neck, and the start of a slender body. The drawing of the head's outline seems to have been done in one movement, all in one go (forehead, nose, mouth, jaw and cheek). The two lines used for the mane are bolder than those of the outline. The upper line is extended to form an anatomically correct dorsal line, while the lower line is continued in the same proportions, but plunges down to the flank.

The second horse is reduced to the head, which is more massive than the first's, and to the neck. It was engraved after the previous one, and faces the opposite way. The top of its neck cuts through the throat of the first towards the right. The head is almost of 'duck bill' type. Its neck is very curved, as if 'coiled', and its nape underlines the first horse's muzzle. The lines are strongly marked and executed in one go. In contrast to the first animal, the head's outline is not precise, but the mane is detailed, and the individualized hairs are spaced regularly. This engraving may be the depiction of a scene, perhaps two horses nibbling each other's withers. These animals display similar features to those on the horses engraved in the Skull Chamber (ill. 94) or the Gallery of the Crosshatching (ill. 101) and recall the proportions of the horses on the Panel of the Horses.

The Brunel Chamber contains a varied collection of cave art, in which both engravings and paintings are found. All of its painted figures are red, except for a small black feline head. The red animals, bears and a cervid, can be compared with those in neighbouring chambers, especially the bears, which are stylistically very close to the one in the Cactus Gallery (ills. 195 and 196). This chamber's greatest originality lies in the large number of its 'dotted' panels.
Dominique Baffier and Valérie Feruglio

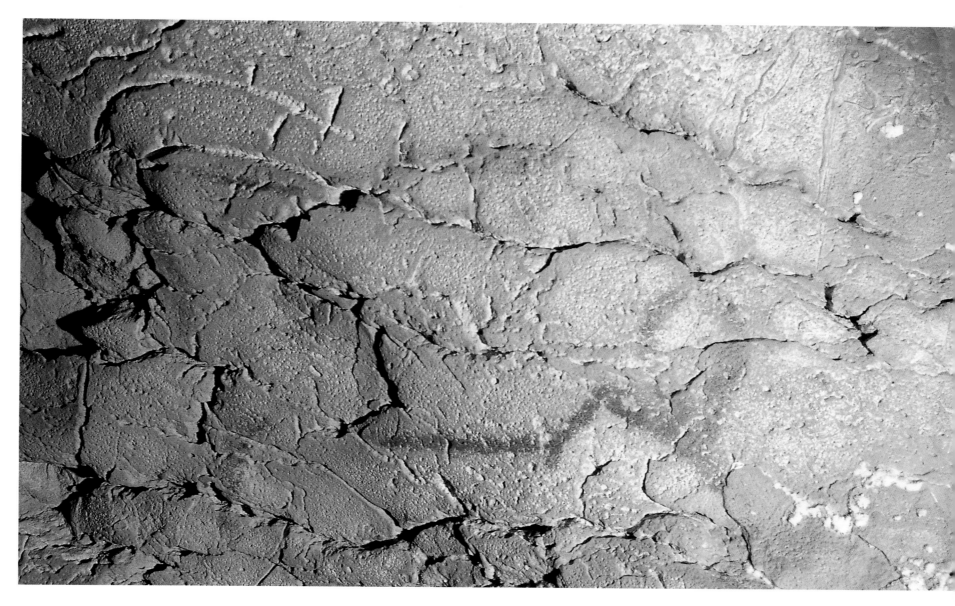

Above

Ill. 65. In the Recess of the Bears, an ibex was drawn in red, making full use of the natural fissures in the rock.

The Cactus Gallery

From the Chamber of the Bear Hollows, the path leads into this gallery on a calcited floor. The hardened film of calcite stops after a few metres, and on the soft clay there remain some bear prints and a few bones. Currently, movement in this area is limited to the path followed by the discoverers, so that most of the walls and the back remain inaccessible and cannot be examined closely.

Just before one goes down into the gallery, the only red figure in the Chamber of the Bear Hollows, on the right wall at eye level, is a rhinoceros head in right profile; its outline incorporates several gaps (ill. 67). Only the base of the horn – albeit the

Fragments of every size have fallen to the floor. The mass of concretions known as the 'Cactus' developed on this collapse, which includes an enormous fragment of stalagmitic floor. A roughly circular space is thus delineated on the floor. While certain huge blocks are scarcely movable, others may have been displaced or set up on edge by the Aurignacians. A flint blade and some plaquettes of raw pigment were deposited in the hollows of one of the blocks. These remains support the hypothesis that this area was adapted by humans. However, according to François Rouzaud, this layout is entirely natural and caused by the floor

Top
Ill. 66. The Cactus Gallery (in pink).

Above
Ill. 67. At the back of the Chamber of the Bear Hollows, just before the Cactus Gallery, on the right wall, there is a stylized rhinoceros head in right profile. One can see its forehead, the beginning of the horns, its muzzle and chest.

determining attribute of the species – is sketched. No use of relief fills in for the interrupted lines.

For the first five metres of the Cactus Gallery the left wall is masked by white or orange-coloured columns, whereas the rest of the gallery is practically devoid of concretions. On the ceiling, traces of extremely ancient fills survive in the form of reddish deposits and stalagmitic floors.

breaking up after the fall of the heaviest fragment from above, which thus determined the tilt of the slabs close by. The debate remains open.

At the gallery's entrance, on a rock pendant (ill. 68), a small red mammoth facing the back is visible and, behind it, a yellow line and five parallel red lines. A little further, three vertical red lines mark the edge of a slight hollow.

At a height of 4 m (13 feet), a very eroded red animal can be interpreted as a bear. It is clear that this figure was deliberately placed in an isolated position: in order to draw it, the artist had to climb the wall, which does provide some easy climbing places, up to a ledge about 1 m (over 3 feet) beneath the animal (ill. 69). Below, a rock shoulder positioned along the gallery's axis sticks out of the wall. On the vertical face of this formation, the artist took advantage of one shoulder to place two mammoths, which make great use of the reliefs of the wall.

Close by, on a vertical rocky protrusion, a brown crook-shaped mark, doubled with black outlines, is cut by a horizontal red line. It can be seen as an original type of sign or as a sketch of a mammoth that would thus form a frieze with the two previous ones; this hypothesis is all the more plausible if the three figures are considered from the back of the gallery. In this sector red signs and a black animal are visible, but cannot be reached.

On the opposite wall, a panel of red paintings is particularly eye-catching. It includes the forequarters of a bear, which, through its stature and the quality of the drawing, dominates the sector (ill. 195). The animal is reduced to an outline, but the sensitivity of the line suggests many details: rounded muzzle, hanging lower lip, curled-up hair beneath the jaw, small round ears. The frontal stop and the carriage of the head identify it as a cave bear. A slight bit of shading spread the paint towards the interior of the outline.

Under this animal's throat, a head with a concave forehead and a small ear has a pointed front leg. After well-marked withers, the back fades away to the right, while the belly is excessively extended and joins up with the forequarters of a feline. The latter's tail and thigh fit the belly of the previous indeterminate animal. The two animals thus seem to be combined into one two-headed creature (ill. 194).

The Last Figure, Placed in Front of the Big Bear, is a Feline

Immediately to the left, after a fault in the wall, begins the second decorated panel, this time in black. Despite the calcite, it is possible to follow the outline of a feline head with a thick muzzle, its mouth half open.

The main figure is a mammoth, 2 m (6½ feet) high. Of its head, only the vertical trunk and the rounded forehead can be made out. The arched belly gives it a lanky appearance. The wall is used to express the volume of the hind leg.

Finally, a figure was placed 4 m (13 feet) above the floor opposite the rock pendant with the little red mammoth, described above. On a pendant from the ceiling a red bear, its back highlighted with black, is clearly visible from the floor of the gallery; but the only way to reach it involves crossing a mass of concretions.

Below the bear, a ledge leading to a crawlway emerges into the niche, close to the red signs. It has not yet been possible to explore this area, which may perhaps contain some human traces.

In total, more than thirty figures have been recorded in this gallery. They include fifteen animal images, eleven of which are identifiable (four mammoths, four felines, three bears). It is notable that there are no rhinoceroses.

As for signs, there are simple marks, short lines in groups of two or three. Three short lines together occur five times (mostly on the right wall). A yellow line on the rock pendant at the entrance can be related to the horse heads in this same colour in the Brunel Chamber.

The layout of the cave art is balanced: animal figures are concentrated on the left side, signs dominate to the right. It is also worth noting that all the animals, except for the red mammoth, emerge from the gallery's depths towards the entrance.

Carole Fritz and Gilles Tosello

Previous page
Ill. 68. The rock pendant of the mammoth, the first figure discovered in the cave, at the entrance of the Cactus Gallery.

Above
Ill. 69. In the Cactus Gallery, the supposed position of the artist when drawing a little red bear, 4 m (over 13 feet) up on the right wall.

The Red Panels Gallery

The deep part of the Chamber of the Bear Hollows is marked by a more modest, trapezoid-shaped extension, the Red Panels Gallery (ill. 70). At its right-hand side, a large stalagmitic mass, together with collapsed blocks, marks its entrance; opposite, a keel-shaped rock blade emphasizes this transition. This sector extends for 30 m (98 feet). Its width varies from 7 to 14 m (from 23 to 45 feet), from the threshold to the entrance of the Rouzaud Chamber, the final axial development of the passage. The ceiling is quite high for the first few metres, but then its height decreases in an irregular fashion towards the back. A large quantity of concretions hang from the walls and floors, as in the Brunel Chamber or the Cactus Gallery, sectors that belong to zones around the Chamber of the Bear Hollows, which itself has no concretions.

The sequences of parietal graphic images occur especially on its right wall, in several panels: in succession, they are Signs, Hand Prints, Hand Stencils, the Little Bear. On the opposite wall, only the first few metres are decorated, with the Panther Panel as their main element. This unequal distribution is caused largely by the morphology of the very irregular support. In fact, a fan-shaped stalagmitic cascade occupies the second third of this area. It is followed by a vast mass of rubble in the final third of the gallery. This is next to the entrance of the Rouzaud Chamber. It is necessary to cross this chaos in order to reach the deep part of the sanctuary.

As an introduction to this sector, two graphic collections of unequal importance are located on the left wall – the Panther Panel and then, slightly to one side, two small groups of residual figures.

The Panther Panel
It is fitted on to a thick rock blade that descends from the ceiling. Its keel-shaped morphology is emphasized by an overhanging profile due to the dip of the geological strata that exceeds 30 degrees as regards the horizontal. This stratified structure has caused some discontinued areas, which have resulted in the wall being cut up into several registers. The surface is hollowed out into broad cavities. These formations placed limits on what the artist could actually do there.

About ten drawings are arranged over an area 5 m (16 feet) long and 1.5 m (nearly 5 feet) high (ill. 71). It is possible to recognize the outlines of three bears, two felines – including the panther – two ibex and three, unidentifiable, incomplete animals. At the base of a wide and deep oblong hollow, a red dot, 8 cm ($3\frac{1}{8}$ in.) in diameter, was made with the palm of the hand, judging by its scalloped edge.

In the centre, the panther and two superimposed bears stand out. The outlines of the bodies are precise, with the ears, the details of the muzzle and the tail. Only the extremities of the legs are missing. Two animals have the part representing the body (inside the outline) filled with spots. It is quite justifiable to see this as an evocation of the coat in the case of the feline, with the spots scattered in a very close representation of reality, above the ventral area. The same cannot be said for the animal immediately above, which can be interpreted as a bear. Its speckles show some resemblance to those of the hyena, but their distribution does not conform to that of the present-day species, in which they are missing on the forequarters. The method used to represent the body here could be attributed to a graphic process and be a substitute for a flat tint, or it could depict fur that is thicker in certain places. The formal analysis of the drawing provides further details: the dorsal line curved at the withers, the presence of a stop marking a break in the nose-line, the relatively heavy forequarters and the massive head – all point towards a cave bear.

These highly developed works provide a contrast with those at the margins of the central group, most of them partial figures whose traits are reduced to essentials but which are nonetheless identifiable, like the second feline drawn under the panel (ill. 72). What is strange is the opposition of the two

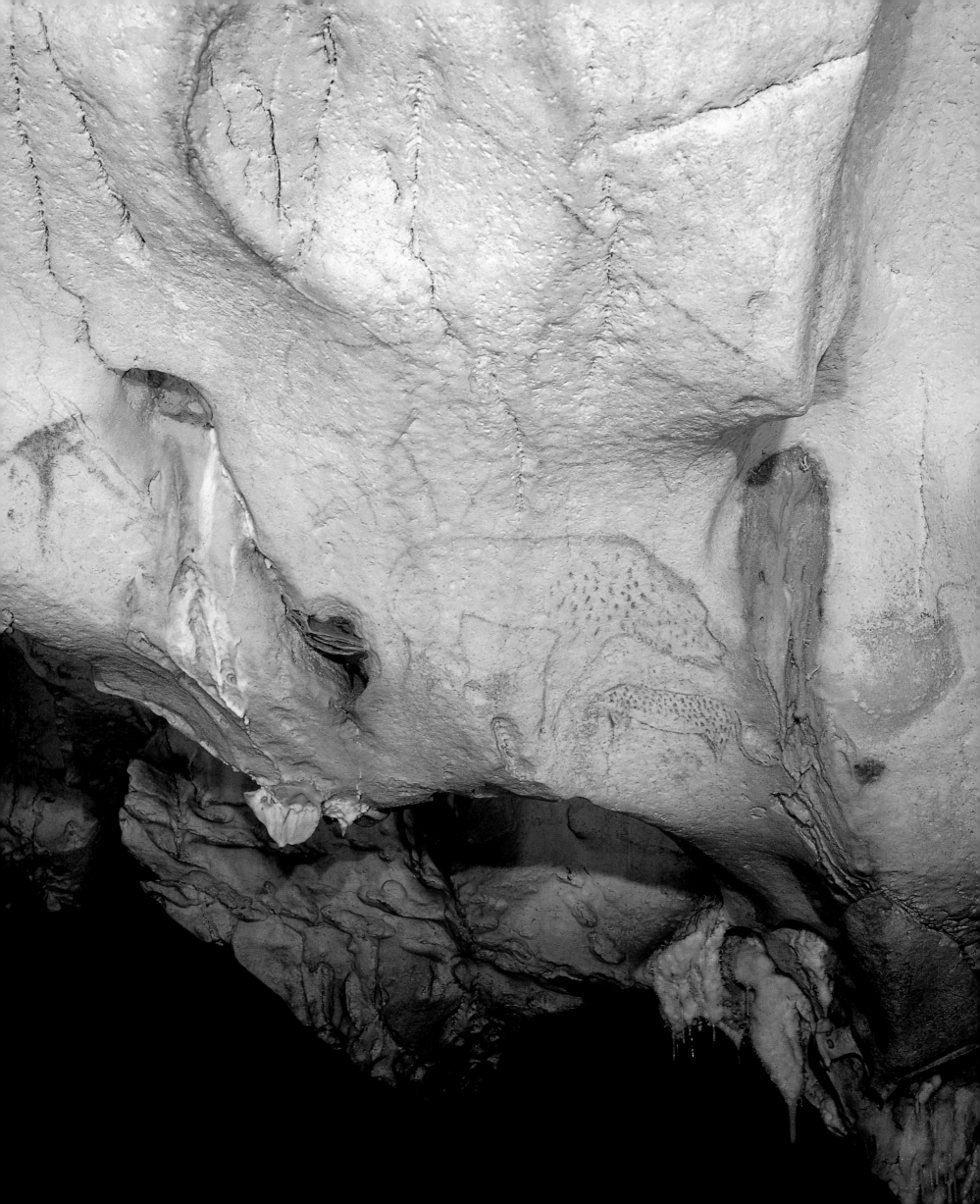

ibex figures, at each extremity of the panel, in which one can recognize the head and horns on the left, and an outline limited to the body on the right.

The numerous rocky ridges between deep cavities contribute to the panel's construction and the direction the figures are facing, particularly those of the ibex and the headless bear.

Four are the result of paw-rubs; a fifth, more precise, reproduces four of the five pads on the front paw, as well as the claws (ill. 47).

A few metres from this major panel, one can see two small groups of figures, one of them comprising engravings of an equid and probable ibex horns, the other drawn in red on an angle of the wall.

The figures are all drawn in red, with a relatively fine line for the bear in the upper register, and a broader line for the two others. It can sometimes evolve into a flat tint, especially where the treatment of the ibex head is concerned. A certain dulling of the colours can be seen because of waterflows, giving these figures a more unobtrusive appearance in comparison with those of the following panels.

Other marks that are visible at the base of the panel are attributable to bears.

These figures have very slender outlines that are difficult to interpret.

On the opposite wall, a passage containing abundant concretions, but no drawings, precedes the long graphic sequence that is announced by the Panel of the Signs.

The Panel of the Signs
It comprises a 4-metre (over 13-foot) length of wall and a stalagmite descending from the ceiling. In fact, the collection of the red signs

Opposite
Ill. 71. The Panther Panel on a keel-shaped rock pendant.

Above
Ill. 72. Newly discovered feline under the edge of the Panther Panel.

can be considered as an introduction to the Panel of Hand Prints and the red rhinoceroses, because the gap between these concentrations of figures is less than 2 m (6½ feet). Some of the works are now buried under calcite.

Following the normal path, one first notices the paintings on the pendant concretion, in easy reach of both hand and eye (ill. 157); besides a small cross and two vertical lines, they comprise two similar signs, in the form of lobes on each side of an axis.

Opposite the pendant, it is easy to make out two collections on the wall. To the right, in a niche at the opening of a low crawl-way that leads to the Cactus Gallery, the intensively leached rock is covered in red or pinkish stains; no shape can be made out here, except for some black marks and fine engravings that evoke the remains of a big animal in right profile.

To the left (ill. 74) the layout begins with some red paintings that are slotted in-between the areas of concretions. When the calcite layer is not too opaque, it is possible to follow the lines painted under the film that covers them; we have been able to count seven double-lobe signs, sometimes flanked by an oblique dash. These specimens recall the sign on the pendant, but the lobes are noticeably more triangular. At the left extremity, on a rock shelf, an engraved animal head is tightly framed on the available surface, which suggests that certain draperies already existed here, even if they were less exuberant than today. With some difficulty one can make out a black animal, emphasized with engravings, that was placed high up; it is probably a bovine (aurochs or bison). In the centre of the panel, a drawing is constructed from a vertical rectangle and six curves that stick out greatly on both sides. The red infill is limited to the bottom two-thirds of the rectangle (ills. 74 and 158).

Some 4 m (13 feet) to the right, in the zone with the most calcite, we have found two red dots and a few engraved lines, indicating the decoration extended much further this way.

Figurative interpretations spring readily to mind for the complex signs: the double-lobe shapes conjure up butterflies or birds in flight; the rectangle looks like an insect,

Above
Ill. 73. The Panel of the Signs.

Opposite
Ill. 74. Mysterious geometric signs that evoke insects.

a millipede or spider. However, the lack of precision in the outline of the 'wings', the absence of a 'head', and the presence of very similar but more geometrical shapes leads us to be very circumspect about any zoological or even figurative interpretation, and to classify these paintings with the abstract motifs. It is worth remembering that it is by no means rare, in any decorated caves, to find thematic spaces reserved for signs.[6]

The Panel of Hand Prints

After the Panel of the Signs, the form of the wall becomes more regular, and the areas with calcite more modest, with a few rare veins and a more massive formation at the foot of the central part of the panel.

Above

Ill. 75. Hand prints, a semicircle of dots, and felines on the Panel of Hand Prints.

The panel extends over 12 metres (40 feet) in length. From the floor upwards, the wall comprises a subvertical segment – surmounted by a joint – then a major overhanging passage, followed by a ridge and the beginning of the ceiling; a second horizontal joint links these last two features.

The smooth wall is scored by a few fissures, with no dominant orientation.

Its base displays areas polished by bears, especially on the right.

Very close to this panel, several stone blocks were brought together by humans. They form an artificial heap that has no obvious explanation (ill. 51).

Despite the remarkable quality of the support, not all of the available wall area was used. The figures are more numerous in the first part of the panel. This corresponds to the overhanging area, and it is only decorated, beyond the halfway axis, by two broad clusters of big red dots, using a similar technique to the one found in the Brunel Chamber, but with a looser distribution. A frieze of five rhinoceroses constitutes the graphic link between the two panels (ill. 76). It is fitted into the top part of the overhang, on a short frontal angle of the wall. A W-shaped sign has been inserted between the last two elements of this frieze.

To the right, the figures are relatively numerous and varied, with six motifs represented unequally. The felines dominate (seven heads and a complete animal). The other animals – horse, mammoth, rhinoceros – only have a single individual each. The rhinoceros, although affected by waterflows, dominates in this context. Several hands, five prints (ill. 75) and two stencils, occupy the centre of this collection. They are underscored by a line made of about ten dots. On the right-hand side of this concentration, a circular figure drawn with a fine line is bordered, both outside it and in the upper semicircle, by a line of twelve little dots, regularly spaced.

In the upper left part of the panel, several painted sketches and marks are lined up in a horizontal series. In succession, one sees a vertical zigzag line, a W-shaped sign (both of these are red), an undetermined figure, and the sketched outline of a rhinoceros (these are the only black figures on this panel), and then, beyond, a hook-shaped line and a cluster of little dots.

This panel's originality lies in the repetition of the motifs, whether figurative or schematic. This is the case with the five rhinoceroses aligned as a horizontal series, the frieze of feline heads, on the right-hand side, the hand prints and dots: in clusters, in a semicircle, or juxtaposed on a polygonal line.

The rhinoceros frieze foreshadows the organization into friezes of the figures that we shall encounter several times in the second part of the cave.

The Panel of Hand Stencils
It occupies a rock blade, a kind of partition, on the back of which is the Panel of the Little Bear. To the right, the wall protrudes as an overhang above the floor. Its surface is affected by several veins of calcite. Conversely, to the left, the concretions are more extensive, and the original rock can

over a length of 4m (13 feet) and a height of only 90 cm (35 in.; ill. 78). At the other extremity, in two juxtaposed cavities with somewhat leached walls, two very weathered drawings remain unidentifiable.

Apart from those drawings, the subjects comprise three red hand stencils, two clusters of dots, and two black animals, an equid and a mammoth. Another black figure, located very close to the central hand stencil, remains unidentified.

Two of the hand stencils are placed inside the outlines of these animals: one on the

only be seen in two hollows. The regularity of the fine-grained support is only disturbed by fossils that protrude slightly.

Most of the decoration occupies the middle and upper registers of the panel,

equid's hindquarters, the other on the flank of the proboscidian. Studies have enabled us to establish that the mammoth was drawn before the hand (ill. 77). The animal is reduced to its trunk and the neck line extended by a short dorsal line, with some very slender marks on both sides of the frontal segment; the right-hand mark, which forms a curve, may depict a tusk.

The drawing of the horse is more complete: head and neck, dorsal line, rump and beginning of the back legs; the tail blends into the wall, through the effects of waterflow. The sketch of the right back leg follows a black line, like the other segments of the figure, but it is extended by an engraved or, more exactly, a scraped line.

In the collection of dots to the left of these drawings, one can see two distinct clusters, differentiated not only by the number of units they comprise, but also by their distribution and their colour. The left cluster has a structure made up of a series of dots, in three vertical lines comprising a sequence of three, then two, then three impacts, some of them circular, but most of them oblong. The construction of the second cluster seems more random, with graphic units of larger diameter. The pigment used is purplish.

The Panel of the Little Bear

On the other side of the Panel of Hand Stencils is the opening to a low gallery with an entrance in the form of an alcove. Within this recess, several red figures were drawn: a bear (ill. 79), a red deer, some residual marks – dot and dashes – and an animal sketch.

There are no concretions here. However, the same network of oblique and vertical fissures can be seen as on the previous panel. The difference in rock texture is caused by the presence of fossiliferous veins, several centimetres thick, which cross the middle part of the panel.

One of the strata underscores a drawing of a bear that is small – 32 cm (12⅝ in.) long by 18 cm (7⅛ in.) high – in relation to the other bear figures in the cave, although it is similar to them in every respect, both in the technique of its lines and in its feeling of animation.

In front of the bear, a small cervid head is visible. The antlers are short, and the facial angle acute. Two converging lines mark the position of one of the front legs, 20 cm (7⅞ in.) below the head. The link between these two segments is provided by an oblique fissure which, from the animal's neck, makes

Above
Ill. 77. Red hand stencil and partial outline of a black mammoth.

Opposite
Ill. 78. The Panel of Hand Stencils.

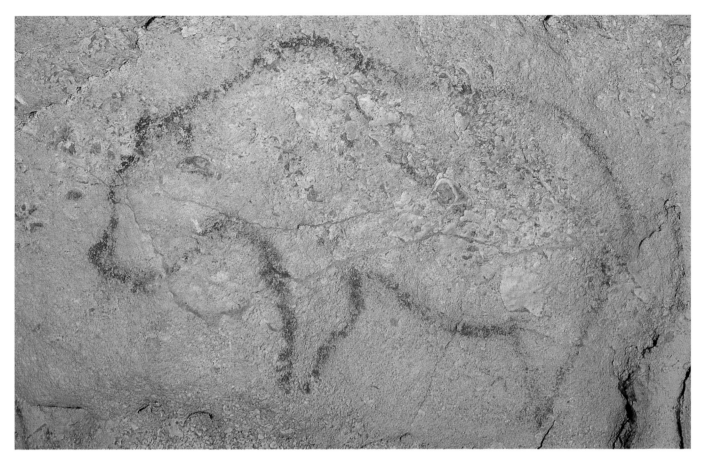

Above
Ill. 79. The Panel of the Little Bear behind the Panel of Hand Stencils.

Below
Ill. 80. The Rouzaud Chamber (in pink).

the chest and then the ventral line materialize. The network of horizontal fissures contributes to the construction of this figure by extending the head by the neck, then the withers and the back. This is one of the most striking examples that exists of the use of reliefs. The wall plays a major role in this drawing.

Some 60 cm (23 in.) in front of the red deer an unobtrusive red stain can be seen and, below it, 80 cm (31 in.) from the distal extremity of the front leg, another drawing could be a second bear, with a ventral line and a leg at each extremity. On the right-hand part of the panel, only a dash and a curved line survive.

The Red Panels Gallery ends the first part of the cave, and marks the transition to the deep areas of the network. Beyond here, engravings and then black figures take the place of the red drawings that have been so very predominant until now.

Norbert Aujoulat and, for 'The Panel of the Signs', Carole Fritz and Gilles Tosello

The Rouzaud Chamber

The natural progression into the Red Panels Gallery leaves to one side, on the left, the low ceiling that enables the visitor to enter the Candle Gallery, and then to skirt the Panel of Hand Stencils (ill. 81) and enter the Rouzaud Chamber.[7] The floor rapidly rises, and it is no longer possible to stand upright. A big chamber extends northwards through a gallery made up of a succession of gours. It is the most humid sector of the cave; water frequently gets in here. It is one of the rare places where it is possible to envisage a continuation of the gallery that was accessible to Palaeolithic people, but is now blocked by the thick recent calcite that covers the floor. The prehistoric artists penetrated this gallery, and left on its right wall the black mark of the dorsal line of an unidentified animal, associated with traces of pigment that are blurred or covered by a film of beautiful white calcite.

Yanik Le Guillou

The Candle Gallery

The Candle Gallery's floor is more than 1.5 m (5 feet) lower than that of the previous chamber. The topography – like the archaeology – separates them, and makes this the beginning of the second part of the cave. It starts immediately after the threshold and provides access to the Hillaire Chamber. It is irregular and measures 20 m (65 feet) along its main axis. The ceiling is high in places, and very low elsewhere, and the contorted walls have numerous concretions of different ages that make the passageway smaller; among the active, sparkling ones that did not exist at the time of the prehistoric visitors is a stalagmite that gave the gallery its name.

The floor is often covered with calcite. Some bear hollows, paw prints, clawmarks and bones, including some skeletons still anatomically connected, bear witness to bears having stayed here. Visits by people took place in the chamber's principal axis, which is marked at its low extremities by reddish dots and marks. Numerous torch wipes and residues, as well as a small heap of charcoal covered by six plaques of limestone that were brought here (ill. 37), have made it possible to obtain radiocarbon dates. A fragment of stalagmite floor was picked up by the prehistoric people and placed at the entrance of the Hillaire Chamber (ill. 39). Although there were numerous accessible and regular surfaces, only a single animal figure can be seen. This small, quite crude mammoth head, imprinted into the limestone's weathering layer on a rock pendant that was within easy reach, foreshadows the white drawings of the Hillaire Chamber: the Candle Gallery is thus a veritable antechamber of the richly decorated deep network. This contrast between a decorated sector and a merely frequented zone had already been recognized in the Ardèche, in the Grotte des Deux-Ouvertures.

Bernard Gély

Above
Ill. 81. The entrance of the Rouzaud Chamber. To the right, the Panel of Hand Stencils.

Left
Ill. 82. The Candle Gallery (in pink).

The Hillaire Chamber, Around the Large Collapse

The Hillaire Chamber measures about 30 m (100 feet) in diameter. The entrance, from the present-day access, is low; the ceiling has few concretions and is up to 17 m (56 feet) in height. Three chambers and galleries converge here. In the centre, a depression has created a collapse of the fill that is 10 m (32 feet) in diameter and 4 m (13 feet) deep. This subsidence partly postdates the decoration, because some figures are now located above the void.

The circular appearance of this chamber is suggested by the concentric distribution of alluvial banks. Humans left some traces of their visits on the floor, especially towards the entrance: wood charcoal, a block brought here to serve as a step (ill. 39), and others piled up further on.

The walls and ceiling display numerous indentations and step faults that are very smooth in shape. The surfaces are sometimes naturally stained with light-brown and vermiculated clay. In places, the limestone of the walls, weathered to a depth of several millimetres, unctuous and perfectly white, is suitable for working with a finger or a tool.[8] Some drawings in wood charcoal, below the entrance of the Megaloceros Gallery, can be linked to this collection.

The decoration is mostly limited to the areas where it is easy to move around,[9] and at both sides of the entrance. The parietal layout is divided into sectors, one of them on the left wall (ill. 85), the others in the axis of the present path towards the next part of the network.

Sector I, On the Left

Two panels, with an equal amount of decoration, converge towards an area with few engravings or paintings that is marked with fragments of stalagmitic floor piled up by humans, without any obvious link with a particular decorated surface. The decoration is at eye level. The figures, including twenty-eight animals, are engraved with a finger or made by scraping. A few torch wipes can be

Above
Ill. 83. The Hillaire Chamber (in pink).

Right
Ill. 84. Forequarters of an aurochs engraved as if it were emerging from the hollow in the rock.

Opposite
Ill. 85. The left wall just before the Large Collapse has many rock pendants whose soft surface was covered with numerous engravings.

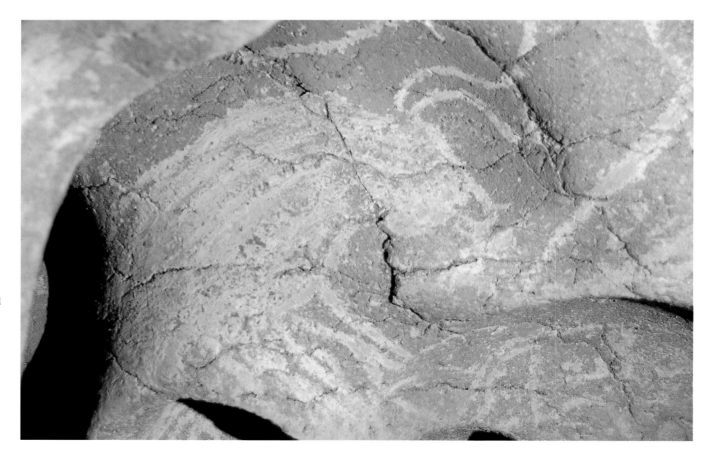

seen, especially in the first few metres, at the opening of the Candle Gallery, a passage that is marked by a small red dot.

The Panel of the Rhinoceroses
It is made up of fairly broad engravings, with twelve animals, spread over a length of about 6 m (19 feet), on four planes: three rock blades come down from the ceiling, offset from each other and parallel to the wall, which is itself decorated. The fairly marked erosion makes it impossible for the moment to know in which order the complex figures were produced. The non-animal drawings tend to occur in the upper and lower registers, whereas the animals are at eye level, which argues in favour of a general organization of the layout in three friezes parallel to the floor. The best place from which to see the whole panel would be the centre of the chamber.

The first rock blade bears two succinct tangled-up mammoths, while the second has three interwoven animals. A scraped bear is the largest figure on the panel. The forequarters of an aurochs emerges from the dark, an illusion that is reinforced by the whiteness of its body, which is likewise scraped (ill. 84). A mammoth with its tusks pointing upward faces it; below, a rough aurochs head is in an apse. On the third blade, four clearly individualized rhinoceroses follow each other and recall the red frieze on the Panel of Hand Prints. On the chamber wall, a large rhinoceros emerges from the back of an alcove (ill. 86).[10] Its head is drawn carefully, and on the belly some vertical scraped lines recall the enigmatic stripe known on other animals of this species.

The Intermediate Zone
The intermediate zone corresponds to some pendants from the ceiling, towards which the principal panels converge. It is not possible to obtain an overall view of the decoration, which is not high up and is very unobtrusive, consisting basically of curves, and series or clusters of lines. The animal figures are: a possible bear head, its muzzle pointing downwards, placed on an evocative and central pendant; the cervico-dorsal line of a small mammoth; and, evoked by

a surface whitened by scraping, the head of a horse whose nose seems natural.

The Panel of the Engraved Horse
Made up of engravings and finger tracings, including thirteen animals, it covers the wall for a length of more than 6 m (19 feet; ill. 88).[11] The figures are within easy reach from the present floor, which was originally clay. This panel, as long and as rich as the Panel of the Rhinoceroses, is more complex, with numerous overlaps. The drawings are remarkably well preserved. The artists exploited both the clay film and the weathered limestone. The stigmata caused during production can be seen: the direction and order in which the marks were executed, excess material pushed to the edges of the lines, residual grooves, accidental touches by fingers. At the level of the large horse's chest, the clay film was lightly rubbed to avoid having the underlying white show through. This peculiarity will be seen again in figures on the Owl Panel.

Finally, some animals are tangled up or linked, with some segments in common. This work, which was originally quite simple, was disturbed by later acts – by scraping, which destroyed some of it, and by adding three schematic mammoths. The animals face left; a large horse is framed, on the right, by two mammoths and, on the left, by a couple of bison and another figure that was rendered unidentifiable.[12] The small horses of the lower register also seem to have been added at a later date.

To the left, a crude mammoth is in a vertical position, which is rare in this cave. Some vestigial traces, including two ball-shaped feet, disappear beneath some large scraped surfaces. The same applies to a couple of bison that are following each other. An indented circle was later engraved on the back of the second. Three mammoths, reduced to simple cervico-dorsal lines made with the finger, are superimposed. The third, the highest, seems to be the last figure to have been drawn on the left section of the panel.

Next, a big horse gives the panel its name. The care given to its head and neck contrasts strongly with the rest of the body, which is not drawn as well. This difference in treatment recalls that which can be seen on the equids in the Panel of the Horses. Two big mammoths are nested, with a shared ventral line forming a deep arch.

On the lower register, three cervico-dorsal lines of horses evoke the little yellow heads of the Brunel Chamber. The left wall then bends. It is covered with bear clawmarks, on which some long, sinuous vertical lines have been engraved, a reminder of the clawmarks that probably inspired them (ill. 87).

Sector II, in the Axis of the Path

It comprises the pendants from the ceiling in the axis of the path, over a length of 10 m (over 32 feet) and within easy reach from the present floor. The drawings, often covered by a veil of calcite, were made with broad scraped lines and finger tracings, with big sinuous lines. The sixteen animals recognized are nine mammoths, two or three horses, a rhinoceros, an ibex, an owl (ill. 90) and one indeterminate. The organization of the parietal layout is less obvious than in Sector I, but seems to comprise two collections.

The first is especially visible in the direction one walks, over a length of 3 m (9 ¾ feet), with three mammoths and an ibex, the latter also whitened by scraping. Several signs (cross associated with dots, double-lobe signs similar to that in the Panel of Hand Prints, alignment of thirteen small vertical commas) and some pairs of torch wipes characterize this group.

The second comprises ten animals, the biggest in the sector, located on both sides of a vast upward sweep of the ceiling. Here again there is a balanced organization in two panels that converge towards undecorated but accessible surfaces. As for Sector I, the best viewpoint must have been in the centre of the chamber.

To the left of the path, three parallel rock blades were engraved facing the back of the chamber. The animals are spread out, which makes it easy to see them.

On the first blade, after a small red dot, a big animal was obtained by shallow scraping; as its head is missing, its identification remains risky, but, on its trunk, four vertical scraped lines recall the stripe noted on the big rhinoceros on the

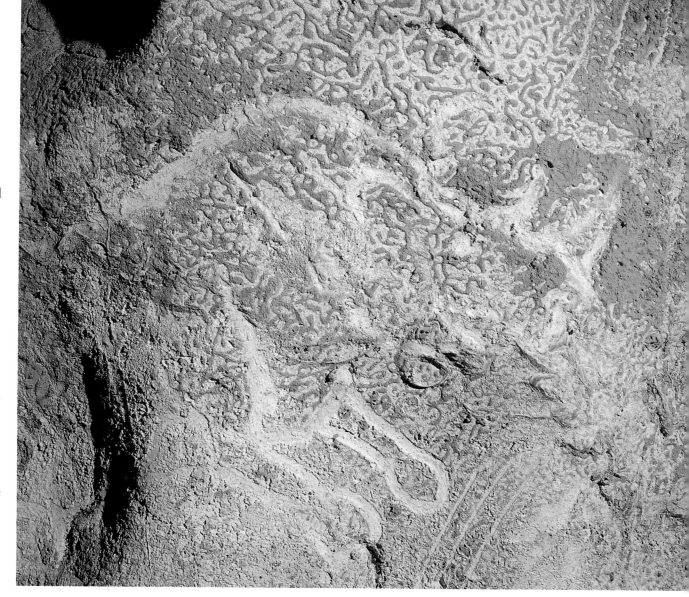

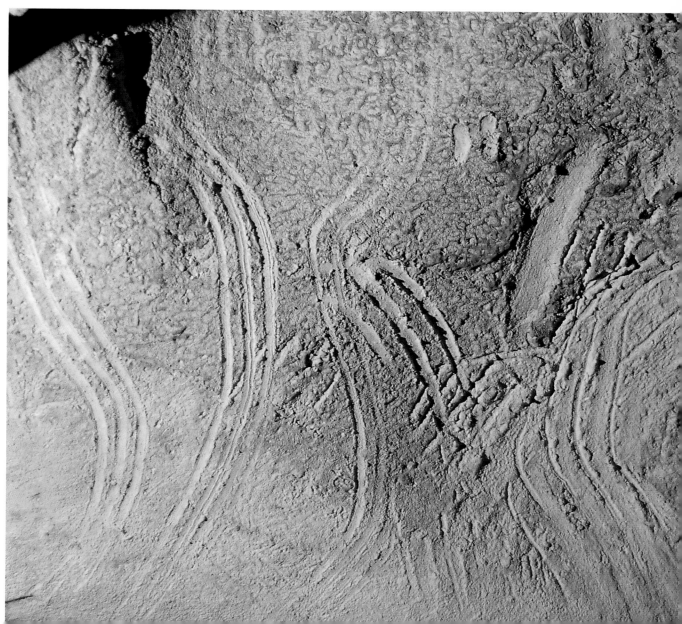

Panel of the Rhinoceroses. Finally, a horse head is not very detailed.

The second blade is decorated over a length of 5 m (16 feet). A scraped mammoth is overlapped by two others, which are reduced to cervico-dorsal lines. From there, the figures, including the owl (ill. 90) and a small mammoth, are above the void.

The third rock blade is the furthest from the observer. A superb horse is drawn with the finger; it has a 'duck-bill' muzzle and its erect mane is indicated by a succession of little dashes perpendicular to the neck.

The Panel of the Scraped Mammoths comprises five animals to the right of the path: a big rhinoceros with a massive shoulder presents a contrast between the lightness of the scraped rock and the sepia of the untouched wall; a possible horse and

an indeterminate animal are next to it; elsewhere, two mammoths follow each other towards the end of the chamber.

Sector III, in the Extension of Sector II
A simple transition to the abundant works found a little further on, this sector has hardly any engravings or paintings. Its vestigial decoration, the victim of erosion and clawmarks, is linear like that in the start of Sector II. The figures are far apart, although the rock was well suited to being worked without difficulty. Some engravings are located at more than 3.50 m ($11\frac{1}{2}$ feet) above the floor (which has not changed) and thus pose the problem of the tool used (pole, spear?). Three black animals announce the following panels (entrance to the Megaloceros Gallery, Reindeer Panel and

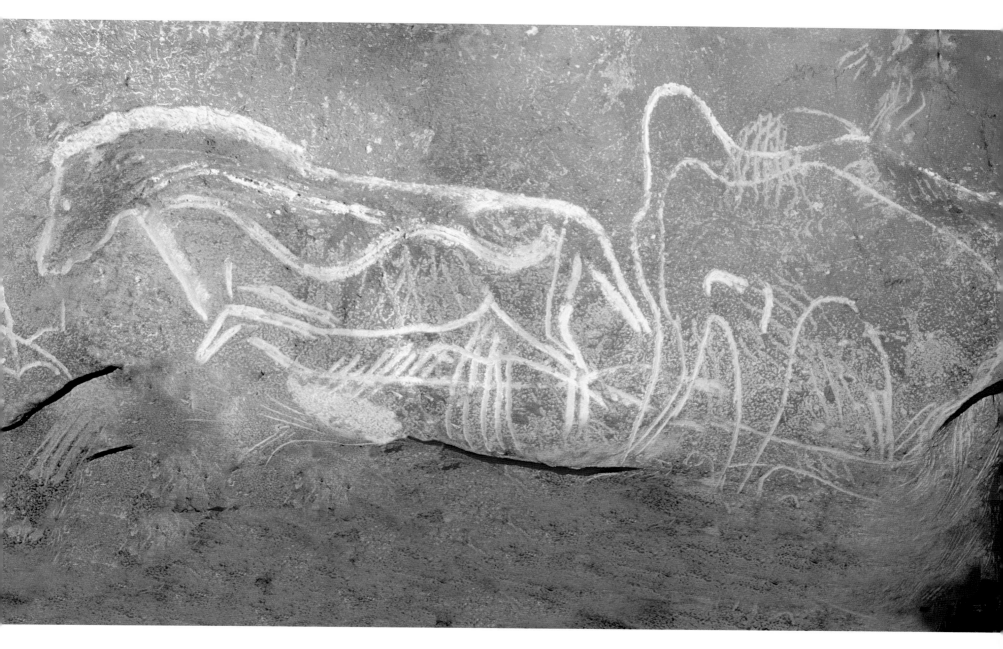

Panel of the Horses). Contrary to Sectors I and II, all these black drawings are visible from a point located towards the zone of the Big Blocks.

A fine black bear was produced as a stump drawing on the facets of a ceiling pendant, which gives the animal volume (ill. 91). Among some clawmarks, the engraved forequarters of a headless animal can be made out. The cervico-dorsal line of a black mammoth is stumped. In front of the entrance of the Megaloceros Gallery, a red dash marks the end of this sector.

In conclusion, out of about 100 graphic units, 49 animal figures have been counted. The animals depicted are varied (8 species) with a clear predominance of mammoths (20 individuals, that is 40%), then rhinoceroses (6 or 12%) and horses

(between 4 and 6 individuals). The absence of felines and cervids is noteworthy, especially as they are plentiful on the other side of the chamber. It is also worth noting the almost total absence of drawings (one possible black feline) on the long left wall of the Hillaire Chamber, perpendicular to Sector I.

After the red drawings in the first part of the cave, almost all the animal figures in this area were engraved before arriving at the black depictions in the rest of the cave. The distribution of the works here is diametrically opposed in terms of colour: white drawings distributed at the entrance, and black drawings at the end of the chamber. This kind of contrast can also be seen on the walls of the Skull Chamber.

Norbert Aujoulat and Bernard Gély

Above

Ill. 88. Panoramic photograph of the Panel of the Engraved Horse, in which the engravings are superimposed on bear clawmarks.

Opposite

Ill. 89. View of the Panel of the Engraved Horse, with, in the foreground, the Large Collapse.

Opposite

Ill. 90. The long-eared owl was engraved full face, whereas its body is seen from the back (feathers and wings).

Above

Ill. 91. This bear is one of the rare black figures in this area.

Double page overleaf

Ill. 92. General view of the Skull Chamber.

The Skull Chamber

After walking round the Large Collapse in the centre of the Hillaire Chamber, one arrives in the Skull Chamber. It differs from the previous chamber in a very distinct reduction in the height of the ceiling at the entrance. The left wall is only partially visible, masked by a rocky mass, the Big Blocks. A sparkling white calcite, which forms high stalagmites in places, has developed on these blocks on to which Palaeolithic people climbed to draw a mammoth by finger on the ceiling.

On the right, one's eye is drawn by a summarily engraved bison head that precedes three black and engraved mammoths. The following part of the composition develops on rock pendants. From afar it is possible to make out two big reindeer drawn in black and with stumping, and another one that is smaller and less detailed. These animals are identifiable from their thick dewlap, their well-developed antlers and their pronounced withers. On the extension of the rock blade, two mammoths with long trunks face each other. The left one only has its forequarters drawn. The second, to the right, has a head and dorsal line drawn in black, with stumping on the head; it is the only one

with tusks. If one steps back a little, one can see another rock pendant on which a black drawing appears very damaged. It is a reindeer, but one can only make out its antlers, the dewlap and the dorsal line, below some red marks. This collection is covered with incisions that were apparently made by finger on decomposed limestone (ill. 94). In this tangle, a succinct horse head can be recognized in right profile and, below it, the left profile of a simply sketched mammoth. It is clear that the aim of this phase of production was to obliterate the pre-existing reindeer.

Continuing towards the back of the chamber, one sees – again, on rock pendants several metres above the floor – a mammoth in left profile, which is unusual in being depicted with its coat, and a big lion; both of them are engraved. Practically at the entrance of the Gallery of the Crosshatching, on the left wall, there is a very rare depiction of a musk ox, easily identifiable because of its horns pointing downwards (ill. 199) and, close by, some black drawings that are too far out of reach to be identified (ill. 171).

The Skull Chamber resembles an amphitheatre, the 'tiers' being made up of banks of grey clay that seem to surround it on all sides. In fact, a low passage leads to the Gallery of the Crosshatching. The maximum height of these banks indicates the original floor level, which, over the millennia, has gradually sunk down in this part of the cave; this process is clearly visible at the foot of the first panels on

Below
Ill. 95. Bear skull placed on purpose on a stone that had fallen from the ceiling in the Skull Chamber.

Below
Ill. 96. In the niche immediately after the Panel of the Horses, in the Skull Chamber, a horse head was sketched very roughly, with the end of a torch, on top of an engraved aurochs facing left.

Opposite
Ill. 97. The niche of the ibex and aurochs (left) and the niche of the Panel of the Horses (right), when water starts to enter the Skull Chamber.

the right wall, whose base is more than 40 cm (15¾ in.) above the present floor. A crust of orange-red calcite, of variable thickness, today covers the Skull Chamber's floor. Some gours occupy the largest part of it, forming little islets of grey clay all over the place, some of which preserve animal and human prints.

On the clay banks, there are surviving bear traces, human prints coming from the Gallery of the Crosshatching and, in a small

In the chamber's centre, a skull placed on the flat surface of a block fallen from the ceiling provides a startling spectacle in the light of the lamps (ills. 95, 204 and 205).

On the right wall, made up of protrusions and alcoves that have been heavily clawed by bears, several surfaces are occupied by drawings made vigorously with a finger: in the first recess, on the other side of the Panel of the Horses, a group of ibex (ill. 200); opposite, two aurochs and a horse head (ill. 96), sketched with wood charcoal in three movements, which resembles its fellow at the base of the Reindeer Panel. On moving a few metres forward, one can admire the Panel of the Scraped Mammoths, which extends for more than 4 m (13 feet) in length and 2 m (6½ feet) in height. Scraped on the soft rock with sweeping gestures, three mammoths face each other, with natural pillars evoking their massive limbs (ill. 98); the one on the left is drawn in a dynamic pose, its hindquarters raised, its tail up, as if it were leaping above a niche.[13] In contrast, the two pachyderms that face it seem motionless. This monumental collection is in an extraordinarily fresh state: the pushed-up material can be seen along the edges of the lines, and white particles that fell while it was being created are still in place on the floor below the wall. A few metres to the right, on the rock pendants that hang from the ceiling,

Double page overleaf
Ill. 98. The Panel of the three big Scraped Mammoths, in the Skull Chamber.

depression, the coprolites of a wolf whose paws have left clear impressions in the hardened clay a few metres before. Many bear skulls and bones can be seen, some of them almost drowned in the concretions.

there are some engraved depictions, inaccessible at present, including an ibex (ill. 187), a very schematic horse head and some indeterminate marks.

Carole Fritz and Gilles Tosello

The Gallery of the Crosshatching

Top

Ill. 99. At the back of the
Gallery of the Crosshatching,
this horse and these two mammoths
were sketched on the ceiling.

Above

Ill. 100. The Gallery of the
Crosshatching (in pink).

After climbing the two high steps that enable
the visitor to reach this gallery, the path
naturally leads along the axis of a roof
channel, under which it is more convenient
to walk than in the low parts to the sides.
The marks on the ceiling or on rock
pendants are concentrated in this easier
passage, and in the only two chambers
where it is possible to stand upright.

Some 3 m (about 10 feet) from the
gallery's entrance, the ceiling rises between
two rock pendants, providing an area in
which to circulate that is much wider
(12 m; 39 feet) than it is long (4 m; 13 feet).
On the two pendants that face each other,
perpendicular to the gallery's axis, there is a
great deal of evidence that prehistoric people
passed by. There are torch wipes, black lines
and lines incised into the very eroded rock,
and a few big lines, some of which could
be the remains of three or four realistic
drawings. Overhanging the natural path, at
a place where the visitor has to stoop in order
to continue, the base of a pendant is marked
with a horizontal alignment of seven little
red dots, next to a series of almost twenty
black dots. Twelve metres (39 feet) further
on, it is possible to stand up again on
emerging into the cave's final chamber. Here
too, there are numerous black marks and
incisions. At the back of the gallery, the
slanting ceiling almost reaches down to the
floor. This is where the only real decorated

panel of this gallery can be found. Perhaps
the artist deliberately wanted to draw at
the far end of the cave, or perhaps he or she
simply chose, out of the walls of this gallery,
the only large flat surface that was easily
accessible, or perhaps it was a bit of both?

The wall is covered with a fine yellow
coating, the result of an ancient
decomposition of the rock surface that
then broke up into numerous little
vermiculations. The spotted surface was in
an identical state when the drawings were
made. It was on this soft surface that an artist
– probably just one – used a finger to draw
a big horse (ill. 101), near more schematic
mammoths, and with a few additional lines
(ill. 99). The technique is always the same:
a finger, and, more frequently, two fingers
joined in the same gesture; in two cases, it
may be all four fingers of the hand; the lines
can go from left to right, or vice versa, but
always from top to bottom. Despite several
resumptions, there is an obvious mastery in
these movements. No error was possible,
because nothing could be rubbed out
without destroying the soft support.
The artist's position, which was the same
as the present-day visitor's, was scarcely
comfortable. The wall slants, with a slight
overhang. The height of the drawings above
the floor required the work to be carried
out sometimes kneeling or crouching, and
sometimes upright, but with the head always

bent backwards; and while the drawing was being done, it was never possible to have an overall view of the panel.

The horse faces right, and is about 1.30 m (over 4 foot) long and 0.70 m (2 foot) high. The join of the head to the neck is very narrow. The drawing was constructed from that point, from which there is a divergence of a line for the mane and the back line, a double line for the chest going down to the bottom of the front legs, a line for the nose, and a double line for the well-marked cheek. The two front legs were added with four double lines, but no difference in plane makes it possible to distinguish them. Only the back leg in the foreground is depicted. Apart from a few lines that perhaps depict the mane, the animal is reduced to its simple outline.

Under these two animals, and drawn after the previous one, a second mammoth faces right. A few details differentiate it from most of the mammoths in the cave. The cervico-dorsal line is not done in one go, but with a first line for the back and a second for the head. The multiple vertical lines drawn on the head could represent hairs.[14]

The other two mammoths are simply shown by their cervico-dorsal line. They frame the composition: one, at top right, faces right, the other, at top left, faces left.

It is uncertain how this panel can be integrated into the cave's homogeneous Aurignacian universe. Associated with a few scattered drawings,[15] it could be the only decorated composition that can be linked to the final phase of human activity, perhaps in the Gravettian.[16]

A sketch of a mammoth faces the horse, drawn before it and at the same height. This is a simple cervico-dorsal line and a probably ventral arch that is somewhat off-centre. On its body, a big sign in the form of a horizontal arch was drawn in one sweep, from the right lower extremity to the right upper extremity.

Apart from this decorated panel, this gallery stands out for having preserved, under large expanses of low ceilings, a Palaeolithic floor on which traces of human visits have been protected from destruction by bears or the discovery of the cave.

Yanik Le Guillou

Above
Ill. 101. Big engraved horse in the Gallery of the Crosshatching.

The Horse Sector

Located more than 190 m (624 feet) from the present entrance, a group of about fifty animal figures marks the transition between the Megaloceros Gallery and the Skull Chamber (ill. 52). It is therefore situated within the field of vision of any visitor moving towards the back of the cave,

urge one to leave the Megaloceros Gallery to the right. This is precisely what happened during the first exploration, which explains the fact that the End Chamber was discovered a week after the Horse Sector.

This cave art triptych, mostly made up of black figures, unfolds over about 15 m

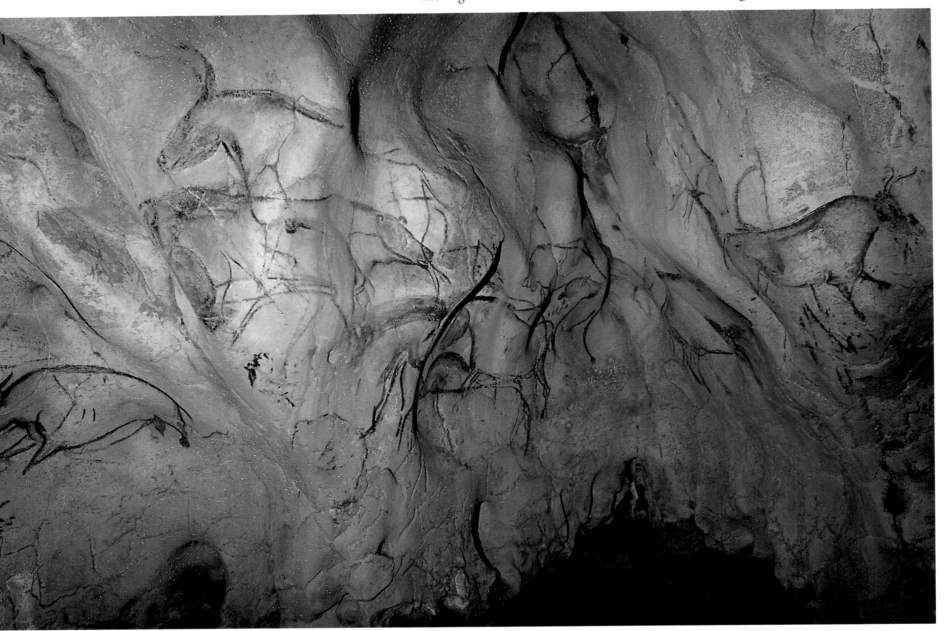

Above

Ill. 102. The Horse Sector: the Alcove of the Lions with its irregular walls marks the centre of the three-panel composition, with the horses on the left and the reindeer on the right.

whether towards the End Chamber or towards the Gallery of the Crosshatching. The drawings stand out against the light rock background and are visible from a distance of more than 30 m (99 feet). In particular, the aurochs and the horses irresistibly lure one towards the left, as they are lit in the beam of the lamps, and they

(49 feet; ill. 109). It can be divided into three panels that are closely related to the wall's morphology. The Alcove of the Lions (ill. 102) is a recess, about 2 m (6½ feet) deep and with a maximum width of 1.30 m (4½ feet), framed by two overhanging rock surfaces, the Panel of the Horses on the left and the Reindeer Panel to the right (ill. 104).

There can be no doubt that the symmetrical effect was perceived by the artists and used in the composition.

It should be added that, just before the Reindeer Panel, there is a little recess occupied by a single animal, the Alcove of the Rhinoceros.

At the foot of the Panel of the Horses, the floor is covered by orange gours, whose origin lies in the alcove, because

widely over the floor of the Skull Chamber (ill. 97).

This water explains the absence of any archaeological remains on the surface at the foot of these richly decorated panels: the possible charcoals, fragments of tools and pigments, and footprints of humans or bears were destroyed, carried off by the water or buried in the calcite crust. The hardening of the floor beneath the

a flow of water at floor level explains the thick concretions that also hide the floor of the Skull Chamber lower down. When heavy rains come, this spring comes back to life, as was the case during our stay in the cave in October 1999. The water flows and fills the first gours to the left of the Panel of the Horses, before spreading

Panel of the Horses and in the alcove has had the benefit of allowing visitors to approach the wall without causing any detrimental effects. By contrast, beneath the Reindeer Panel and in the Alcove of the Rhinoceros, the clay floor is not covered by any calcite deposit and has bear hollows dug into it.

Above
Ill. 103. The rhinoceros (left) and the mammoth (right), engraved at a height of more than 2.5 m (8¼ feet), are the remains of an early phase and were effaced to prepare the black drawings.

Double page overleaf
Ill. 104. The Reindeer Panel.

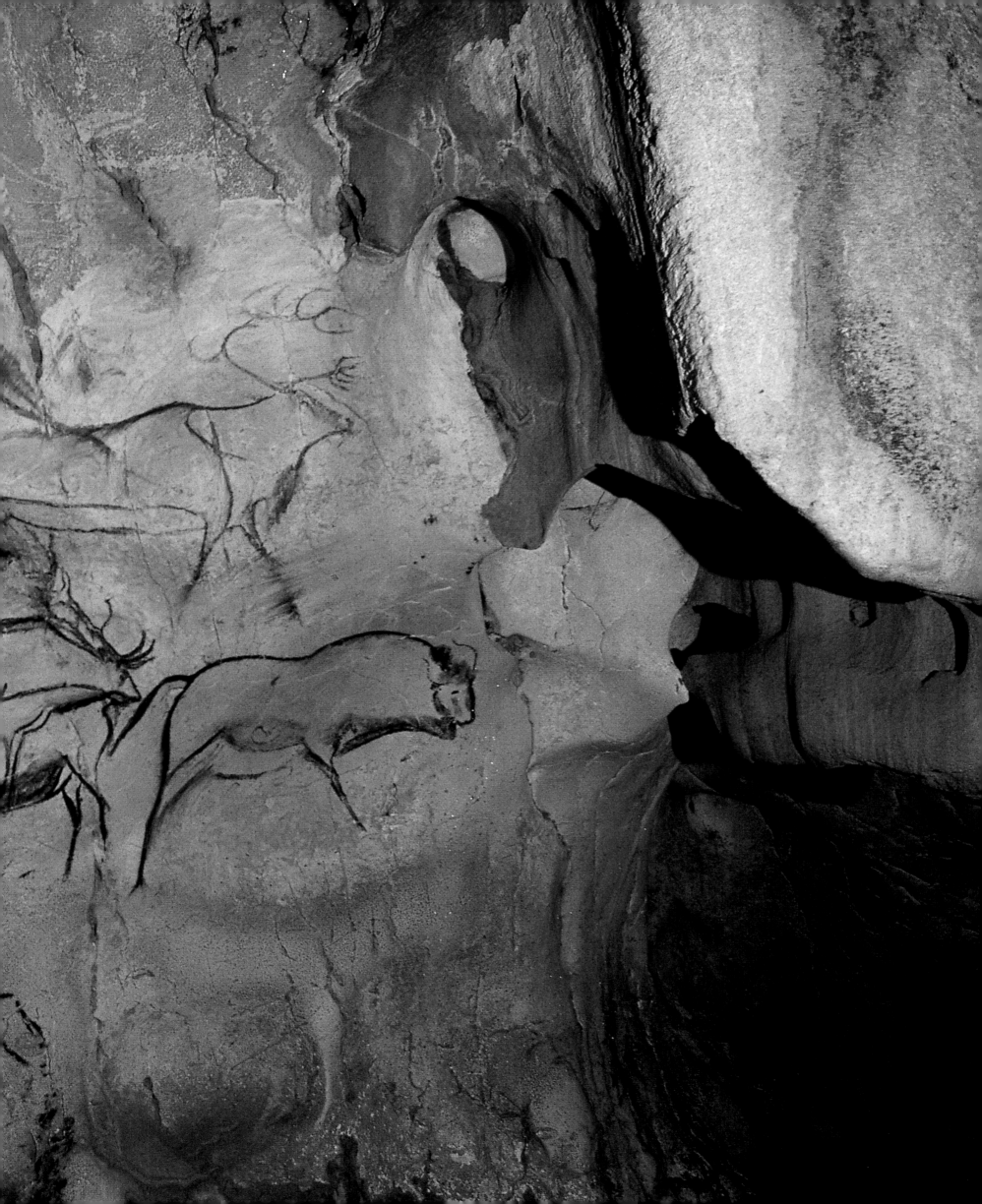

For the moment, our study conditions are thus not identical for the three panels: for the Panel of the Horses and the alcove, observation of the wall (including using a binocular magnifying glass) can be made without any major difficulties. By contrast, visitors have to keep at least 2 m (6½ feet) away from the Reindeer Panel, especially its central part. We shall have to wait for walkways to be installed in order to achieve the same degree of precision in our observations there. Our study of this

top, to the right, hidden by the rock pendant mentioned above, an aurochs head overlaps that of a little horse. To their left, the whole surface has been scraped or smoothed by hand, bringing out the whiteness of the wall and obliterating clawmarks or earlier drawings, as shown by the engraved remains of an animal at a height of more than 2.50 m (8 feet). Two red deer stags, facing in opposite directions, are identifiable by their antlers, and occupy the centre of the panel (ill. 104); they are framed, to the right, by a

Above

Ill. 105. Tracing of the confronted rhinoceroses.

Opposite

Ill. 106. As can be clearly seen in these photographs, the rhinoceros on the right is distorted to a greater or lesser degree, depending on the angle of vision. The central photograph, which is the least distorted, corresponds to the view of an observer seated on the ground, facing the cavity of the wall; this was probably the artist's position.

sector is currently underway, and only the Panel of the Horses has been the subject of an in-depth analysis; we shall present its first results below.

The monumental composition begins on the right with a big black rhinoceros, with an exaggerated long horn that curves strongly backwards. It seems to spring from a fold in the rock, just at the corner of the Megaloceros Gallery (ill. 173).

Towards the left, a very ancient stalactite that descends from the ceiling is marked with torch wipes, indicating that a prehistoric visitor walked 1 m (over 3 feet) from the wall; these traces mark the start of the first panel, the Reindeer Panel, which contains thirteen animals (ill. 104). At the

strange bison with an equid body, and to the left by an aurochs surmounting another stag followed by a big red stripe (ill. 192). Beneath the stags, at 50 cm (19⅝ in.) from the floor, there are more isolated black marks and a very schematic horse head sketched with four lines.

The upper frieze of the panel is as high up as a standing person could reach. It comprises a stag head, a drawing that was obliterated on purpose and made illegible (ill. 207), and a horse head placed between two reindeer fleeing in opposite directions. The right-hand reindeer has the distinctive characteristics of the species: antlers curving markedly to the front, brow tine with several points, a very thick dewlap below the throat.

Its left front leg was obliterated with the flat part of a hand (ill. 191).

The left edge of the panel with the torch wipes is none other than the start of the Alcove of the Lions, a restricted space large enough for only one person and yet containing seventeen animals.

In the continuation of the Reindeer Panel, the right wall of the alcove is occupied at its entrance by an aurochs with fine horns, whose hindquarters are superimposed on a horse head and a lion, both of them drawn as if falling. The major figure in this place is a bison with eight legs and a double back line, which is centred on a cavity. The animal is galloping; this sense of movement is reinforced by numerous limbs.

On the left wall, a couple of lions overlap (ill. 177): one of them looks threatening, with its lips pulled back; four horses in differing stages of completion seem to be superimposed on the body of one of the lions (ill. 183). In fact, a break in the feline's outline has made it possible to integrate it with the panel after the horses had been drawn, thus forming a complex but remarkably balanced composition.

On returning towards the left, a lion, an aurochs, a horse and a possible megaloceros (with its head obliterated but its withers very clear) form an inextricable tangle. When one tries to decipher a figure, one's eye is constantly led to another by the pattern of overlapping curves. It is as if the artists deliberately created this graphic exuberance, seeking abundance rather than the individual. The horse's nose is formed by a rectilinear rocky edge, just at the exit of the alcove. Below, close to the floor, a mammoth profile and a lion head are evoked by a few curves. On this wall, the details of certain animals are underscored by fine engraving. The lions and two horses are marked with red dots and yellow smudges on the shoulder, the throat and the muzzle.

The Panel of the Horses

On emerging from the alcove, one finds oneself facing the Panel of the Horses. Twenty animals are grouped on this surface of about 4 square metres (about 43 square feet), most of them facing left as if heading towards the Skull Chamber nearby. Their

exceptional state of preservation has made it possible to reconstruct the chronology of events (ill. 111); we shall therefore describe the figures in accordance with the main phases of work, at least those that we have been able to establish.

The initial state of the panel, before any intervention by humans, is impossible to reconstruct because the surfaces are scraped or occupied by figures almost everywhere. However, through comparison with other panels in the vicinity, it is likely that a fine film of yellow clay originally covered the limestone, probably lacerated by bear clawmarks. In this sector of the cave, the rock has decomposed into mondmilch

Above
Ill. 107. Horse Sector: evocation of the entrance of the Skull Chamber with, on the right, the Panel of the Horses and, in perspective, the projections of the wall.

Opposite
Ill. 108. The Panel of the Horses: the last two horses of the quartet. This close-up view makes it possible to appreciate the complexity of the activities that took place one after the other on the wall.

through the action of bacterial and chemical agents, that is to say, the surface layer – to a depth of only a few millimetres – has a soft texture and a dazzling whiteness. This natural phenomenon, frequent in very humid caves, transforms the local hard limestone into a malleable material, which can be incised with fingers, but, if the surface is scraped, the hard rock beneath reappears.

The Aurignacian artists had, of course, noticed this property, which presents some drawbacks, but also provides some opportunities. Although, on the one hand, it becomes impossible to produce fine engravings (the burin sinks in too deeply,

and the lines are blurred and imprecise), it is possible, on the other hand, to play with contrasts and colours with very little effort. By smearing the charcoal (probably crushed or crumbled beforehand) on the ochre clay, the mixture produces a palette of sepias or browns. If the charcoal is applied on to the white rock after the clay has been removed, shades of grey dominate. It is thus easy to understand how stumping is used so much in the cave, notably on the horses (ill. 108). This technique, so rare elsewhere, was here imposed on the artists, but did they see it as a constraint or as a stimulus to creativity?

There is another consequence of the wall's malleability: the possibility of altering the colour of the background by simply scraping the wall with a hand. The immediate legibility of the black outlines on a white background and the spectacular reinforcement of contrasts that result from doing this were perfectly perceived and exploited, as is demonstrated by the group of horses and aurochs.

As on the Reindeer Panel, the oldest drawings are engravings at a height of 2.50 m (8 feet). The only works surviving from this phase are a mammoth with downturned tusks on both sides of its trunk, a rhinoceros with its arc-shaped ears (ill. 103) and a group of oblique lines. The vigour of the incisions, with their jagged edges, the high-up position of the drawings, and the absence of superfluous details suggest that a crude tool (wooden stick, bone?) was used and held at arm's length.

In a second phase, the high and middle parts of the wall were vigorously scraped, obliterating engravings and clawmarks. According to the superimpositions, five animals (two rhinoceroses, a cervid, two mammoths) – all of them underlying the big figures – were placed at different levels, although it is difficult to determine whether this was done in a planned way.

The third great phase corresponds to the production of the fighting rhinoceroses (ills. 105 and 154), in the lower part of the panel at an average of 60 cm (24 in.) from the present floor.[17] The left animal is located on a portion of flat, vertical wall, while the hindquarters and limbs of the right-hand one are drawn

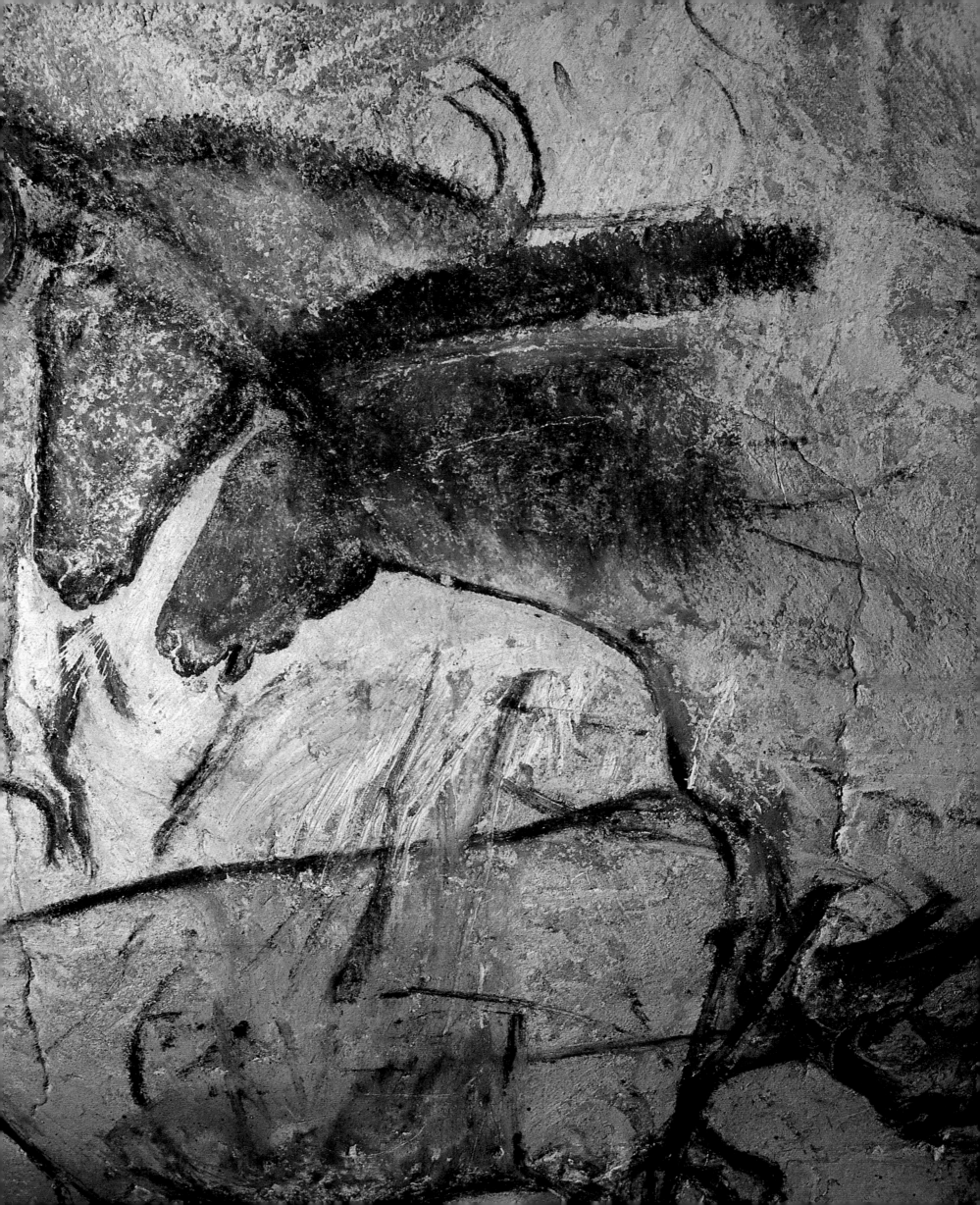

on a cradle-shaped wall; depending on one's viewpoint, major distortions affect it (ill. 106). The least distorted view is obtained by a spectator sitting at the foot of the panel, which was probably where the artist was.

In Palaeolithic art, narrative depictions are very rare; this conflict between two rhinoceroses is a unique work, with no comparable work in contemporary or later iconography.

Although there is no doubt that the two animals are the actors in a scene, the nature of their relationship is less clear. Is this a confrontation between two rival males or

drawn with a finger, are barely visible. Taking into account the artist's evident wish to make this first animal disappear, could it not be interpreted as an initial sketch for the right-hand animal in the actual version of the confrontation? Or did the artist only think of this scene after having drawn an isolated rhinoceros? He or she would then have modified the composition, trying to obliterate the sketch by incorporating it into the drawing of another rhinoceros.

The panel's fourth chronological stage corresponds to the drawing of the aurochs, in the upper left corner. The three heads

a prelude to a coupling of a male and female? Both types of behaviour exist in present-day African rhinoceroses. In the absence of a dimorphism or of clearly indicated sexual characteristics, the problem remains unanswered.

In this duo, the left rhinoceros has a grey-sepia middle stripe, obtained by rubbing with fingers and mixing the surface clay of the virgin rock with the black line of the head of a pre-existing figure, that of a rhinoceros in left profile – other surviving parts of it include the curved extremity of the long nasal horn, the back, the jaw and the chest. The animal's thigh and belly,

display obvious similarities, in the direction they are facing, in size and in their graphic conventions. The elegantly curving horns, very sinuous and projecting forwards, are a good example of this (ill. 186). According to the superimpositions, the central aurochs was the last to be drawn.

The four horses mark the last important phase (ill. 182). The first, limited to the head and the dorsal line, is located high up, at the limit of a standing person's manual reach, as if the artist had wanted to make the most of the largest possible surface in order to place the animals as he or she pleased. The second is complete. However,

Above
Ill. 109. The Horse Sector: overall view of the monumental composition that stretches for more than 15 m (49 feet). Note the different states of the floor at the foot of the panels.

Opposite
Ill. 110. Detail of one of the horses in the Alcove of the Lions.

the body is simply sketched by a black outline, whereas the head has numerous details. The ears folded back on the neck and the lowered head evoke anger, an impression that is underlined by the spray of lines that were energetically incised in front of the nostrils, as if the animal were breathing or spitting.

The whole surface below the neck is striated with fine engravings aimed at bringing out the white of the limestone. This meticulous finishing touch, now hidden by the third horse's head but visible with slanting light, constitutes in our view strong evidence that the composition was temporarily halted. Even if the artist had, from the start, intended to depict four figures, did he or she have second thoughts for a moment about the initial project, when only two horses had been finished? In any case, the artist then chose to add the third horse, with its fine juvenile head (ill. 108). As with the previous horse, the forequarters are detailed, while the rest of the outline is evoked with a few curves; a hesitant ventral line leads to a back leg in an aberrant anatomical position, as if the animal's body was open, around a cavity in the wall.

Once again, the surface was carefully scraped beneath the throat, which suggests to us a moment of reflection, or perhaps doubt: once the third horse was finished, the artist looked on the work with a critical eye. Following the initial project, he or she then decided to complete the composition, to finish it off by adding the fourth animal, which would partially mask its fellow. The last horse is unquestionably the most successful of the group, perhaps because the artist is by now certain of his or her inspiration. This fourth horse was produced using a complex technique: the main lines were drawn with charcoal, the infill, coloured sepia and brown, is a mixture of charcoal and clay spread with the finger. A series of fine engravings perfectly follow the profile (ill. 143). With energetic and precise movements, the significant details are indicated (nostril, open mouth). A final charcoal line, dark black, was placed just at the corner of the lips and gives this head an expression of astonishment or surprise.

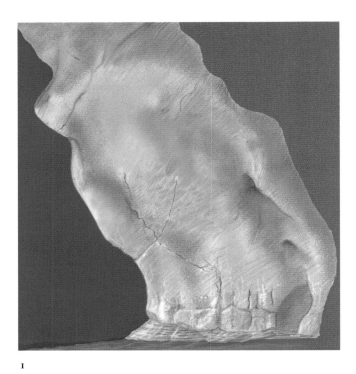

I

Opposite

Ill. 111. Panel of the Horses: reconstruction of a possible chronology of the composition, according to the superimpositions of lines. The initial state of the panel and the presence of possible bear clawmarks (**1** and **2**) can only be assumed through comparison with the nearby panels. Preparing the surface (**4**) subsequently caused the engravings to be partially destroyed (**3**); small black animals (some of which cannot be replaced in the superimpositions) seem to form the next phase (**5**), just before the confronted rhinoceroses (**6**) and the aurochs (**7**). The four horses were produced in a final stage (**8** to **10**).

The Panel of the Horses:
A Few Conclusions

The panel's general structure follows a diagonal axis, marked by the alignment of the horse muzzles. This group, the most spectacular, was the last to be set in place, after the fighting rhinoceroses and the aurochs; moreover, the bovines are intimately linked to the horses, as they extend the dynamics to the left.

Although the horses were the final figures, it was only because the space had been reserved for them in the general conception of the decoration. A few older animals – not very many, in our view – were obliterated (mammoth, cervid). It is thus possible to observe the genesis of the decoration from the margins towards the centre and even the heart of the panel, marked by the most expressive horse. Moreover, the movement of the heads, the harmonious curve of the necks, inevitably lead one's gaze towards it.

With regard to form, the horses – which were all done by the same hand[18] – share a family likeness, but also differ from each other in numerous details: the proportions of the head and neck, the drawing of the eyes and ears, the postures, all make them individual. The same applies to the aurochs: the general structure of the figure remains identical, but the mouth is open or closed, the eye is sometimes almond-shaped, sometimes V-shaped. By way of contrast, the image of the rhinoceroses seems more stereotyped, less expressive; in their case, the only differences are limited to the variations in shape and size of the grey or black stripe that divides the body.

Finally, analysis has confirmed that this collection is, above all, a masterly composition, a work of art produced by not only inspiration but also experience. After close observation of the wall, we have been able to understand the artist's tentative efforts and reworkings to achieve a more harmonious composition. It is impossible not to see in this the fruit of an artistic approach in the most contemporary sense of the term.

Carole Fritz and Gilles Tosello

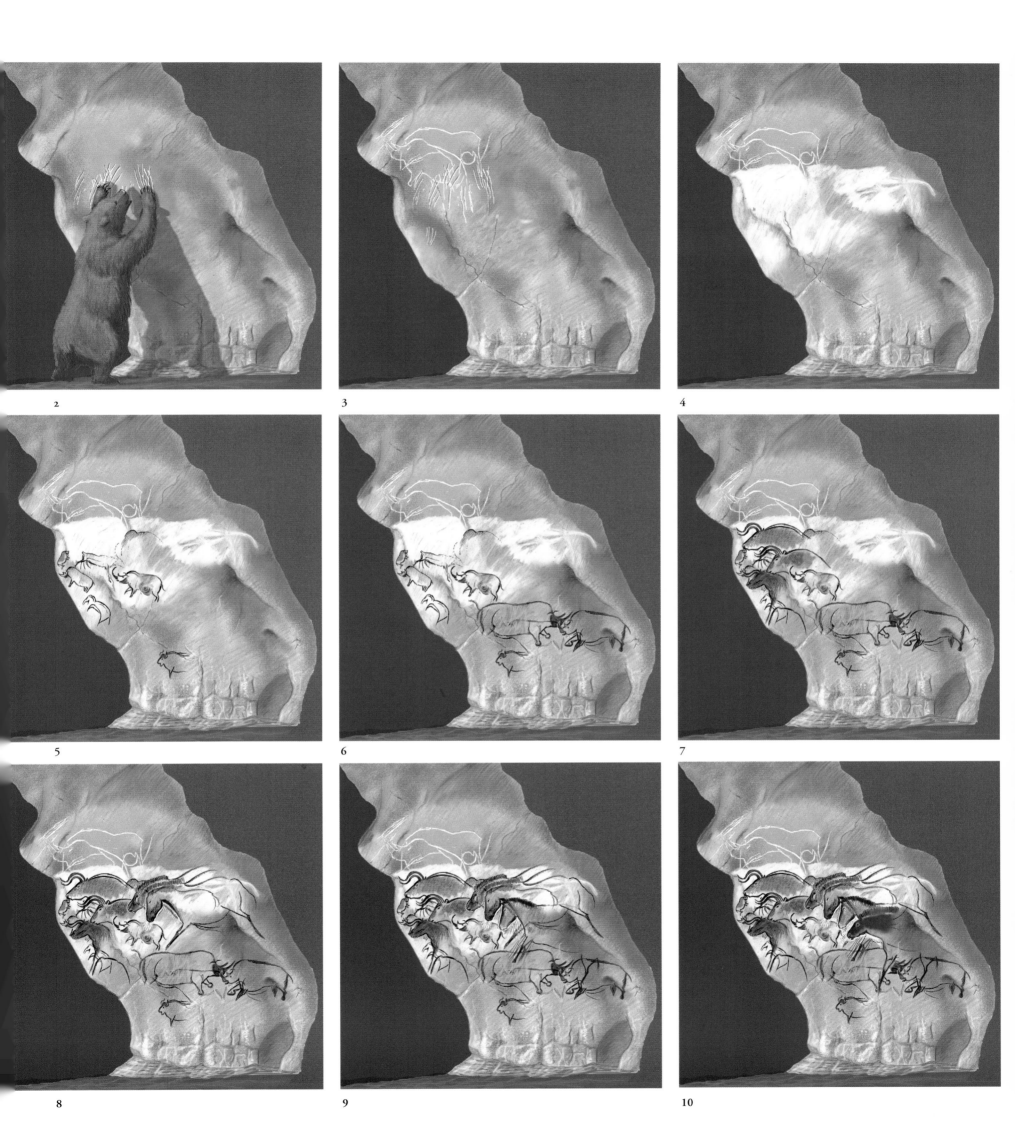

2

3

4

5

6

7

8

9

10

The Megaloceros Gallery

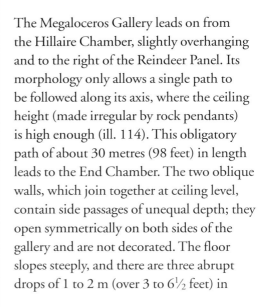

The Megaloceros Gallery leads on from the Hillaire Chamber, slightly overhanging and to the right of the Reindeer Panel. Its morphology only allows a single path to be followed along its axis, where the ceiling height (made irregular by rock pendants) is high enough (ill. 114). This obligatory path of about 30 metres (98 feet) in length leads to the End Chamber. The two oblique walls, which join together at ceiling level, contain side passages of unequal depth; they open symmetrically on both sides of the gallery and are not decorated. The floor slopes steeply, and there are three abrupt drops of 1 to 2 m (over 3 to 6½ feet) in

hearths, lit and maintained, blackened or dirtied the walls in different parts of this corridor. At the level of the last terrace, they were probably used for producing charcoal, the raw material for the black frescoes. Heaps of large pieces of wood charcoal, located in the alcoves or along the walls directly below the paintings, seem to be reserves of this material. The freshness of these remains gives the impression that, when we intruded into the cave, we interrupted the Aurignacians in their task and caused them to flee abruptly.

At the entrance, two decorated panels face each other (ill. 114). Near the ceiling is the white fossiliferous limestone that is gradually covered towards the bottom by a film of yellow clay. On the walls, the repeated and alternating passages of people and big bears can be seen. To begin with, black drawings, using broad lines, were produced directly on the clay film, which was not affected by this activity because it must have been protected by a thin veil of calcite. Then the bears came and left the mark of their claws on the wall. Next clawmarks and paintings were obliterated by vigorous scrapings, but some large portions of drawings still survive and sometimes make it possible to identify the species depicted.

To the right, they may be rhinoceroses and a megaloceros (ill. 115); to the left, the forequarters and the cervico-dorsal line of two big mammoths. The scrapings by finger, made possible by a process of natural weathering of the surface layer of the wall, brought to light the white, chalky support. This support is mixed with grey or ochre traces that result from the combination of limestone with the charcoal of the paintings or with the clay carried out of fissures. The end of the joined fingers dug shallow grooves edged by little rims of soft limestone that help reconstruct the direction and order of these gestures. These scrapings, which seem to indicate a desire to prepare the wall for new decoration, differ from others that succeeded them, and seem to be clearly organized. The later scrapings

Top
Ill. 112. The Megaloceros Gallery (in pink).

Above
Ill. 113. Two small rhinoceroses facing in opposite directions, at the entrance of the Megaloceros Gallery. The one at the top left is limited to the line of the back and the characteristic ears.

Opposite
Ill. 114. The entrance and first part of the Megaloceros Gallery.

height that delimit terraces. Three graphic collections can be distinguished, at the entrance, middle and end of the corridor. Black paintings, organized into panels, are only found at the two extremities, whereas engravings are distributed at the entrance and in the centre. The intermediate areas are purposely bereft of decoration, even though their walls were just as suited to it as the rest.

This gallery is the only place in the cave where traces of humans on the floor, which are well preserved and scarcely covered in calcite, are strongly linked to, and directly related to, the parietal art. An alignment of

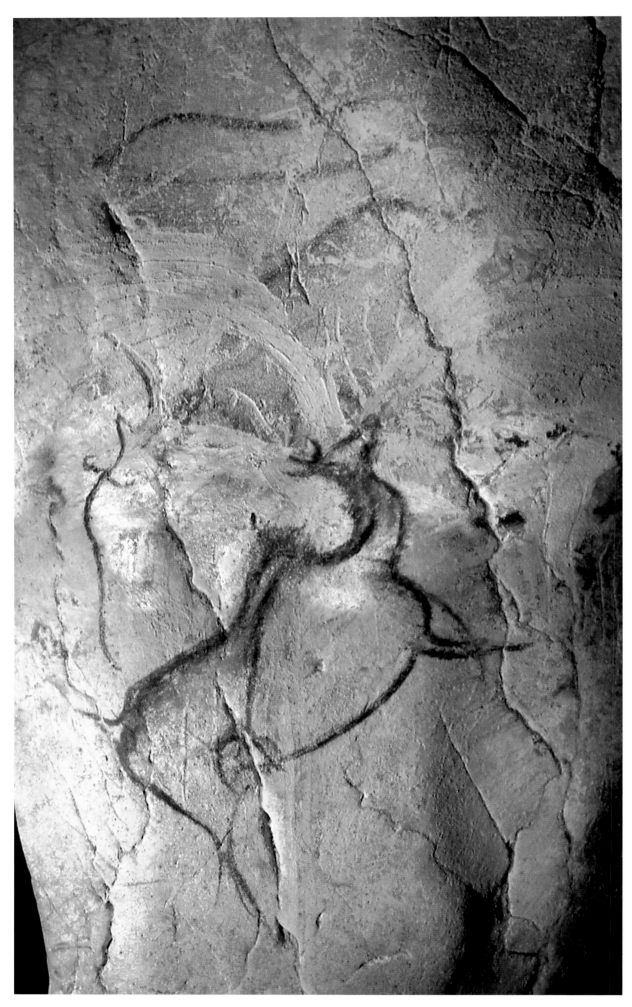

Left
Ill. 115. The Panel of the Megaloceros, on
which one can see quite clearly the different activities
that took place one after another: black paintings,
clawmarks, scrapings and black drawings.

take the form of semicircular lines, in opposite directions, in the form of a 'sheaf', two on the right wall and a larger one on the left wall. In their organization, these three similar figures recall the sign painted in red and surmounted by a cross on the Sacred Heart Panel in the Brunel Chamber. The similarity in shape between signs

mammoths, the reindeer (ill. 94) and other weathered marks on the rock pendants in these two chambers are similar, in the nature of their hardened support and their graphic technique, to the first black paintings in the gallery entrance. They likewise had engravings, finger tracings or clawmarks superimposed on them.

executed with different techniques in two remote sectors of the cave raises a question about the possible synchronicity of these depictions. The last phase is that of the currently visible black paintings.

The chronology that has been interpreted from these two panels sheds light on other parietal collections in the Hillaire and Skull Chambers. The black bear (ill. 91), the

It is therefore possible that the Hillaire and Skull Chambers and the entrance of the Megaloceros Gallery contained a group of black figures in the same style, though only a few of them have been preserved.

Stylistically, the first black drawings differ noticeably from each other. The mammoths are different from those made with finger tracings. The reindeer have more

Above

Ill. 116. Rhinoceros with the black stripe on its middle, drawn after obliterating another one whose horn and ears can still be made out.

harmonious proportions and greater care has been taken in the detail and in the characterization of certain parts of their coat. The bear does not follow the conventions for the red bears in the first part of the cave. These differences do not necessarily mean that these figures are much older, but nevertheless they do show that the had grown softer, then black paintings again. Only by evaluating the time necessary for the rock surface to be weathered would it be possible to understand how long had passed between the two successive phases of decoration; radiocarbon dating of the pigments from such ancient periods would certainly not bring this out.

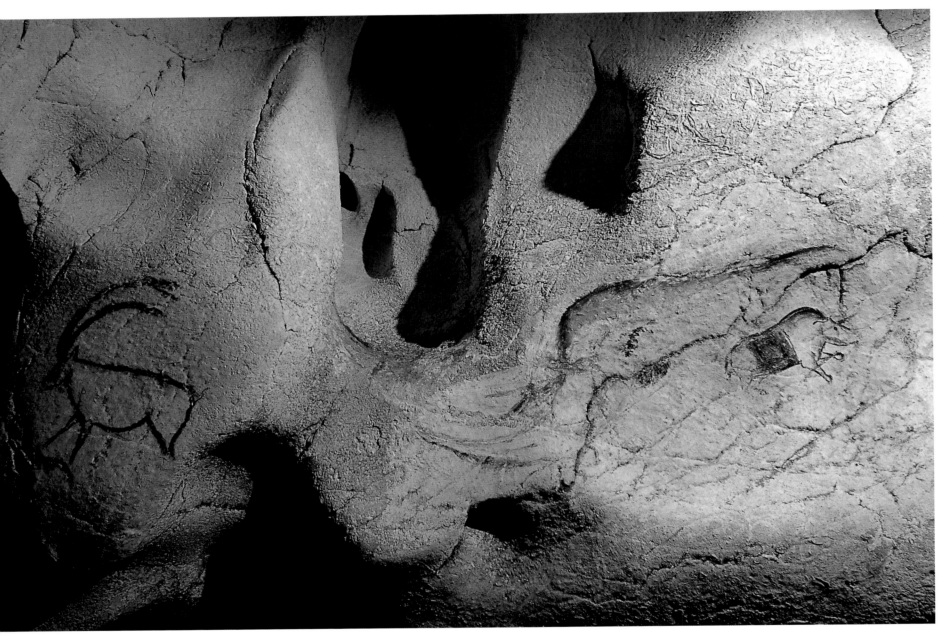

Above

Ill. 117. The Panel of the Rhinoceroses, with, on the left, the little ibex (see ills. 8 and 121).

group of artists who made these images was different from the group responsible for the more recent depictions.

One thing is certain: there were several incursions to produce art that was the fruit of different inspirations; the chronology could be as follows: black paintings on a hardened support, animal incursions, natural weathering of the support, engravings and scrapings on a wall that

The Megaloceros Panel

In the central part of the right-hand panel, a very graphic megaloceros (ill. 115), drawn in charcoal, was completed with some stumping. About 50 cm (nearly 20 in.) long, it faces right, in an oblique position, its lines drawn rapidly and confidently. The lines of the silhouette are sometimes doubled and relatively broad, though they become finer at the ends. The anatomical characteristics conform to those of the majority of other known megaloceros images: small head, supple neck, short tail and legs, represented with one per pair, that are relatively spindly in relation to the body. The withers are shown most distinctly, and are further emphasized by the line, stumped towards the top, which evokes a tousled

has a broad slightly curving line running across it from the dorsal hump that could be an attempt to depict the different colour of the hide. This schematic separation is also found on one of the megaloceroses at the back of the gallery and on those in Cougnac, which are believed to date to the Early Magdalenian or the Solutrean. The colour

coat. Curiously, although this animal, which disappeared more than 10,000 years ago, had impressive antlers, they are not represented here, and only some short excrescences grow from the top of the head, as in the Grande Grotte at Arcy-sur-Cure, at La Grèze, and on certain megaloceroses at Cougnac, Cosquer or Roucadour, in different periods. A crescent-shaped line surrounds the groin region, while the body

was spread by stumping, from this line and that of the back, over the top of the body, but also on the neck and chest, and it clearly expresses volume. The crushed pigment is mixed with the limestone and forms flat tints shading into grey.

Above the rump of the megaloceros, an incomplete rhinoceros, limited to the horns, forehead and cervico-dorsal line was drawn vertically, with its head facing

Above
Ill. 118. Pubic triangle with vulva (top left) and feline facing left, engraved with broad lines.

upwards, on the left of the panel (ill. 152). The drawing of its two ears as a 'double arc' is typical for the rhinoceroses of Chauvet Cave. The outline was drawn as a continuous line with a crumbly piece of charcoal of unequal hardness. Some small charcoal particles can be seen on both sides of the line, inside which are fine parallel longitudinal striations, the marks left on the soft wall by the harder or less carbonized elements contained in the charcoal.

The Panel of the Rhinoceroses

On the left wall, two rhinoceroses are facing in opposite directions (ill. 113). One of them is incomplete, being reduced to the sinuous cervico-dorsal line and the two 'double arc' ears; the other, facing right, is complete. The frontal horn is drawn stiffly, set perpendicular to the line of the forehead. On the abdomen, a broad stripe, which may depict one of the thick skin plates, is fully painted black by stumping, as is often the case at Chauvet.

The Engraved Panels

The middle of the gallery is devoted more particularly to engravings. After two deep alcoves, and shortly before the second change in floor level, three pubic triangles with the vulvar cleft marked are engraved opposite each other, two on the right and one to the left (ills. 118, 165, 166 and 168). They are comparable to those painted in the End Chamber. The one on the left wall is associated with a feline covered in oblique striations (ill. 118); the other two, on the right, are close to a group of parallel lines. The engraving of these two collections is broad, produced with a finger or with a flat-ended tool on the soft support; some little heaps, like clay commas, are found in places along the edges of the lines, or congregate at their ends, displaying the successive movements of the engraver.

The Last Painted Panels

The last painted group contains the largest number of depictions. It is located just before the big drop in floor level that separates the gallery from the End Chamber. Through its quality, it prepares visitors for

Opposite
Ill. 119. Torch wipes on some topographic features of the Megaloceros Gallery.

the emotional shock that the big panels are about to give them.

To the right, four rhinoceroses are partly painted and engraved. One of them, barely visible, seems to be a bad sketch. Two others, with traditional 'double arc' ears, are quite small, and have their belly circled by a broad black stripe (ill. 116). The last one is the biggest, albeit incomplete, and is limited to the upper part of the body (ill. 117). A big ibex with imposing horns was drawn on a rock pendant and dominates the group (ill. 121).

On the left wall, part of the surface is naturally peeling. Preparatory scrapings can only be seen beneath the body of the big megaloceros. The animals are far more numerous (12), and the organization more complex. Four species are grouped here: 6 horses, 2 bison (ill. 120), 2 megaloceroses, facing left, are close to 2 little rhinoceroses facing in opposite directions. Each of these species, except for the rhinoceros, is represented by at least one complete animal. The other figures are incomplete, cut short (megaloceros), reduced to the cervico-dorsal line (horses) or to the simple depiction of the head (bison). The complete horses are remarkably well drawn (ill. 38). One of them, in particular, is surprising because of the way it has been treated. The contours of the body and of the head are conveyed through stumping, but the end of the muzzle is not, and appears in a light colour. The mane and chest are drawn with a double line. The four legs are moving, and are offset through perspective and rest on the bottom edge of the wall, which makes the ground line materialize. The big megaloceros, painted and engraved for most of the back line and the rump, is comparable to the one at the entrance. Its antlers are not depicted. The head is fine and the spindly limbs are stiff and 'crutchlike'. Its flank is likewise crossed by an oblique line and its neck is decorated with a stripe that is totally blackened by stumping (ill. 189).

The walls that link these different panels do not have any drawings on them, although they are regularly marked with short black lines grouped in a random fashion and of varying importance, which

Above
Ill. 120. A bison from the Megaloceros Gallery, drawn with a piece of charcoal that engraved the wall at the same time.

Opposite
Ill. 121. A male ibex in the Megaloceros Gallery.

are generally visible when one walks from the gallery's entrance towards its end. Eight have been counted on the left and nine on the right, all located about 1 m (over 3 feet) above the floor, mostly opposite each other. However, one black mark was placed at a height of 2 m (6½ feet), in the centre of the gallery, on a stalactite above the first step (ill. 119). These charcoal spots, morphologically similar to torch wipes, seem to play the role of direction panels here. They are characterized by the way they are repeated in a rhythmically structured way and by their locations, linked to the gallery's topography, close to irregularities of the floor or to niches.

This gallery contains a total of 24 animal depictions. Rhinoceroses are most in evidence (10); then come horses, mammoths, megaloceroses, and finally 2 bison, 1 feline and 1 ibex, 3 vulvas, groups of parallel lines and 'sheaf-like' signs. The way the space is occupied gives the impression that the gallery is hardly decorated, whereas in fact the number of depictions is high for this restricted area.

The black figures at the two ends display the same characteristics. Some of them are relatively well worked, while others are reduced to simple bodily segments. This schematization of animals can be found in all the gallery's painted panels. The constant symmetry in the organization and the layout of the figures, which can even be seen in the charcoal marks, makes this one of the most original spaces of the cave, a topographically strong place, as it forms the junction between the two most spectacular compositions, and the site of intensive activities, as revealed by the remains abandoned on the floor.

**Dominique Baffier
and Valérie Feruglio**

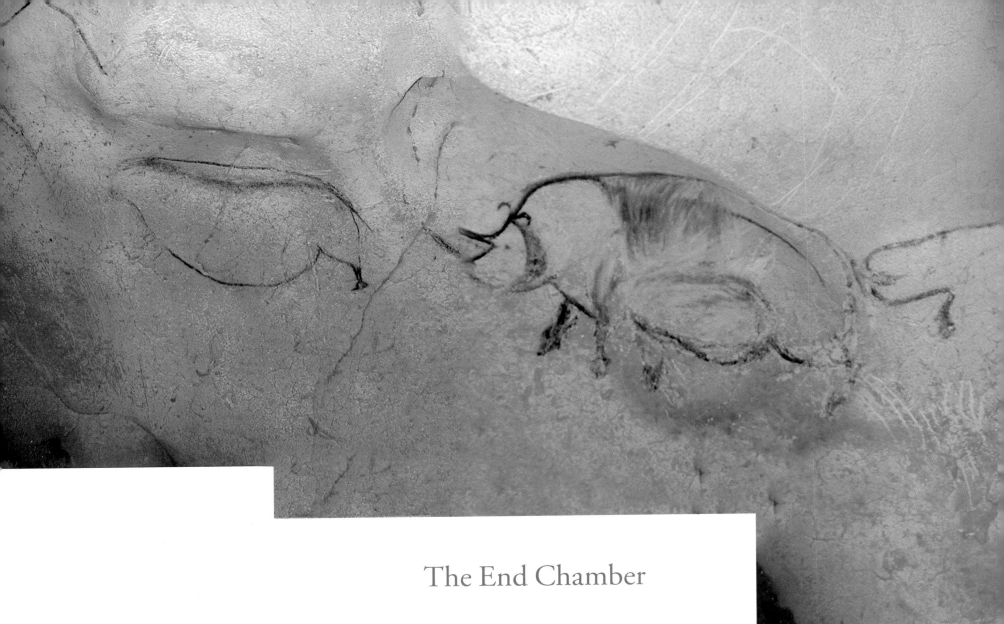

The End Chamber

Top
Ill. 122. The left wall in the
first part of the End Chamber.

Above
Ill. 123. The End Chamber (in pink).

From the Megaloceros Gallery the visitor emerges into the End Chamber. The entrance is relatively narrow – about 5 m (16½ feet) – and is marked by a major drop in floor level. A succession of irregular terraces have been created by waterflows and by depressions in the thick fill. Enormous bear hollows are dug into them, and in places accentuate the differences in the reliefs. One thus descends about 4 m (13 feet) to the level of the Panel of the Big Lions and the Panel of the Rhinoceroses.

The End Chamber comprises three major parts. Everywhere the ceilings are impressive, from between 5 and 6 m (16½ to 19½ feet) up to 12 m (39 feet) high, with rock pendants that have fine, light surfaces.

The first part, still following the direction of the path from the entrance, extends for a length of about 15 m (49 feet). Its separation from the second part is marked by the end of a big shelf, 5 to 6 m (16½ to 19½ feet) long, interrupted by an abrupt drop that obliquely cuts the chamber, from the left wall, shortly before the big lions at the far left of the main panel, to the right wall, immediately beneath a large engraved lion. At this point, the chamber is about 12 m (39 feet) wide.

The second part is the most richly decorated. It occupies the whole left-hand area, from the wall to a very abrupt relief with an irregular profile, forming a drop in height of about 3.50 m (11½ feet). The clay floor seems horizontal; in fact it slopes very slightly towards the back of the chamber. The whole chamber contained a thick fill of sediments, but they now only survive in the first and second parts. They gradually became fissured and collapsed, before being leached and disappearing in depressions.

The third part is practically undecorated. It provides a contrast with the rest through its numerous concretions, with big reddish stalagmitic masses that disappear into the darkness. In the middle of this deep space, a high and slender stalagmitic column that joins the ceiling and floor is marked with a few large red stains.

The Organization of the Panels in the First Part of the End Chamber

The Right Wall
The two walls are decorated in an unequal way. Most of the right wall was not decorated, apart from an isolated indeterminate head and geometric sign, although its surfaces are just as usable as those of the wall opposite, and there does not seem to be any particular erosion that might help explain the possible disappearance of figures. So this absence of drawings, here as elsewhere, must be the result of deliberate choices.

The only real panel on the right wall, about 4 to 5 m (13 to 16½ feet) long above a shelf, occurs before the drop in floor level that ends this first part of the chamber. All the figures are located within manual reach. Some pieces of charcoal are scattered on the floor here and there, and this panel is dotted with numerous torch wipes.

This panel comprises: three rhinoceroses and three lions drawn in black or engraved, a black bear, a big engraved bison head. A pubic triangle in black flat tint (ill. 167), but with its vulva kept white, recalls the engravings in the Megaloceros Gallery and the genitalia on the Sorcerer Panel.[19]

Some rock pendants descend to barely 3.50 m (11½ feet) from the floor, and could have been as accessible as others that were decorated elsewhere. However, none of them was touched.

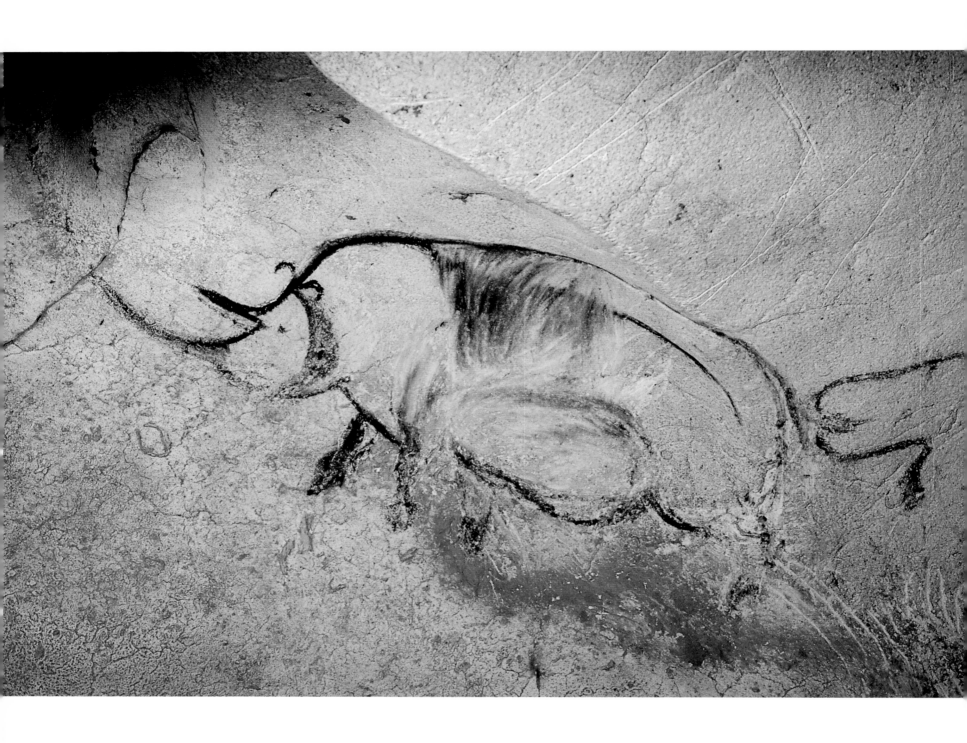

Above
Ill. 124. A big rhinoceros with all the
conventions used for this species,
on the left wall at the entrance
of the End Chamber.

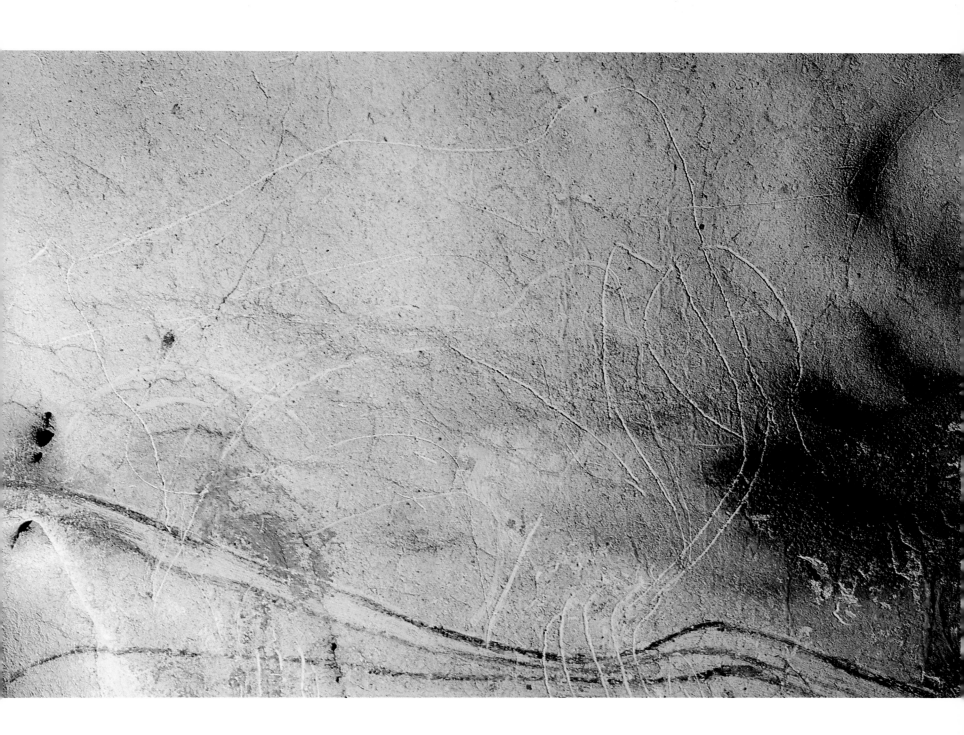

Above
Ill. 125. Mammoths engraved above the couple of lions, on the left wall at the entrance of the End Chamber.

Foldout
Ill. 126. The left wall of the End Chamber.

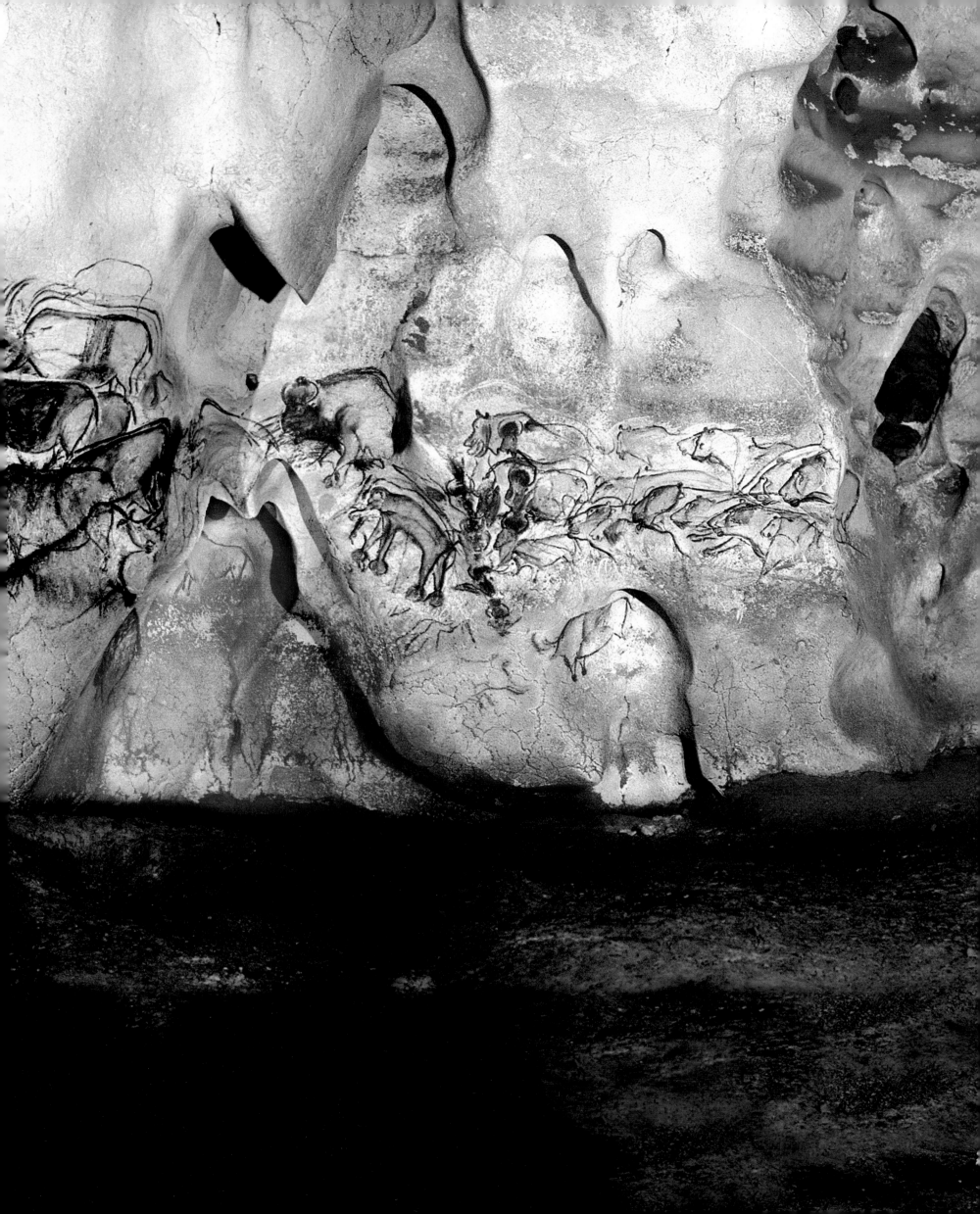

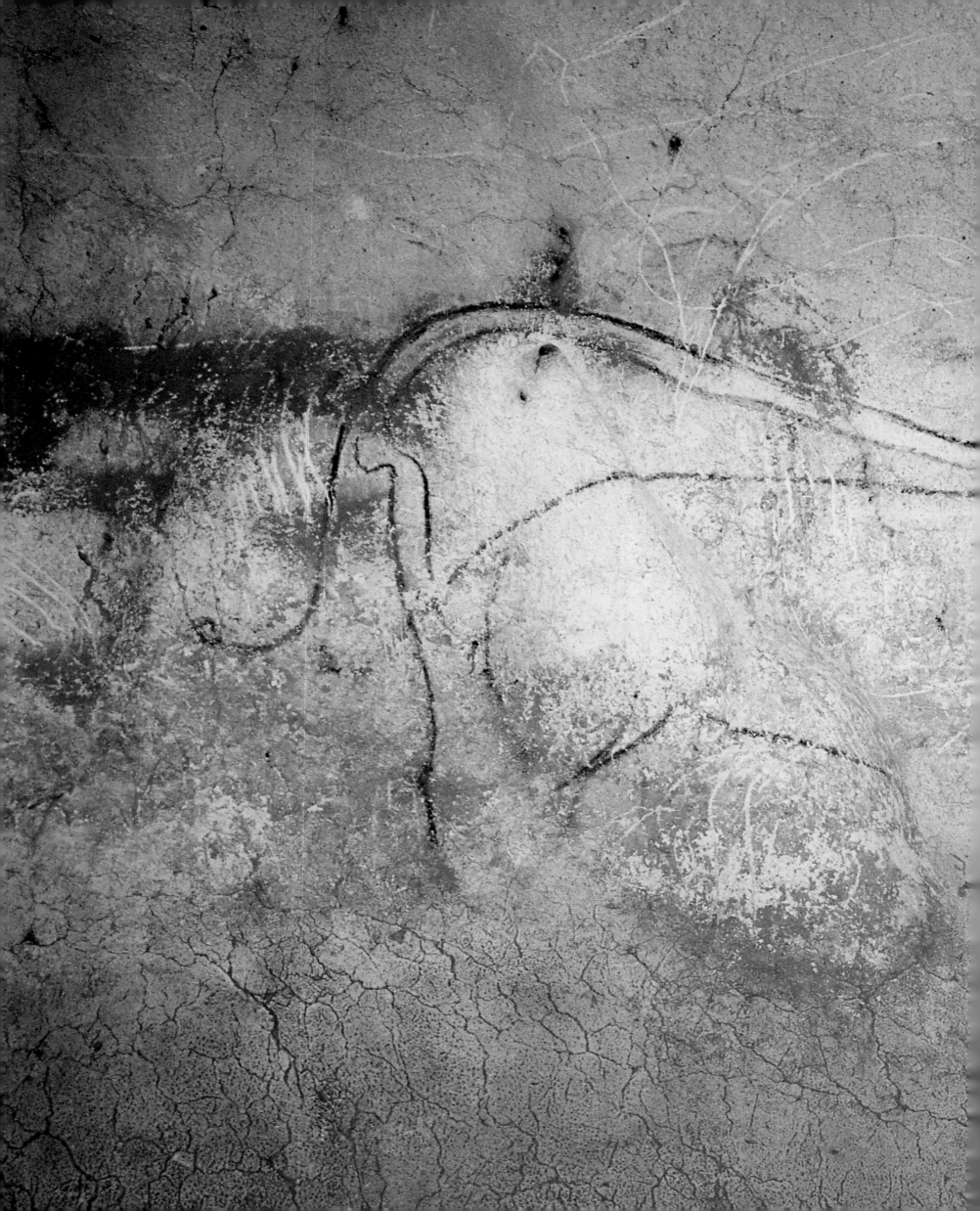

Previous double page
Ill. 127. These two lions, side by side
(2.5 m; 8¼ feet), on the left wall of the End
Chamber, represent a male, with its scrotum
marked, drawn in the background, and a
female rubbing against him.

The Left Wall
The left wall (ill. 126) comprises three major groups of figures separated by empty gaps of differing size. The centre of the *first group* features a big black rhinoceros preceded by a horse (ill. 122); high up, a mammoth and an indeterminate animal are engraved; there are two crude black feline heads, one of them overpainted with red, and a few black and red signs or marks.

plausible explanation in this specific case is that a red line was used to position the drawings, that it was drawn beforehand in order to mark the place for the drawings of the two big felines, one above it and the other below it. This argument presupposes a conception of the whole, and a real artistic project. This panel also includes three engraved mammoths (ill. 125) and multiple torch marks.

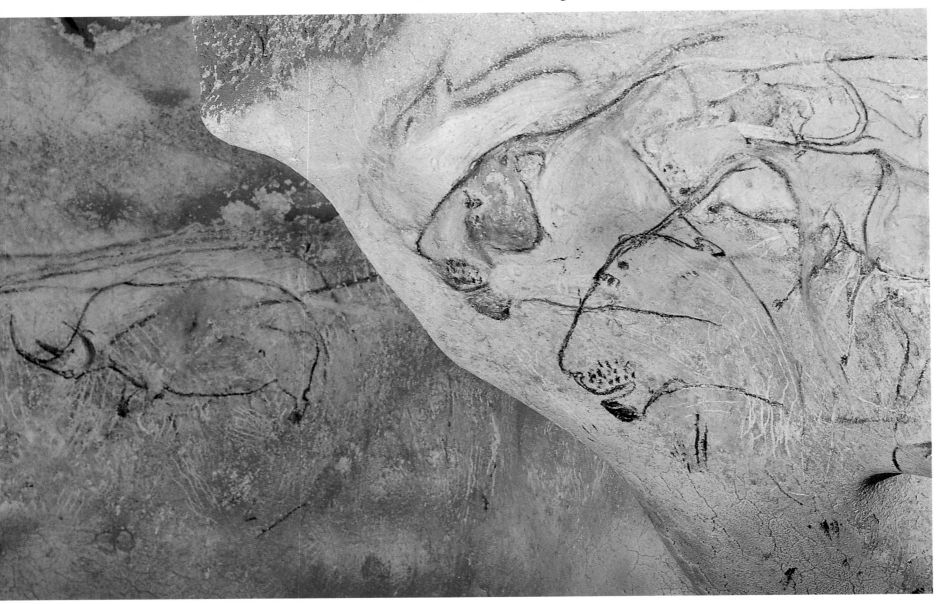

Above
Ill. 128. The big lions on the left of the panel in the End Chamber. In the middle distance, on the left, a big rhinoceros superimposed on bear clawmarks.

The *second group* is separated from the previous one by a gap of 1.30 m (4½ feet) on the wall, but it is at the same relative height as the other depictions. It is dominated by two big black lions, side by side (ill. 127). The male (2.47 m; about 8 feet) is identifiable by his scrotum. This animal's body seems to have been doubled by a red line that follows the outline of the hindquarters, the back and nose. The most

The *third group*, located 2.50 m (8¼ feet) from the previous one, is structured in a similar way to the second. It comprises three big red lions facing left, and two rhinoceroses (ill. 128), one of which is partially engraved. It is therefore possible that there were two groups of lions with more or less parallel back lines, facing each other on both sides of a space that was deliberately left empty.

All the animals in this area (except for one mammoth engraved in a high position) are located at a height that is within reach of a person from the floor; there is nothing to indicate that this floor has changed considerably since the visits by prehistoric people. At the foot of the decorated panels, it is relatively horizontal and regular. It is possible that these characteristics played a role in the choice of places to decorate.

The Organization of the Panels in the Second Part of the End Chamber
Only the left wall was decorated, except for certain rock pendants, one of them at the level of the present passage, in the right-hand area of this part of the chamber, more or less opposite the Big Panel. This pendant contains a natural hole in the middle. An indeterminate animal, perhaps a bear facing right, with about ten vertical lines

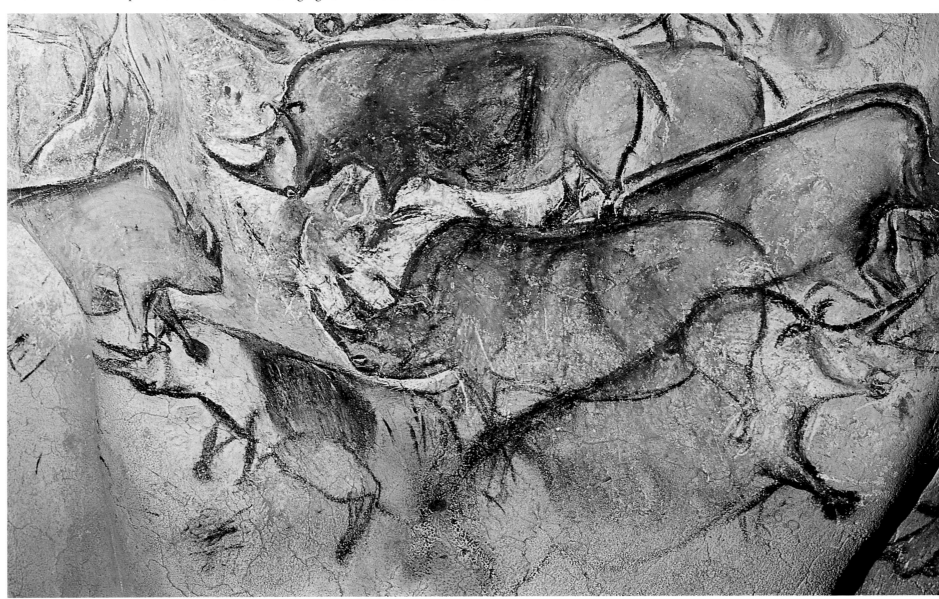

All the accessible walls in the first two parts are covered with bear clawmarks, most of them predating the works of art, but sometimes superimposed on them, which means that bears also frequented this chamber after the humans.

superimposed on it, was engraved to the left of the hole, at about 3 m (nearly 10 feet) from the floor.

The left wall extends for about a dozen metres, with beautiful smooth surfaces. On its far left, it projects forward a little, thus marking a separation from the previous part (ill. 128). The major element is a small niche, at 3 m to 3.50 m (9¾ to 11½ feet) from this projection (ill. 131). It measures

Above
Ill. 129. Lower part of the Panel of the Rhinoceroses in the End Chamber. The rhinoceros on the left seems to emerge from a cavity in the wall.

Next double page
Ill. 130. A troop of rhinoceroses have their horns represented in true perspective, but the lines of their backs in false perspective.

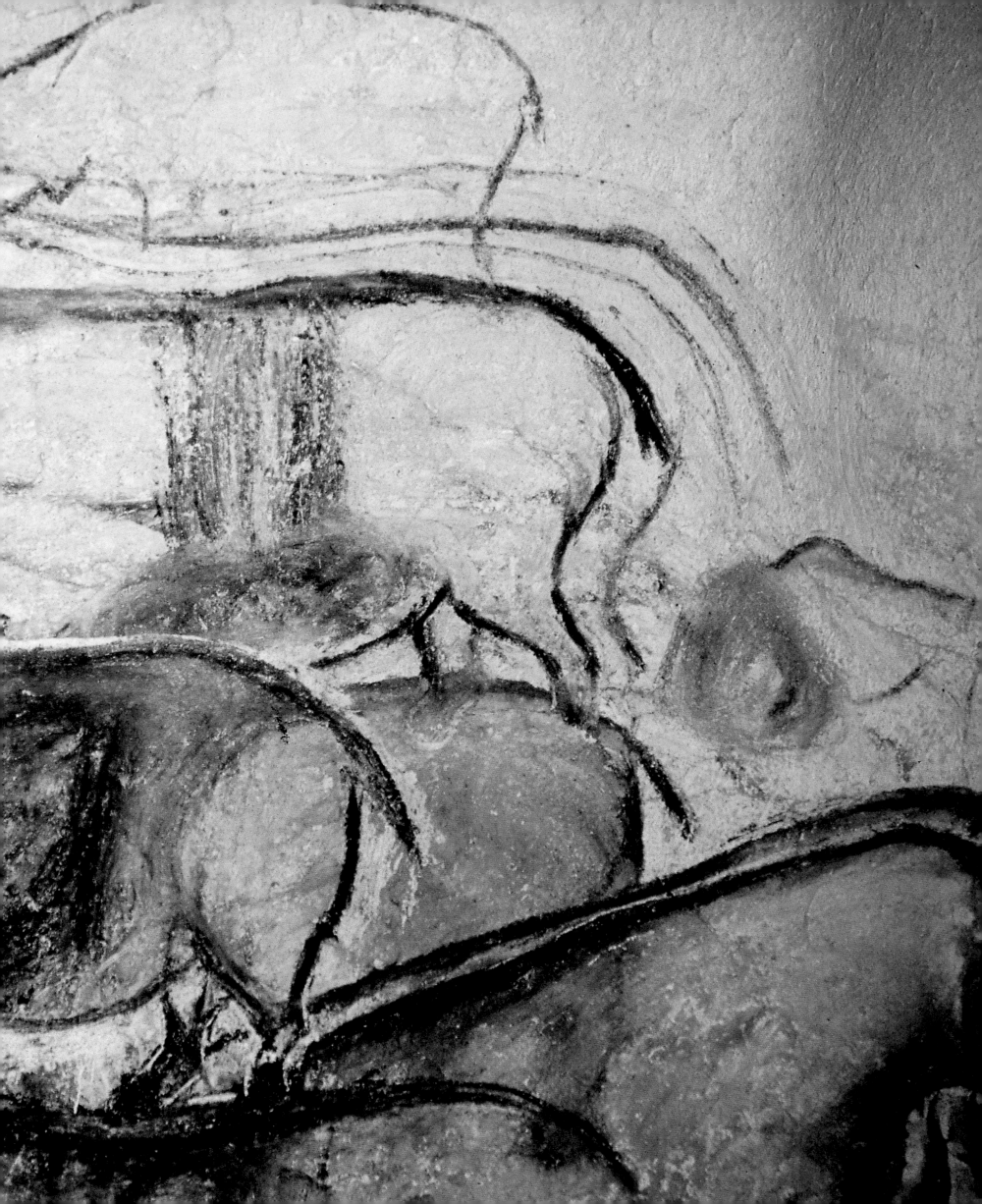

about 2 m (6½ feet) long by 1 m to 1.50 m (3¼ to nearly 5 feet) deep, and 1.70 m (5½ feet) high. The two sections of the decorated Big Panel unfold on both sides of this alcove.

The Left Section of the Big Panel
In this section, two groups can be distinguished. The first one, the *left*

The *Rhinoceros group* constitutes an impressive and relatively homogeneous group, immediately to the left of the niche, with at least seventeen rhinoceroses, all comparable in size and technique, a small bison and also a bison head, seen full face. Such a herd of rhinoceroses is unique in Palaeolithic art, as hitherto only about

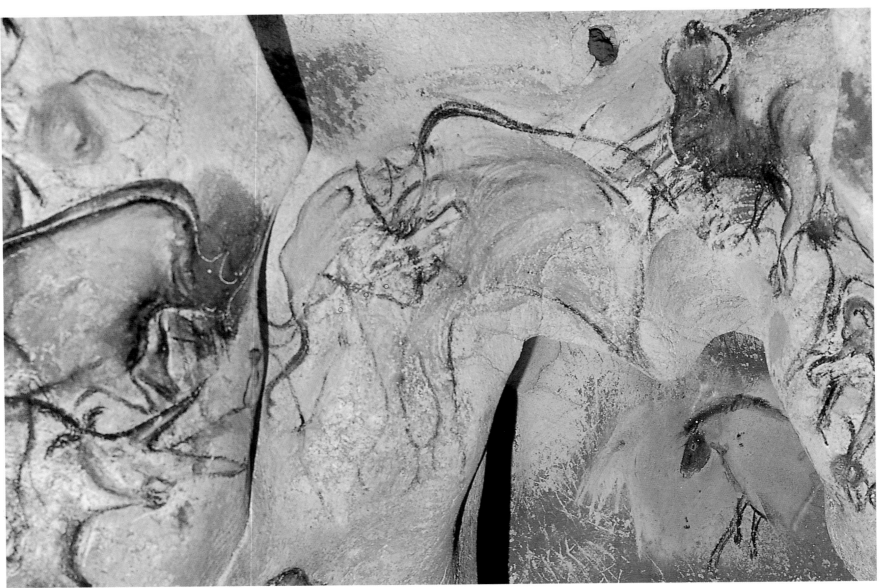

Above

Ill. 131. Niche in the centre of the Big Panel of the End Chamber. On the right, at the back of the niche, part of a horse can be seen. At the top of the niche, a rhinoceros is superimposed on a mammoth. On the top right, a bison seems to emerge from the wall.

panel, known as the Panel of the Big Lions – 4 m long (about 13 feet) – subdivided into two in the middle by a deep cavity at its far left, comprises three series of depictions.

In a first phase, five felines were drawn, together with a series of big dots, at the top right, following the wall's cavity. All these figures are red and faded, as are a series of about ten little dots and dashes. These red depictions are partially or totally covered by black ones, which comprise four big lions and a six-legged reindeer (ill. 128).

twenty parietal rhinoceroses were known in all the European caves and shelters, from all periods.[20] The study of superimpositions has made it possible to determine six phases in the panel's production. They were executed in fairly quick succession,[21] whether they result from a conception of the whole – the artist wanted to create a rhinoceros herd right from the start – or from successive additions.

Certainly, apart from the fact that it is the main species on the panel, there are numerous characteristics that are shared by these figures. All the animals, which are more or less complete except for the last one drawn, have their body shaded by the stumping technique (ills. 129 and 130). When the ears are portrayed, they are drawn using the usual convention, as two joined arcs on both sides of the skull line. The jaw is depicted by an identical arc of a circle on five rhinoceroses. Two peculiar artifices should be noted: on the one hand, the decreasing perspective of the horns for the rhinoceroses at the top (true perspective) and their superimposed back lines (false perspective), whether this technique was meant to depict a herd side by side or movement (ill. 130); on the other hand, the outlining of certain silhouettes, which gives them remarkable depth (ill. 129).

The Central Niche

It comprises several parts: at about 2 m (6½ feet) from the floor, two black rhinoceroses and a black mammoth occupy a sort of pediment (ill. 131); the niche's left wall forms a shallow cavity where a big black rhinoceros was drawn as if it were emerging from the hole (ill. 174); the niche's back wall itself has a horse-shaped scraping, with a sketch of the head and even a black eye. However, the black horse drawn in this spot was placed right at the back, its tail encroaching on to the beginning of the right wall. Seen from the front, its hindquarters are masked by the relief (ill. 131). There is an impression of an animal emerging from the depths of the rock. The same feeling is evoked by the massive forequarters of a bison, drawn in the right-hand cavity of the niche's sides, above another animal. Three mammoths, a bison head, a small rhinoceros and the forequarters of a fantastic animal (ill. 169) complete the panel. Its composition seems to be the result of successive drawings being added from top to bottom. Finally, the right-hand ridge of the niche was decorated with four bison heads one above the other (ill. 132).

The Right Section of the Big Panel: the Panel of the Big Lions

After the ridge, a large collection can be divided into two, the left part being dominated by bison, and the right by lions.

At the foot of the wall, in a small recess, a heap of charcoal can be seen, although there was no hearth in this spot (it was probably material kept in reserve for drawing).

The *left zone* is defined by a double cavity with two lions among five central bison and two rhinoceroses (one of them engraved), one at the top and one at the bottom of the

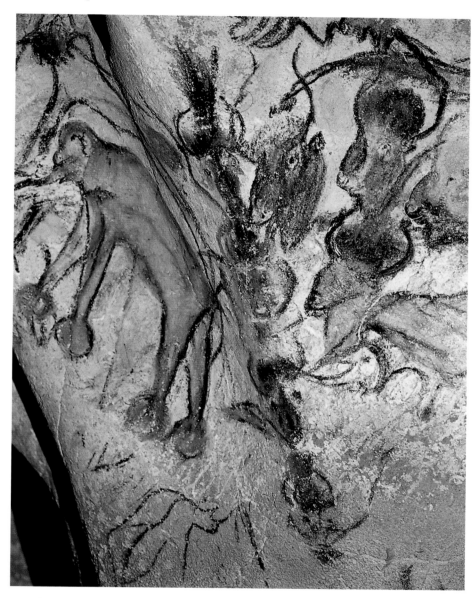

panel. The five bison are laid out in three superimposed registers. All these animals face left, except for one lion. So numerous figures are accumulated in this restricted space, but without any of their predecessors being obliterated or destroyed. This panel was executed from top to bottom.

The *right zone* occupies a broader cavity than the preceding one. This is the famous scene of lions hunting (ills. 133 and 203). Above it, 2.80 m (over 9 feet) from the floor, is a schematically engraved mammoth. In this zone, there are a bison, fourteen lions

Above

Ill. 132. To the right of the central niche, four bison heads were drawn on a ridge in the wall.

Next double page

Ill. 133. In the End Chamber, a whole group of lions appears to be hunting bison and seems to be stretching towards them.

and an animal with an elongated body which could be a lion or a mustelid (wolverine, otter). The wall was sometimes prepared by scraping, adapted to the subject that was to be drawn.

After this presentation of the Big Panel in the End Chamber, it appears that it was carefully constructed, as there is not only a symmetry in relation to the central niche, but also the two main parts of the panel have

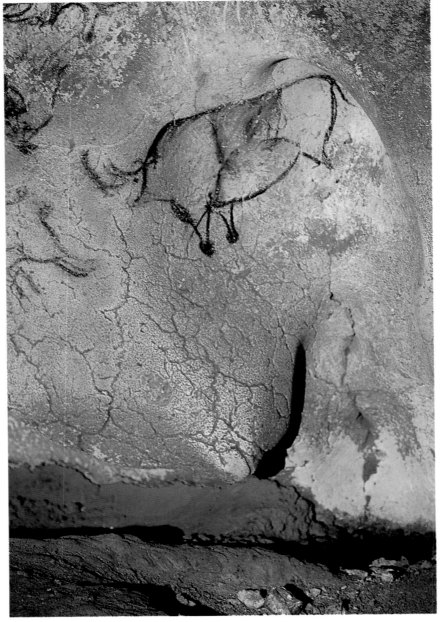

Above

Ill. 134. A rhinoceros in a cavity of the wall, below the Lion Panel.

a double construction, determined both by the shape of the wall and by the subjects drawn. This fact, added to the constantly repeated conventions for the depiction of the animals (stumping, outlining, rhinoceros and lion ears, bison heads), is an argument for the black figures being seen as a unit and for the panel being produced in a limited amount of time.

The Second Niche and its Surroundings

The Big Panel ends on a ridge made by a recess in the wall that forms a kind of second niche, this time shallow and with a very splayed profile. There is the possible front of a black bison, a complete black rhinoceros that seems to emerge from the recess (ill. 135), some torch wipes, the back line of an indeterminate animal. On the opposite wall (ill. 136) a bison was drawn with its head on one plane, seen full face, and its body in profile on another, at 90 degrees. The effect of perspective is astonishing. Below the bison, a deep triangular cavity is decorated with two black lion heads, on a black background which was either deliberately prepared or on which an earlier animal was obliterated by the spreading of pigment. The forequarters of a third feline, facing right, which was the first to be drawn, can scarcely be made out on the right part of the cavity. At more than 2 m (6½ feet) from the floor, a big black rhinoceros, drawn on a vast area that was scraped beforehand, has red colouring on its jaw and its two horns (ill. 137). In addition, a fan-shaped arrangement of red lines seems to come out of its mouth, and two other red lines are drawn on its flank.

A wide rock pendant follows and accentuates the start of this point where the ceiling descends towards the middle, until it is perpendicular to the right wall. Most striking are three big lions and a strange head on its internal surface, visible from the chamber (ill. 175). As for its external surface, it was equally well suited to drawing, but it could only be seen from the Bison Panel. It was not touched. In this instance the artist evidently made a choice in favour of the spectacular, a selection of places meant to be seen. This pendant also bears another schematic lion head and an engraved horse head, neither of which are very visible.

Just before the ceiling descends, a protrusion of rock stands out from it and descends vertically to end in a point 1.20 m (nearly 4 feet) from the floor. This is the so-called Sorcerer Panel or pendant. It has four faces, even if there are links between them: the one opposite the rhinoceros marked with red; the one showing the so-called Sorcerer, perpendicular to the previous one (ill. 138);

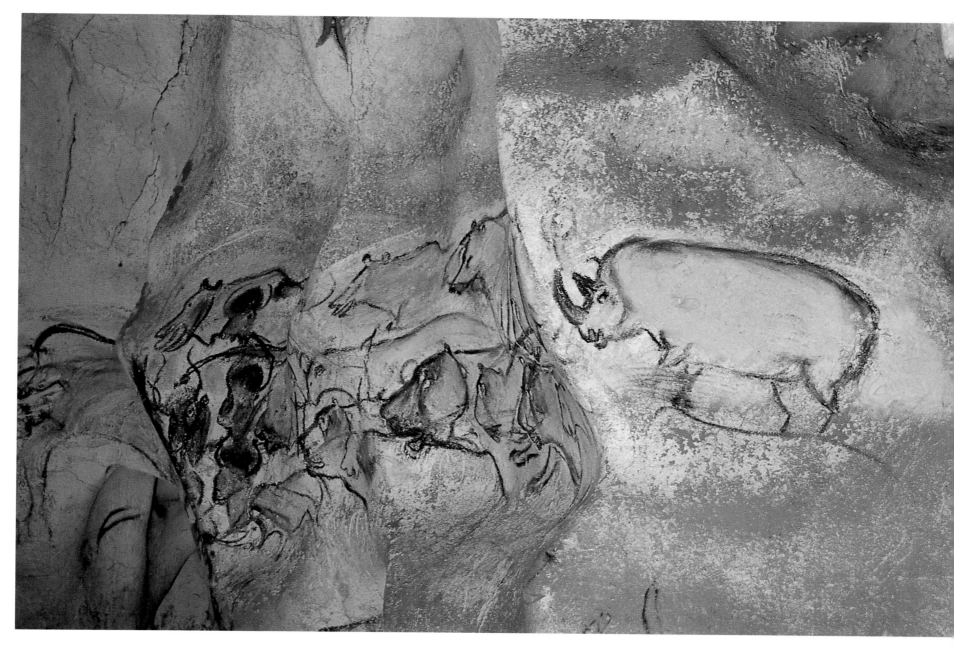

Above

Ill. 135. A rhinoceros drawn after preparation of the wall by scraping, on a wall perpendicular to the great Lion Panel.

the one opposite the present passage; and the one in front of the big bison at the back. They are all richly decorated, which indicates that particular importance was accorded to this geological irregularity.

As soon as one enters the End Chamber, one is immediately faced by this spectacular relief, and one can make out the forequarters of a bison on top of what have been interpreted as human legs (ill. 138).

Between its head and its knee, a big black triangle with internal filling, crossed by a little vertical engraving at its lower point, greatly resembles the engraved pubic triangles in the Megaloceros Gallery and was interpreted in the same way. Quite recently, Yanik Le Guillou, after photographing all faces of the pendant, noticed that this vulva was not isolated, but associated with two legs that evoke

Above
Ill. 136. Two animals, a rhinoceros on the left and a bison on the right, have been drawn as if they were coming out of this recess, to the right of the great Lion Panel.

The thick black lines are identical at the top and bottom. The same internal smoothing has been applied to the hump and the thigh. No comparable smoothing can be seen on the rest of the panel. This being was first interpreted as a composite creature, half-bison for the top of the body, and half-human for its general upright stance and the bottom of the body.

the bottom of a woman's body (ills. 162 and 163).

Perpendicular to this face, a black head of an indeterminate animal can be seen, full face, on both sides of the pendant's ridge, and, at more than 2 m (6½ feet) from the floor, a finely engraved mammoth that makes use of the wall's contorted relief.

Above

Ill. 137. Rhinoceros drawn after preparation of
the wall by scraping, on a wall perpendicular
to the great Lion Panel.

The face opposite the Bison Panel bears finger tracings and three animals, a black horse head and two lions. Finally, four animals were sketched on the pendant's hidden face, opposite the rhinoceros marked with red: two incomplete black lions, a mammoth's forequarters and a complete musk ox, also in black, identifiable from its downward curving horn (ill. 198), as well as some indeterminate engravings.

Beyond the rhinoceros marked with red, the left wall continues to the Sacristy via a

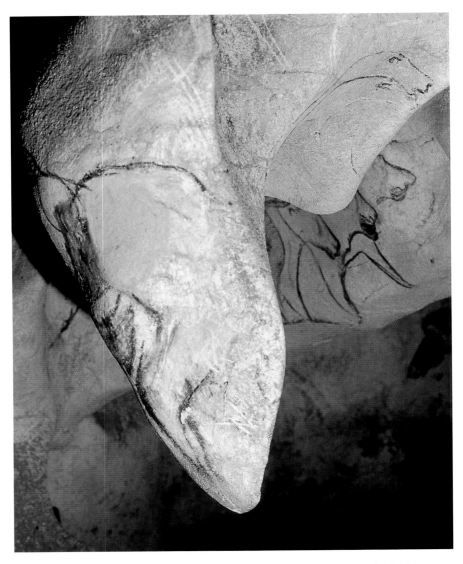

Above
Ill. 138. The Sorcerer Panel, seen from the entrance of the End Chamber.

Opposite
Ill. 139. Forequarters of a big bison, which has been dated to 30,340 ± 570 BP.

corridor that is barely 1.50 m (5 feet) wide at its entrance. Here one can see the forequarters of a beautiful horse, the rest of whose body is masked by an enormous descending rock, 3 to 4 m (9¾ to 13 feet) wide, which develops perpendicular to the left wall. This is the Bison Panel.

The Bison Panel

This gigantic pillar, with its black bison (ill. 1), can be seen very clearly as soon as one enters the End Chamber. It is a vast panel, covered with clawmarks, and with areas of corrosion that predate the drawings. Apart from the three big bison, it comprises the cervico-dorsal line of an isolated mammoth, engraved at arm's length. A sample taken directly from the central bison (ill. 139) gave a date of 30,340 ± 570 BP.

Among various lines, engravings and scrapings, three horse heads can be made out. A fossil present in the wall was used for the eye of one of them. These animals were engraved before the black drawings, which also comprise a big black feline facing left, earlier than the big bison.

Beyond the End of the End Chamber

The Sacristy

The Sacristy is an annex-gallery, perpendicular to the End Chamber. The walls are vertical and the ceiling reaches 8.50 m (27¾ feet) . The gallery's width diminishes regularly as one progresses through it, from 3.50 m (11½ feet) at the entrance to no more than 50 cm (nearly 20 in.) after 8 m (26 feet). In order not to destroy the floors covered with animal prints, we made the decision not to go to the back of the chamber. The morphology of the place makes it possible to dismiss any true continuity here, but we cannot see certain little walls or niches, even with our systems of indirect prospection by means of a camera at the end of a pole.

A small lateral corridor that opens at the left side at the back of the End Chamber is the easiest way to reach the Sacristy. The Aurignacians probably preferred going this way rather than passing via the bottom of the End Chamber, descending three steps of almost 50 cm (nearly 20 in.) and climbing three others of at least the same height. This corridor, about 4 m (13 feet) long and 1 m (over 3 feet) wide, was used, as it is decorated.

On the left wall, a beautiful black horse, already mentioned, faces the End Chamber, from where only its forequarters are visible. On the right wall, facing it, and likewise pointing towards the End Chamber, an oblique rhinoceros is sketched with firm lines. Apart from the characteristic ears, only

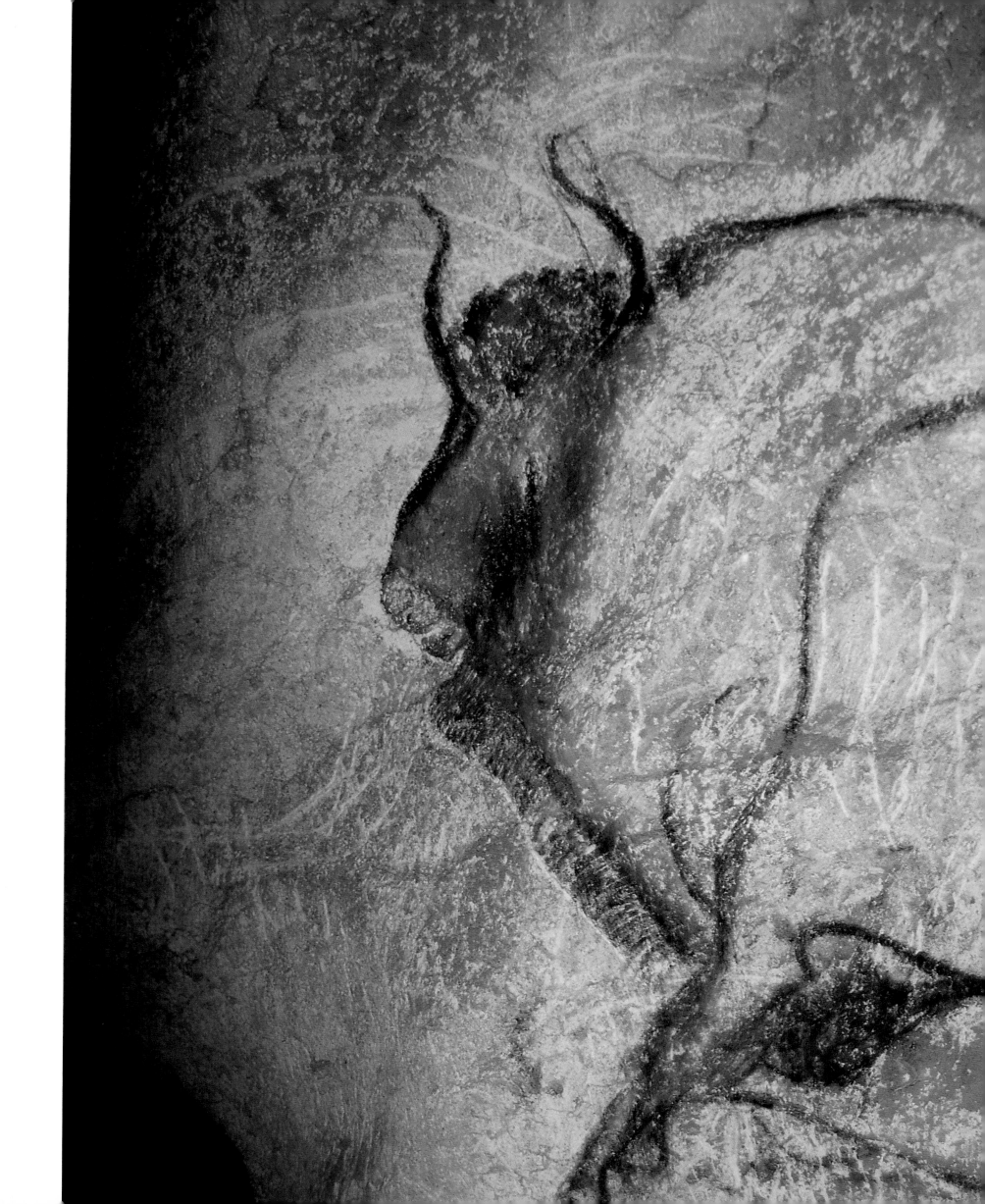

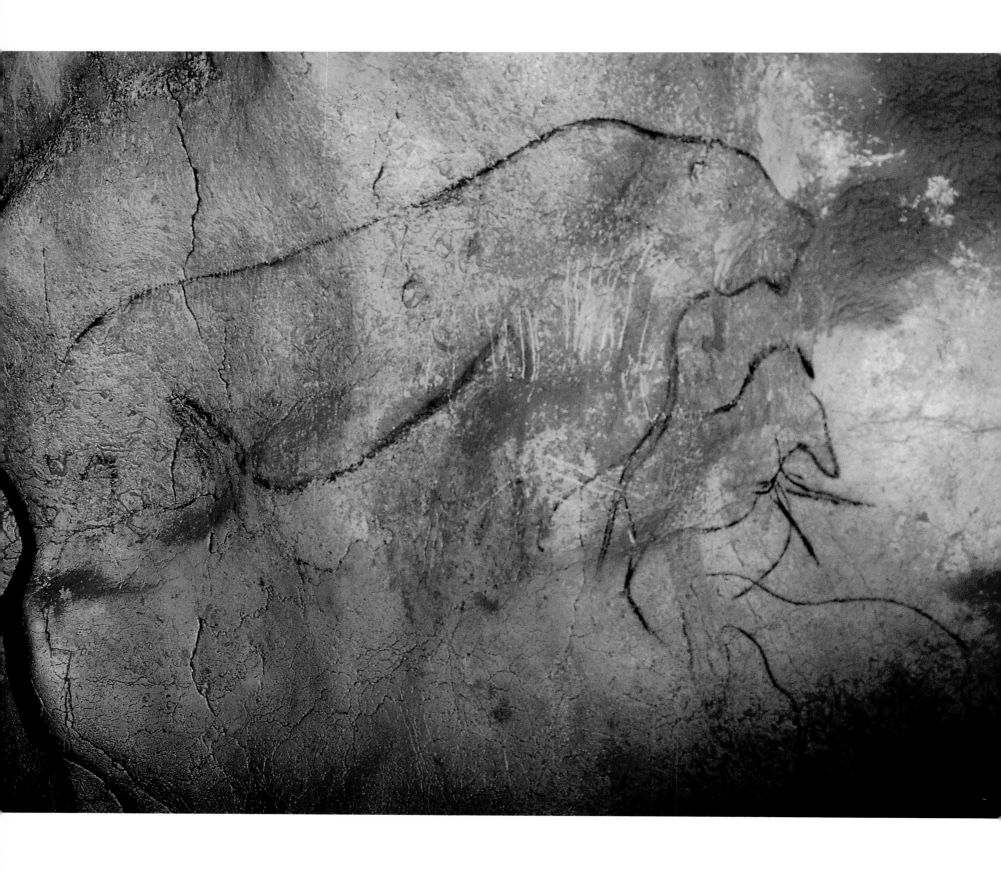

the horn, the forehead and the back line are depicted. About 1 metre (3 feet) behind it, but facing the other way, a unique little mammoth is both painted and engraved at a height of 1.80 m (nearly 6 feet; ill. 179). Perhaps there is some similarity between this horse and the one in the niche of the End Chamber, because both of them appear to the spectator to be isolated in the background, emerging from the hollows. The corridor's floor is horizontal, like that of the Sacristy, of which it is the continuation.

At the entrance to the Sacristy, drawn at a person's height, two decorated panels face each other. Each of these compositions is constructed around a big feline facing the exterior. The right-hand panel is 2.80 m (9 feet) long (ill. 140). It is the more complete of the two, but the appendage drawn at the level of the crease of the groin has not yet been interpreted. It is associated with two smaller horses. The lower one faces left; the other, facing right, has its head just under the feline's chin. On the feline's rump, a structured series of little incised lines is very blurred.

The composition of the left panel is richer but not as well preserved. It is an association of black lines, engravings and scrapings. The feline, 2.60 m (8½ feet) long, is represented by its head and dorsal line. Under its nostril, a black horse head, facing left, was drawn in the same situation as the one facing it on the other panel. Much later, a finger, covered in ochre clay, reworked the head and the start of the chest, in a style that recalls the little yellow horses[22] or a horse head on the Reindeer Panel. A small feline is to be found on the body of the big one, facing the opposite direction. Just above, two small ears, a triangular head, a hump and a chest, all clearly marked, make it possible to identify a megaloceros, through analogy with the cervids in the Megaloceros Gallery. At the same spot, before that animal was drawn, a structured alignment of short engraved lines faced those of the right-hand panel. Above this group, and at a height of 2.40 m (7½ feet), a U-shaped sign, a real open-topped rectangle, was inscribed on the wall, perhaps by using a stick. Further to the right, the last work on the panel is also the most complete and the most carefully drawn

– it is a large bison that was both engraved and scraped (ill. 184).

The Belvedere Gallery

The decorated panel on the right wall of the End Chamber occupies a rock pendant that overhangs the floor by about 50 cm (nearly 20 in.), for a length of almost 7 m (23 feet). When one crawls and slides under this pendant, one discovers on its ridge two unobtrusive little red dots marking out the path before one emerges in the Belvedere Gallery. A prehistoric person went across the whole of this gallery in which it is always possible to stand upright. As soon as he or she could stand up, he or she made two drawings, at a person's height: an engraved quadruped, facing right, and, just to its left, some big scraped curves, perhaps similar to those that mark the entrance to the Megaloceros Gallery.

A few metres further, still on the right wall, and almost out of reach, a mammoth's dorsal line dominates the narrow gallery. It then becomes more difficult to progress. The person made a vertical descent of 4 m (13 feet), using the wall and a calcite flow as supports for his or her body. Then he or she slid into a series of narrows, sometimes no more than 30 cm (11¾ in.) wide, whereas the ceiling often rises to almost 10 m (32 feet). He or she then climbed to a height of 2 m (6½ feet), on a small overhang, a climb that was again accomplished by using knees, elbows, hands and feet. This progress is marked out on the wall by black marks and torch wipes; the residues from the burning torches are present on the floor in the form of small scattered fragments of wood charcoal.

What we are witnessing here are the early beginnings of speleology. Having reached the overhang, the person moved forward to a small opening, the Belvedere which, on the wall, dominates from a height of 2 m the end of the End Chamber. Intentionally, or accidentally through brushing past with his or her clothing, he or she smeared red on the edges of this quadrangular aperture that forms an opening a quarter of a metre square. From there, a suitably adapted lighting system enabled that person to take in with a single look, centred on the

Opposite
Ill. 140. Right wall of the Sacristy. A big feline surmounts two outlines of horses.

horse in the niche, the whole of the left wall of the End Chamber, from the entrance to the back of the Sacristy. Only the corridor leading to the Sacristy and the Sorcerer Panel were hidden from the observer.

These two adjacent and terminal galleries are independent entities, with their own parietal layouts that are highly structured and yet not at all alike. For all that, they cannot be dissociated from the End Chamber, which has its own layout, partly constructed around the central niche and its horse (see above). However, the two adjacent galleries are directly linked to it. This link is not exclusively topographical. It is made certain by elements of the parietal decoration, taking the morphology of the place directly into account.[23] This evidence of autonomous and dissimilar layouts, linked together by original elements in their decoration, sheds light on the function of parietal art. The Sacristy and the Belvedere Gallery had, at least in their decoration, their own particular function in direct relationship to the End Chamber.

The Main Characteristics of the End Chamber
The End Chamber comprises 148 animal depictions, that is, more than a third of those counted in the whole cave, an indication of the importance that was attached to it. The first part of the chamber has far fewer drawings (9 on the right wall and 18 on the left) than the second part, where 107 animals, a woman and a composite creature were drawn, apart from 12 animals in the Sacristy and 2 in the Belvedere Gallery. The numbers reveal the dominance of the felines (52) and rhinoceroses (34), while the mammoths, which are so numerous elsewhere in the cave, only have 14 individuals here and are heavily outnumbered by bison (21). The other species comprise indeterminate animals (10), horses (12), a bear, a reindeer, a musk ox, a megaloceros and a fantastic animal. A pubic triangle, the woman and the composite creature should also be given a mention.

The techniques were also carefully chosen: the red depictions (11) and the engravings (21) are very much in the minority, the other figures being black (106) or both black and engraved (10) when the end of a torch was used.

The geometric signs are more difficult to count than the animals, because they are less visible. They comprise very numerous vertical black lines, commonly called torch wipes, although they could well have been used to mark the wall rather than to revive a light. Among the signs, it is worth drawing attention to the engraved tectiform, the angular engraved U-shape, and some red signs, including the arc of big hand dots, the series of ten dots and dashes, and a few short red lines, simple or double, some associated with animals and others not.

The End Chamber's major characteristic is the spectacular way in which it has been thought out and constructed. In the first part, on the left, the big felines, in two groups of comparable importance, separated by an empty space of several metres, seem to face each other. The Big Panel is organized in a symmetrical way on both sides of the central niche, each lateral section displaying two parts determined by reliefs in the wall, with distinct subjects. The wall of the big black bison figures faces the arriving visitor, as does the Sorcerer pendant.

Even if a 'red phase', earlier than the black, was detected on the left of the Big Panel, the general impression is not that many different additions were made over a long period, but that the whole composition was produced in a relatively short time, when the cave was first visited by humans.

Nor do there seem to have been numerous visits to this chamber. A fire, perhaps for lighting, was made in front of the Sorcerer pendant. Some charcoal fragments in a perfect state of preservation are scattered all over the floor. A heap of charcoal was formed at the foot of the wall, in a small hollow of the Big Panel. If many people had followed each other into the chamber, it is highly improbable that these remains would have survived being trampled on.

Jean Clottes and, for 'Beyond the End of the End Chamber', Yanik Le Guillou

Conclusion

The large decorated caves, such as Rouffignac, Niaux or Chauvet, have an advantage that the small or medium-sized caves like Marsoulas or Font-de-Gaume do not have. It is possible to understand in them the choices made by Palaeolithic people. They did not cover all available walls with their drawings indiscriminately. Moreover, when confronted with the infinite possibilities offered by the walls and their reliefs, they used them in their own way. There are three main elements that play a role and are combined in these choices: firstly, the topography of the cave itself, with its chambers, its galleries and its recesses, its changes in floor level, its open spaces and its secluded places; secondly, the morphology of the walls; thirdly, the techniques employed and the themes selected in relation to the preceding elements.

We note first of all that prehistoric people went everywhere, that they explored the smallest recesses of the cave, except for the high galleries, even if, on occasion (Cactus Gallery, Big Blocks, End Chamber), they sometimes managed to produce drawings at a height of up to 4 m (13 feet).

The second point to emerge from the evidence is that the cave can be viewed as two collections, which were used differently: the first part, up to the Candle Gallery, with the majority of red figures, its panels of hand dots and its bears; the second part, after the transition of the Candle Gallery, with an abundance of engravings and black drawings organized into great panels. Aurochs, bison and reindeer are only found in these deep areas.

Our third finding concerns the empty spaces. Some entire chambers (Chamber of the Bear Hollows, Candle Gallery), some long walls (both sides of the Hillaire Chamber and in the Gallery of the Crosshatching), some apparently favourable alcoves (Megaloceros Gallery) remained untouched by any drawing or almost. If one dismisses the possibility that they were destroyed by natural means, one has to admit that Palaeolithic people deliberately ignored them.

The fourth fact is that the major panels (Panel of the Horses, End Panel) certainly involved several phases of production, but this cave does not have the same abundance of superimpositions that are known in other decorated caves, such as the Sanctuary of Les Trois-Frères or the Apse of Lascaux. The conclusion that can be drawn from all this is that very few people took part in actually producing the parietal drawings.

This deduction is supported by our fifth observation, that is, that the cave was perceived in the same way by those who visited it. Everywhere, be it in the entrance zones or the areas at the end of the cave, the same attention is given to the striking topographic elements in the chambers and galleries; everywhere the artists made use of the hollows, the fissures, the contours of the walls. These parts of the cave either played a determining role in the production of the animal itself or were used as backdrops from which the animal was drawn as if emerging from a hole or the back of a gallery.

Finally, it is worth noting that the animals, be they red, engraved or black, display the same conventions of depiction throughout the cave (see Chapter 6).

We therefore conclude that most figures were drawn by a very small number of people who shared the same ideas, probably during a fairly short length of time, even during the period when the cave was first visited by humans. If their successors, some millennia later, also created a few works, the differences were not so marked that we can recognize them today.

Jean Clottes

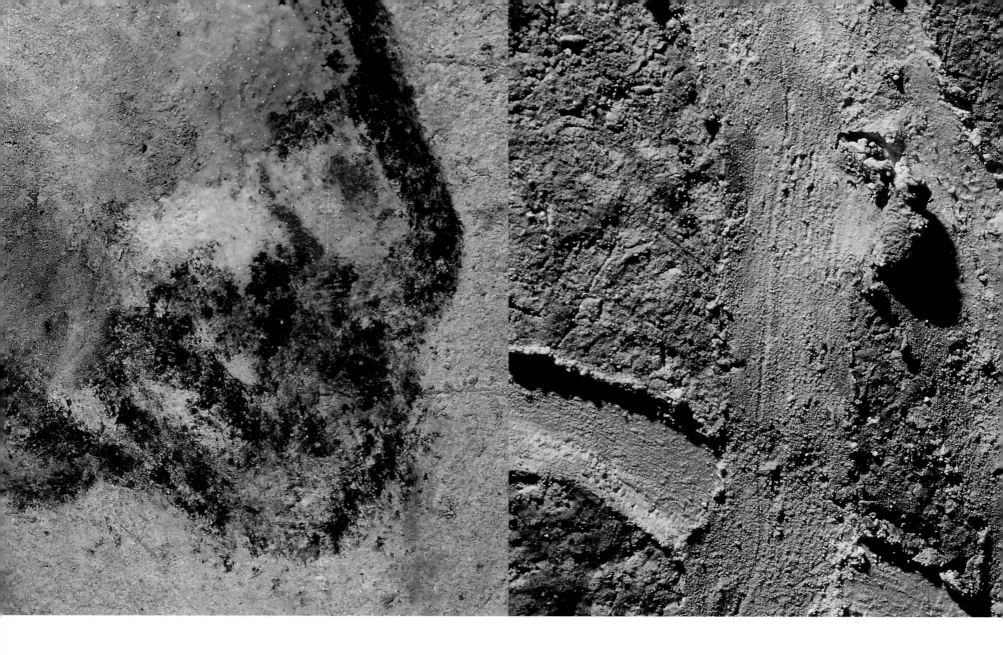

5

Above left
Ill. 141. Detail of a horse head in the Alcove
of the Lions in the Horse Sector.

Above centre
Ill. 142. Superimposition of engraved lines
in the Hillaire Chamber.

Above right
Ill. 143. The head of the fourth horse in the
Panel of the Horses has been carefully outlined by scraping.

THE TECHNIQUES OF PARIETAL ART

All observers have been struck by the sophistication of certain techniques: the frequent use of stumping to represent internal modelling, the spatial perspective, the preparation of the walls and the outlining of certain figures. Some choices became evident in the use of colours, especially red in the first part of the cave, white (engraving) towards the middle, and black in the deep galleries. These observations were confirmed by the in-depth study of the panels, which even reveal the very gestures of the artist, the direction in which the figure was executed, and the thousand details that combine to produce a masterpiece. The way in which the wall was perceived – its surface, its many reliefs and the space surrounding it – was found to be essential for any understanding of the state of mind of the Palaeolithic people.

5

THE TECHNIQUES OF PARIETAL ART

As in most major decorated caves, a very broad range of graphic techniques was used. Generally, in the production of parietal works, two main types of procedure can be distinguished: one consists of removing material from a rocky support of varying degrees of hardness, with this property dictating the choice of tool (engraving, scraping or finger tracing); the other involves applying introduced pigments either by projection (spray painting) or by direct contact with the wall (drawing with a finger, brush, charcoal or crayon). Certain figures combine several of these techniques and display modes of production that differ in accordance with anatomical segments or details (outline, coat, ears, legs, tail, horns or tusks). Our initial distinction by type makes it possible to observe these two major trends among the cave's figures.

According to the counts that have been carried out, half of the animal figures belong to the first category (removal of material), which includes a variety of procedures that arose at different points in the production of the works. In most decorated caves, the surfaces were hardly ever prepared before any drawing was done. However, some cases were already known in the two Magdalenian caves of Altxerri (Guipuzcoa) and Covaciella (Asturias). In Chauvet Cave, many examples of preparing the wall have been found. There

Left
Ill. 144. Finely engraved horses near the entrance.

20 cm

Opposite
Ill. 145. Mammoths engraved on a soft surface to the right of the Panel of the Engraved Horse in the Hillaire Chamber. They are superimposed on bear clawmarks.

Above right
Ill. 146. The hand print on the
Panel of Hand Dots, at the entrance
of the Alcove of the Yellow Horses.

are large areas of manual scraping, sometimes quite vast, which make the wall more regular or smooth before the figures were drawn. These vigorous scrapings, always on relatively soft surfaces, abrade the mondmilch and bring out a very white and more compact graphic space. In a few cases, the purpose of this work was also to obliterate bear clawmarks or pre-existing figures (see the Megaloceros Gallery). Moreover, at the top of the Panel of the Horses, an engraved rhinoceros and mammoth partially escaped the scraping, whereas other figures, of which some traces remain, are completely destroyed. Scraping can also be a graphic technique in itself: in the Skull Chamber, surfaces scraped with the flat of the hand sometimes take on zoomorphic profiles, for example the

Panel of the Scraped Mammoths (ill. 98).

Around the Large Collapse and in the Megaloceros Gallery, some drawings were created with a finger, on a support with a very soft surface, which constitutes the simplest procedure to carry out. In particular, it favours lines with a very broad trajectory, with the fingers always remaining in contact with the wall (cervico-dorsal lines of mammoths). The differences in texture of anatomical segments can be reproduced. Hence, the mane of the big engraved horse (ill. 153) was treated in an original way in order to obtain a more blurred edge, in contrast, for example, with the neck line that is sharper on the exterior and with some gradation on the interior. This modelling is obtained by a lateral variation both in the depth of the incision and in its colour,

through the denser surface film being gradually stripped. This approach made it possible to depict this animal's carotid muscle in relief.

Other engravings with broad profiles were executed on these same pasty surfaces by means of a hard implement, of flint, bone or wood, which sometimes leaves a very precise impression. These drawings display remarkable contours. One of the best illustrations of this is the ibex on the other side of the Panel of the Horses (ill. 200). Fine engravings are noticeably less common; they were executed with a flint point, and are found on hard limestones or on ancient concretions, which have preserved these unobtrusive incisions. They were rarely used to produce figures (engraved horse heads in the Brunel

Chamber), and are essentially found in association with the black pigments employed for outlining animals or anatomical segments and details. The artist emphasizes some graphic elements by playing with the colour contrast between the painting (black) and the background (white). The head of the last horse in the Panel of the Horses is outlined in a remarkable way. At the edges of the black pigment, there are small blows of a gouge around the mouth and chin and big straight lines along the nose and jaw. In this engraving all the artist's skill can be seen (ill. 143).

This technique can be observed on a few specimens in the Megaloceros Gallery (in a very small way, detail of certain anatomical elements) and on most of the figures on the

Above left

Ill. 147. Panel of the Horses: charcoal and fingermark on the rock surface. The very light superficial layer of humidity-filled limestone (mondmilch) has preserved the slightest marks, thus revealing the artists' work.

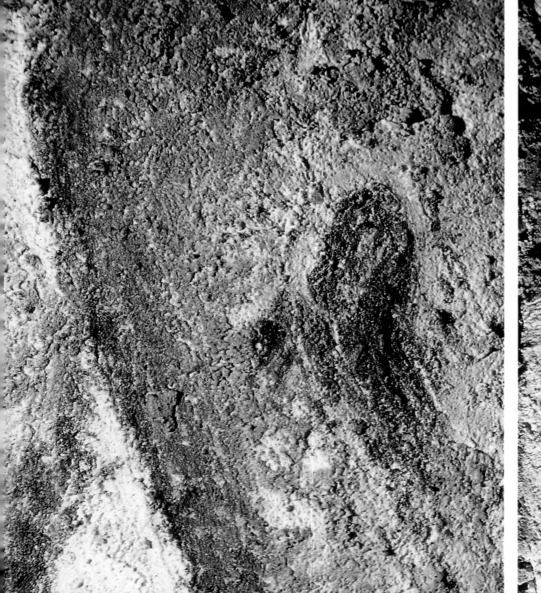

Lion Panel (rhinoceroses, lions). The figures (animal or abstract) that were produced with pigment require a more complex procedure. The use of colouring material clearly demands some preparation in order to obtain a texture adapted to its application (more or less liquid, thick, transformation into a crayon, into a charcoal pencil).

Most of the time, the red paintings needed this transformation, especially through being pulverized and, probably sometimes, being mixed with a binder. For the hand and palm prints, the paste used seems to have a somewhat greasy, thick and compact consistency, as, when the paint was applied, it seems to have run very rarely or not at all. The same is not true for the hand stencils, which were produced by spraying, or for the drawing of the figures on the panel in the Alcove of the Yellow Horses, where the paint seems to have been more fluid. Some dots, especially in the Alcove of the Yellow Horses, were produced with the use of pads; it is possible to see the imprint of plant fibres or animal hairs that lie close by and are sticky with coloured paste.

On the wall, the paint was often crushed by finger in order to stump or unify the outlines, as is evident on the bears in the Recess or in the Cactus Gallery. By contrast, on other figures the line appears 'drier', and the paint does not penetrate the rock's hollows; in these cases it is safe to assume that a different ochre crayon was employed, one that was not retouched by a finger as in the Recess of the Bears or by a brush, like certain animal motifs on the Panther Panel.

Where the black figures are concerned, some analyses (mostly carried out on the Panel of the Horses and in the Megaloceros Gallery) reveal that charcoal was used as a crayon.[1] The sketches were then retouched with the finger: this action improves the legibility of the outlines because any gaps in the charcoal line are thus filled. Some lines that were not retouched by finger preserve the scars left on the wall by the harder or less carbonized nodules contained in the crayon and give the impression that two techniques were employed jointly: drawing and engraving (ill. 152). By stumping, that is, by mixing the pigment with the clay on the surface of the limestone, the artists succeeded in creating volumes, thanks to the numerous shades of greys, browns or sepias.

As our studies proceed, it will be necessary to find out if the charcoal used is only of vegetal origin (which seems probable, taking into account the numerous hearths or charcoal concentrations on the floors close to the decorated wall); however, it is possible that the artists occasionally resorted to burnt bone (possibly reduced to powder beforehand). We will also need to determine if pigment and clay were mixed directly on the wall (as our first observations have led us to believe) or if there was a previous stage of preparation – which would also have made it possible for a binder or extenders to be added. Be that as it may, it will be difficult to establish with any precision the composition of the black pigments on the Panel of the Horses (or other major panels in the Megaloceros Gallery and the End Chamber) because choosing the location for extracting even a very small sample poses a very real dilemma: can an artistic masterpiece be treated as the subject of a scientific study? However, the freshness of the lines and the range of the techniques make it possible, here more than elsewhere, to understand the artists' slightest gestures. The sharpness of the lines, the retouchings, the changes of mind, the hesitations, the affirmations, everything has remained on the walls, and a vast field of observations lies before us.

As in most decorated caves, the reliefs and volumes of the wall were frequently used by the artists. They were able to make the most of the niches and recesses in positioning the figures (for example, in the End Chamber). The edges of ledges can then represent a ground line. Fissures and irregularities in the rock were often integrated in the depictions, and become natural back lines or horns, or suggest the shape of a body and turn the drawing into a three-dimensional image. The use of reliefs is a classic feature of parietal art, but there are some unique examples in this cave, such as the bison in the End Chamber that is placed on a right-angle of the wall (ill. 136), its body drawn in profile on the plane that is perpendicular to the observer, and its head drawn full face

Opposite
Ills. 148, 149 and 150. Panel of the Horses.
Ill. 148 (top): Ears and dorsal line of the small red rhinoceros, placed at the right end of the panel. The highly visible striations in the line indicate that a particularly dense colouring material has been applied using a tool, pastel or brush.
Ill. 149 (bottom left): The second horse's forehead and eye. The black pigment was spread with fingers on the decomposed white limestone along the line of the forehead; the eye is in a darker black and is emphasized with engraving.
Ill. 150 (bottom right): The third horse's muzzle. The outline, vigorously emphasized with engraving, creates an impression of relief on the white background.

(in any case, full-face views of herbivores are very rare) on the other plane, or the scraped mammoths (ill. 98) that are virtually natural sculptures completed by engravings to enhance their reading.

The work of art participates in a decor that is itself inscribed in the cave, and it takes advantage of all possible influences linked to the support. When the wall remains hopelessly flat, the artists use visual processes to give an impression of perspective. In the cave, outlining or breaks in lines are employed to give concrete form to this illusion.

concern for the relative proportions of each element (ill. 177).

On the Lion Panel, perspective is conveyed through the outlining of the animals and the economy of line. The rhinoceroses on the left part or the lions on the right provide a perfect illustration of these techniques. There are the white gaps (of differing widths) as well as the slight staggering between the individuals or certain anatomical segments that produce the succession of planes. In most cases, it is difficult to speak of actual perspective, but the interplay of planes bears witness to a

Right

Ill. 151. Vertical fingermark on an engraved panel in the Megaloceros Gallery.

Opposite

Ill. 152. Vertical rhinoceros outline engraved at the entrance of the Megaloceros Gallery. It was drawn with a piece of charcoal and the wood left its imprint.

Next double page

Ill. 153. Detail of an engraved horse in the Hillaire Chamber. On the mane, which has been thickened by hand, fingermarks are visible.

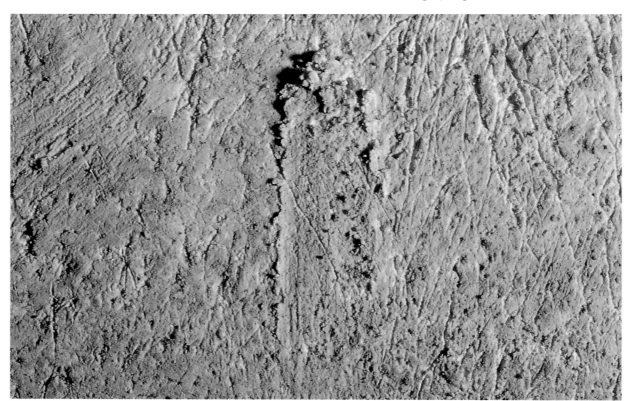

In the Alcove of the Lions, on the left panel, the big central lion was executed after the three horses by arranging gaps in its outline in order not to obliterate the horses' heads. The artist thus creates four different visual planes; however, they are not all completely mastered, as the lion's belly crosses the breast of the horses. There is a desire to place the lion in the background in relation to the horses, but without any

particular attempt at composition that is rarely found in parietal art. Whatever value is given to words, Chauvet Cave leads us to discover every day the sensitivity and perception of these ancient artists, and their inventiveness in conveying reality.

Norbert Aujoulat, Dominique Baffier, Valérie Feruglio, Carole Fritz and Gilles Tosello

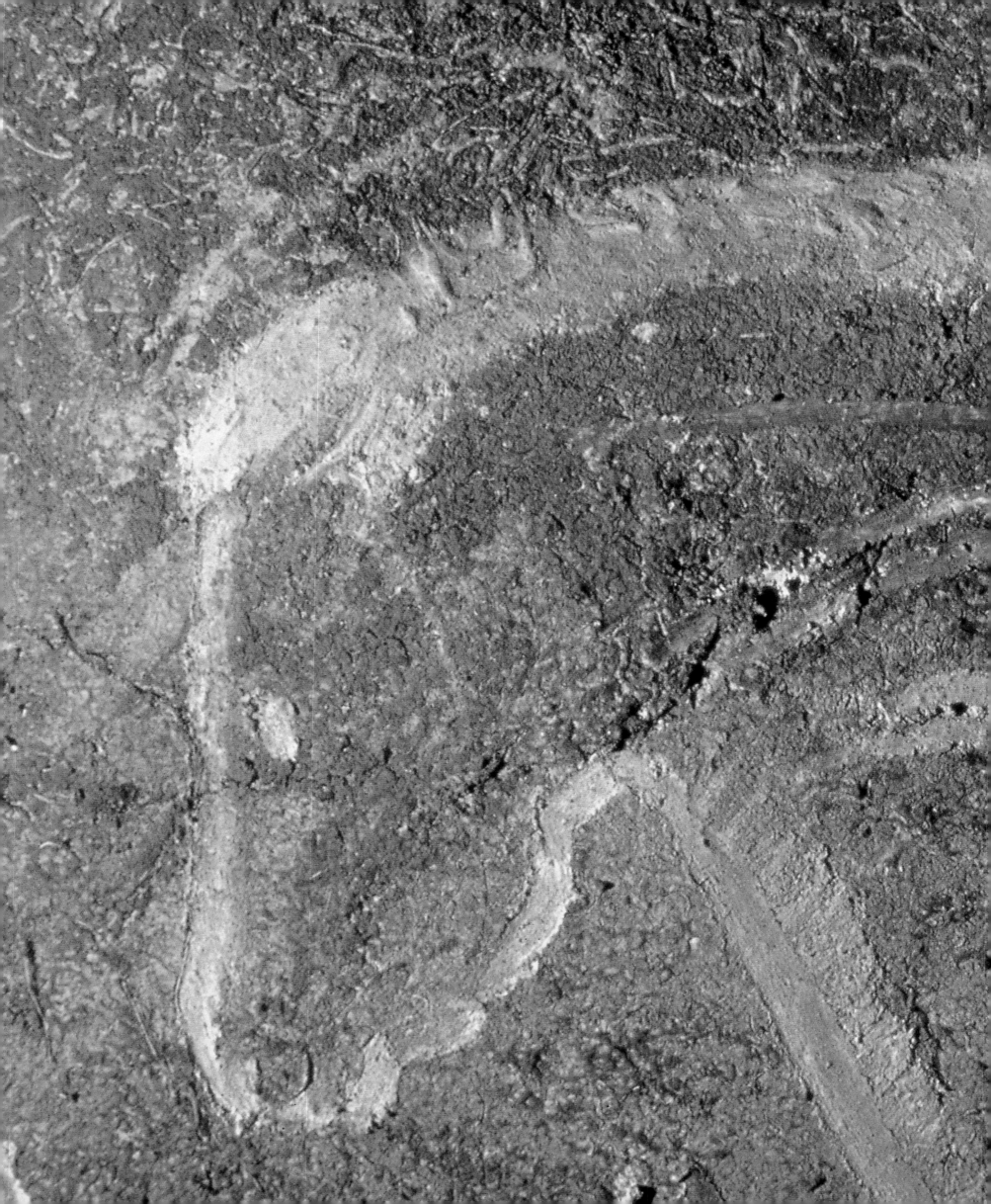

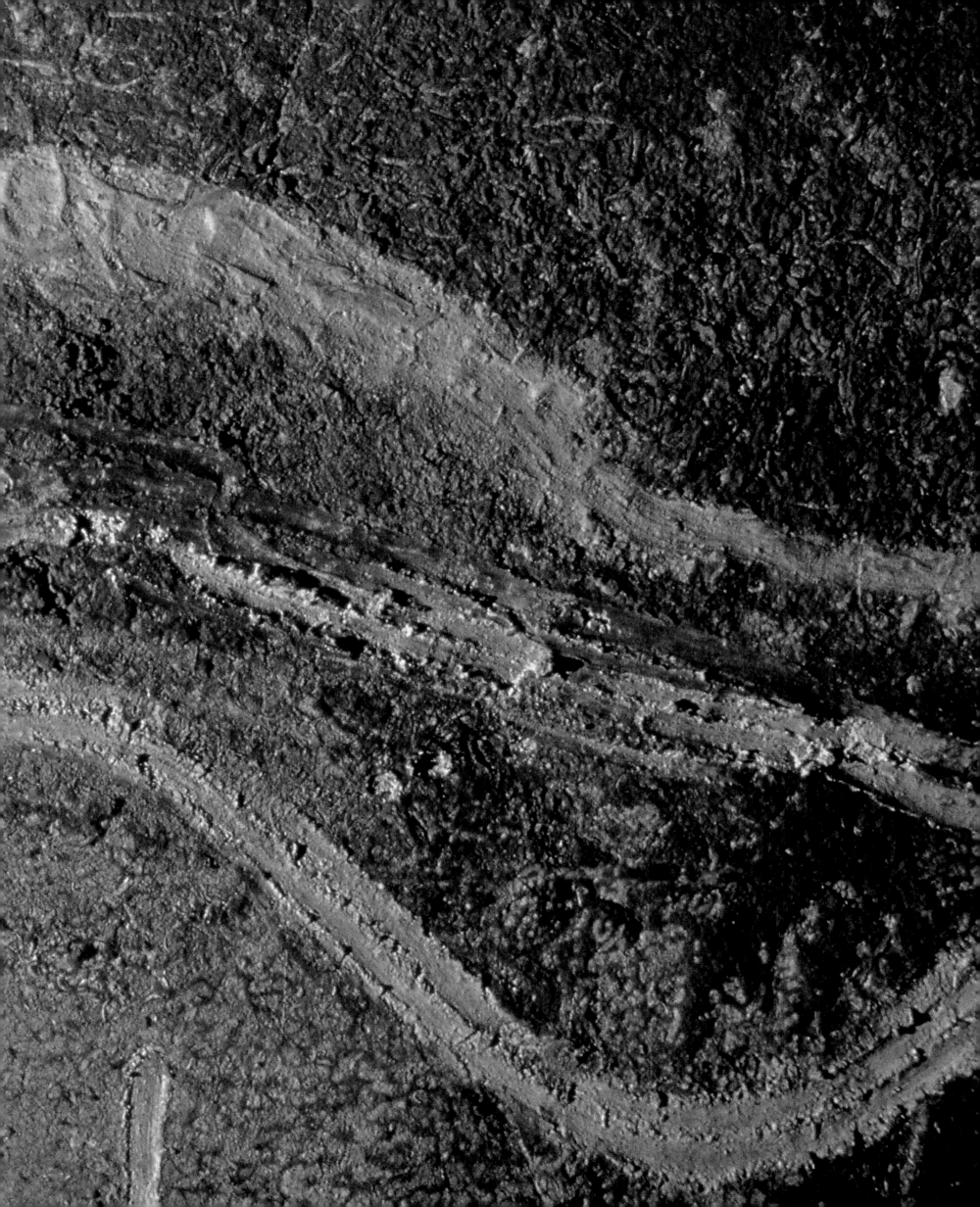

6

Ill. 154. The confronted rhinoceroses constitute one of the most original and most extraordinary images of Chauvet Cave. They may represent the behaviour of two males at the time of sexual display.

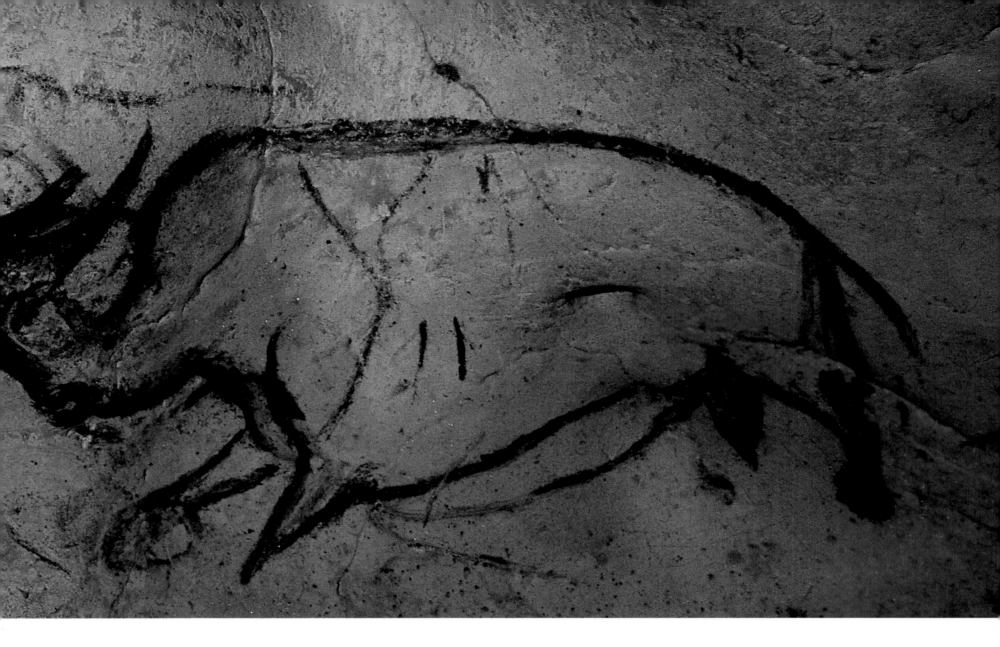

LOTS OF ANIMALS AND SIGNS

The first research carried out in the cave had revealed several important facts about the themes depicted:[1] the diversity of animal species (fourteen); the emphasis on dangerous, non-hunted animals (felines, rhinoceroses, mammoths, bears); the large number of big red dots, especially in the chambers close to the entrance; the presence of bizarre signs that evoke insects or birds; the absence of any human figures, with the possible exception of the enigmatic 'Sorcerer'.

Since then, the list of species has grown, with the musk ox. The owl has been identified as a long-eared owl with its head seen full face and its body viewed from the back. By contrast, the careful examination of the sinuous lines in the same area has led us to abandon the hypothesis of a second bird. Many other details have been brought to light, and the preference for big, non-hunted animals has been confirmed. The production of the big red dots, though not their function, has been elucidated. Apart from the hand prints and stencils, the human theme has been enriched with female pubic triangles and an extraordinary female silhouette associated with a composite being.

We now know more than twice as many animal depictions as we did when the previous book was published. The conventions used in their creation allow us to tackle the problem of the art's unity or diversity with some solid arguments. Ethologists have managed to shed light on some postures of the animals depicted. A reappraisal of the cave's walls, as thorough as possible, given the demands of preserving the vulnerable floors, enables us to obtain a better understanding of the originality of these numerous animals.

6

LOTS OF ANIMALS AND SIGNS

The Dots and Hands

Three categories of dots exist in the cave's different sectors. First of all, little dots, which are common in most Palaeolithic decorated caves, are found either in direct association with the animals or in isolated groups. They are more or less the size of an ochre-covered finger. Most of them are red, even when they are superimposed on black paintings, but in these cases they do not make remarkable anatomical points materialize. They are found on the head or neck of several horses and a feline (ill. 160).

The dots that are not associated with animals can be in groups of two, or organized into curved lines of about ten juxtaposed specimens, or may even form a sign, like the barbed motif in the Brunel Chamber. Other, bigger dots are often aligned or grouped as a cluster. Some of them can be isolated and signify remarkable topographic places. Red in colour, they are primarily distributed in the first part of the cave.

The most surprising category comprises almost five hundred prints of palms covered with ochre, organized in whole spreads, mostly in the Brunel Chamber – nearly 420 dots grouped on four panels (ills. 59–62, 156 and 157). They also occur under the Panel of Hand Prints and as far as

the End Chamber, this time in an arc of a circle above a group of felines. This original technique gives the dots another symbolic dimension, as they are both dots and partial hand prints (ill. 146).

However, six complete hand prints (ill. 75) and five red hand stencils are found grouped (except for a print in the Brunel Chamber) in the Red Panels Gallery, associated with prints of palms covered in ochre. Whereas the palms are all of right hands, two prints are left hands and one hand stencil has its thumb on the left.[2] The technique used is sometimes different, as the hand stencils were obtained by spraying (ill. 77).

This new evidence confirms that hand prints are concentrated in an area around Mediterranean France, especially in the Rhône Valley and its surroundings (Bayol, La Baume-Latrone, Grotte aux Points, Cosquer). Chauvet, which is the first to contain palms covered in ochre, reveals the importance of a theme that was hitherto considered rare in Palaeolithic art.

These organized groupings of ochre palm prints are charged with emotion, because they make it possible to characterize individuals and give the painter a physical reality. The size, sex and

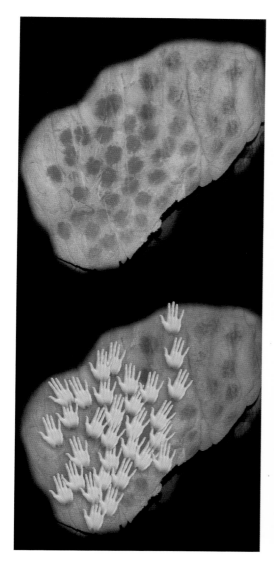

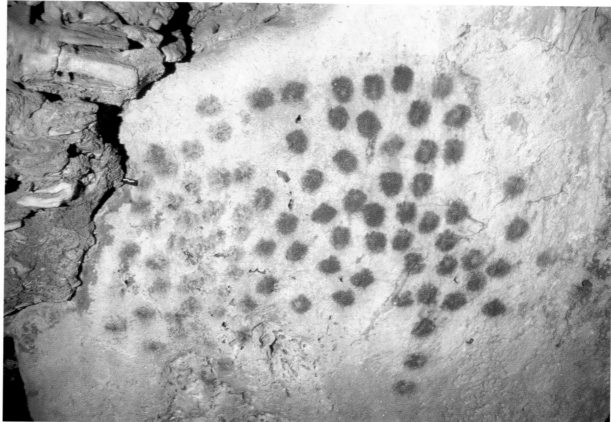

handedness of the creator can be identified. Sometimes, certain physical imperfections can be discerned.

For instance, the man in the Panel of the Dotted Animal has a slightly curved right little finger, which is very visible on certain prints. This characteristic makes it possible to follow his progress in the cave: it is certain that it is the same man who left the hand prints further on, under the Panel of Hand Prints, because he is recognizable from this little finger.

This tracking game of 30,000 years ago makes us conscious that the people are there, they lose their anonymity and reveal themselves to us, certainly through their talent and the different styles they use, but also through a bent little finger.

**Dominique Baffier
and Valérie Feruglio**

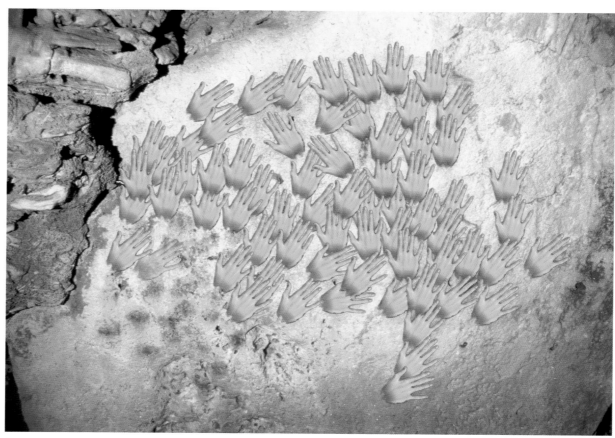

The Signs

In Chauvet Cave, forty-five collections of signs have been counted.[3] This number only takes into account the lines, circles, dashes or broken lines.[4] We shall not go into any more detail about the big red signs that have been described earlier (ills. 158 and 159).

In the whole of the first part of the cave, most of the signs are drawn in red. In the second half, pigments are abandoned in favour of incision, engraving, scraping or drawing with a finger. The technique has absolutely no influence on the theme, as the same subjects are found in every case: dashes or short vertical lines associated in twos and threes; parallel or sub-parallel lines; sinuous lines; vertical lines that seem to mark the base of certain rock pendants or the entrance of galleries such as the Cactus Gallery.

These signs are found in close association with a few animals. In the Red Panels Gallery, two W-shaped motifs are included in a rhinoceros frieze (ill. 76). In the Alcove of the Yellow Horses, dashes are placed close to the little horse heads (ill. 62) and the dots.

Overall, the geometric motifs seem to be modest or in any case very simple, except for the big red signs on the Panel of the Signs. This area of the cave, not far from the passage towards the second part, may play the role of a privileged thematic space, as, over a small surface, the signs are the dominant feature, while animal figures are relegated to the background.

Carole Fritz and Gilles Tosello

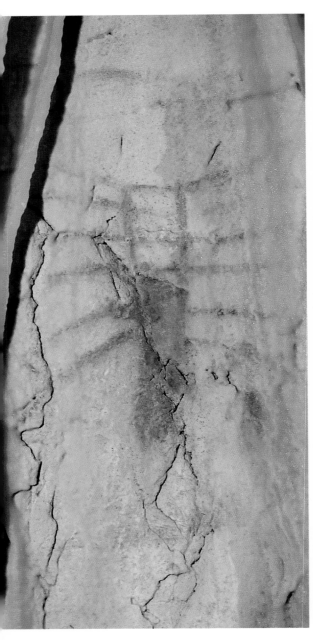 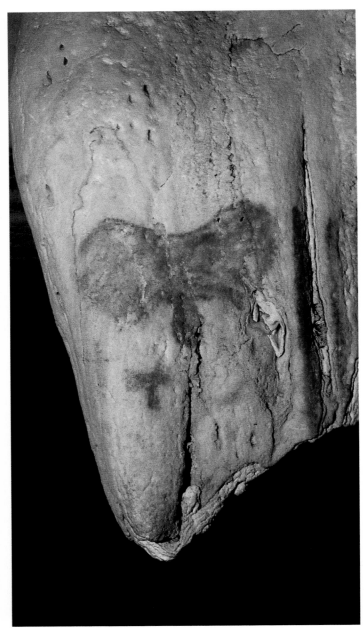

Above left and right
Ills. 158 and 159. Geometric signs reminiscent of insects in the Red Panels Gallery.

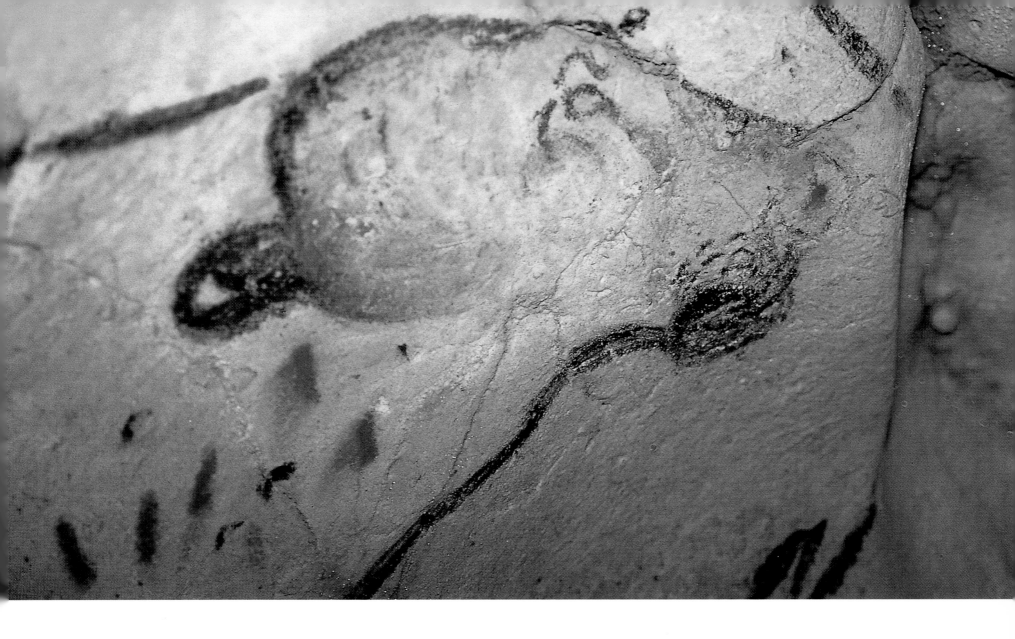

Depictions of Humans

Apart from the hand prints and stencils mentioned above,[5] six other graphic units will be excluded from this section. Two are omitted because of an erroneous reading.[6] The interpretation of four other drawings is more problematical; it is possible that a vulva is associated with the engraved horses of the Brunel Chamber, and three groups of painted or engraved lines on the right wall of the End Chamber could be interpreted as anthropomorphous anatomical segments. However, only depictions that are indisputably human will be considered here. There are six of them.

On five occasions, the Aurignacians depicted pubic triangles on the cave's walls. Although three are engraved and two are black, they are very similar (ills. 166, 167 and 168). All are drawn about 1.80 m (almost 6 feet) above the floor, and are of similar dimensions, slightly bigger than lifesize. The choice of the elements

represented seems systematic. A strongly curving line forms the limit of the upper contour. A continuous line or two unjoined lines at the bottom indicate the fold of the groin. The upper junction of these lines can be open, or closed, as if it were not a major concern to finish them. The vulvar cleft is clearly indicated by a vertical line. These elements are exclusive of all others for the three engraved triangles. After the outlines of the two painted triangles were drawn, a black infill was made, especially in the lower part. The cleft was then engraved. The incision was marked so strongly that it removed both the black pigment and the rock's yellow surface film, thus giving it a white appearance. These five drawings show great cultural similarities. Unless they are the product of a single artist (in which case these similarities are the result of an individual vision and one hand),

Above
Ill. 160. Short red lines drawn on to the forequarters of a lion in the niche of the Panel of the Horses.

Left
Ill. 161. The distribution of human depictions.

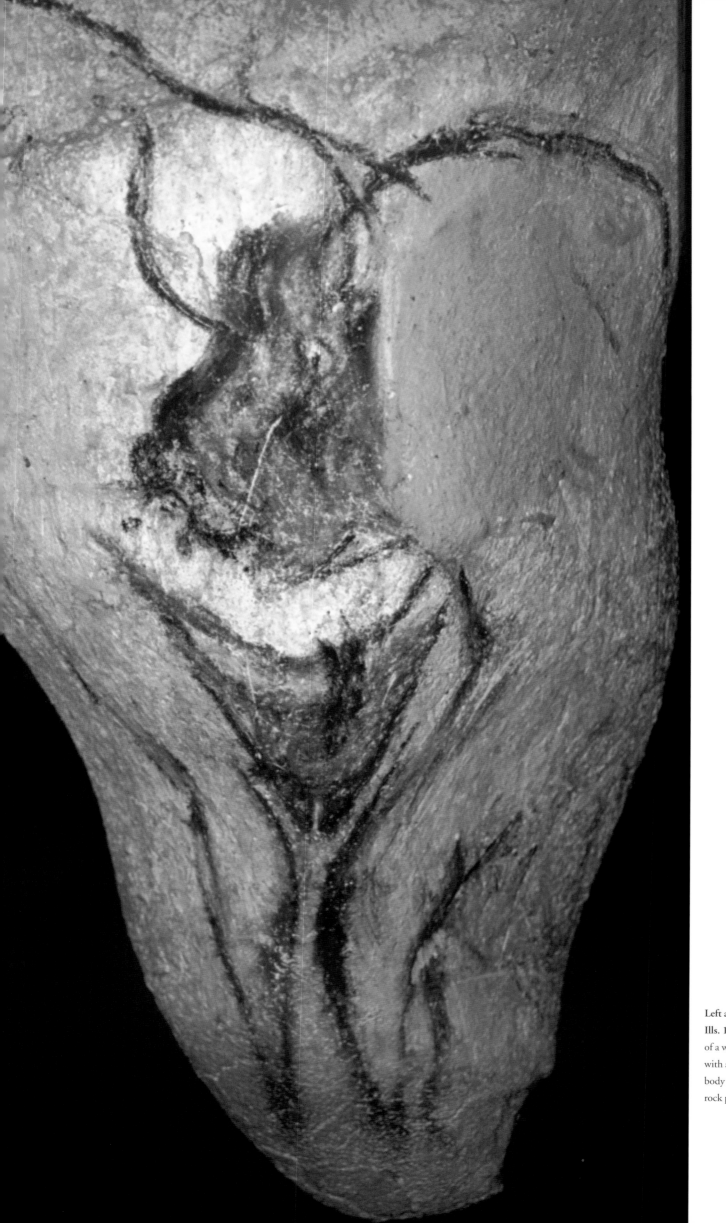

Left and right

Ills. 162 and 163. A composition that links a depiction of a woman, reduced to the lower part of the body, with a composite being, bison in the upper part of its body with a human hand. The conical shape of the rock pendant causes distortions in the photographs.

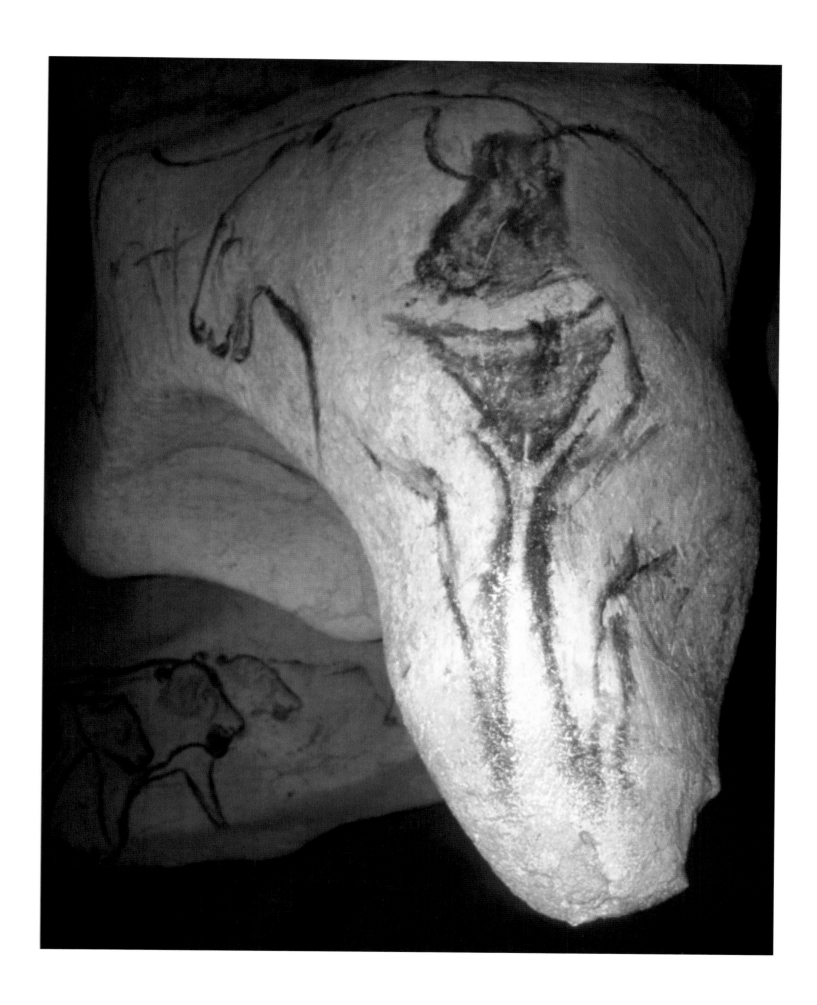

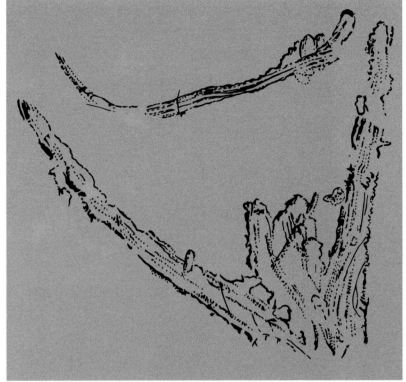

this uniformity of choice and form of lines reveals stereotypes that were deeply ingrained for the theme of pubic triangles.[7] Four times, the triangle is isolated from any other anatomical segment.

In the last case, it is associated with other elements of the body and, quite certainly, with a complex, exceptional, even fundamental composition in the minds of those who came to draw it at the end of the cave. The artist began by sketching a typical 'Venus', bigger than lifesize, seen from the front around a rock ridge (ill. 162).[8] The pubis is clearly marked. The legs, with fleshy thighs, end as points. The feet are missing. All of the upper part of the body is absent, but this may not always have been the case. The buttocks could have been, at least, begun and then obliterated. It is highly probable for the right buttock, which was destroyed by the drawing of a feline later on, and possible for the left buttock, whose position is covered by areas of rubbing and many eroded lines. These obliterations were deliberate, as in the case

of the far left part of the pubic triangle. They are equally selective and relate directly to the depictions that were superimposed on them, such as the main one, a composite being, half-man and half-animal, nicknamed the 'Sorcerer' since its discovery.[9]

The head of a bison is drawn in some detail. The chest and the start of the hump are both depicted. The arm is human, extended by a hand with long fingers that hang downwards.[10] An in-depth study of this composition has not yet been carried out, but will perhaps make it possible to decipher the rest of the body. This whole wall is very eroded and covered with numerous lines (ill. 164), which still have to be interpreted.[11]

These drawings, in relation to the cave itself and to the depictions of animals, were certainly not placed where they are by chance. All of them occur in the network that comprises the Megaloceros Gallery and the End Chamber. The engraved triangles face each other, in the Megaloceros Gallery,

at the entrance of the two main adjacent side passages. The pubis, drawn on the right wall of the End Chamber, is exactly above the access to the Belvedere Gallery.[12] The Venus/bison-man composition occupies a central topographic position in the End Chamber, but it is peripheral to the arrangement of its parietal decoration.[13] Perhaps the depiction of the woman is directly related to the corridor leading to the Sacristy, which opens just behind it.[14]

All the pubic triangles occupy a privileged and perhaps essential position in the construction of the parietal layout. They provide strong evidence for a real thematic structure that is closely associated with the cave's topography.

Yanik Le Guillou

Top
Ill. 166. Pubic triangle with vulva, engraved in the Megaloceros Gallery.

Above left
Ill. 167. Pubic triangle drawn in black on the right wall of the End Chamber, just above the entrance to the Belvedere Gallery.

Above right
Ill. 168. Engraved pubic triangles with vulva in the Megaloceros Gallery.

The Indeterminate Animals

The depictions of indeterminate animals, presented together here for the sake of convenience, in fact fall into three distinct categories. Firstly, the *composite animals* combine anatomical characteristics that are peculiar to different species. Secondly, *indeterminate animals* are definitely animals, but it is impossible to identify them more precisely. Thirdly, *fantastic animals* are partly the result of imagination.

These categories pose numerous problems, which can only be mentioned here.[15] For example, it is sometimes possible to claim that a particular image shows a male cave lion hunting, whereas in other cases one has to be content with a less precise label (feline), without this animal being considered indeterminate.

For some figures, what is obvious to one researcher may not be so to another, and we have sometimes had lively discussions.[16] So numbers for different species, although dry and apparently precise, can never be more than indicative.

The figures may be indeterminate because of external reasons (deterioration after completion, ill. 171) and other causes that were intrinsic to the creation of an ambiguous or unclear image, whether it be the clumsiness of an ungifted artist, our ignorance of certain Palaeolithic conventions, or the artist's deliberate desire for a lack of differentiation (ill. 169). It is not always easy to choose between these causes, even though they are determining factors as far as the artists' intentions go.

The composite animals only include a vertical feline with ungulate legs (right wall of the niche in the Panel of the Horses). We have also only counted a single fantastic animal, to the right of the central niche of the Panel of the Big Lions in the End Chamber (ill. 169).

The indeterminate animals, a total of 78 of them, represent 19% of the animals portrayed. They are more or less complete in 18 cases. Isolated heads or heads and necks come to 17, and there are 37 incomplete bodies, and 6 other figures. In almost half of the cases (34), their indeterminate status could be accidental: bear clawmarks have damaged some figures in the Skull Chamber and made them illegible (ill. 171); some figures have been superimposed; natural erosion has taken place; some figures have been scraped deliberately at a later date.

The topographic distribution of the indeterminate animals shows a few differences in the percentages for the animals counted in each of these places, not so much between the first part of the cave (23% indeterminate) and the second part (18%) as between the whole of the Hillaire Chamber–Skull Chamber–Gallery of the Crosshatching (26%) and the Megaloceros Gallery–End Chamber group (11%), as there are nearly two and a half times more indeterminates in the first group than in the second.

These differences do not seem to be caused just by the techniques used, even if the engraved figures (39 or 50%) are much more numerous than the red (12 or 15%) or the black (27 or 35%).

These observations reinforce the idea that it was not the same artists working in the different chambers, despite the use of the same conventions for the animal depictions. In many cases where we are not sure, where we have to put up with classifying particular figures among the indeterminate animals, or even the 'undetermined' figures, and thus with omitting them from the statistics for the animals, it must have been obvious for the artists, and perhaps for their contemporaries, that it was a rhinoceros, a lion or a mammoth.

Jean Clottes

Below
Ill. 171. An indeterminate animal at the back of the Skull Chamber. In this case, the figure is classified as indeterminate by accident, because the whole of this panel has been spoiled by bear clawmarks that postdate the drawings.

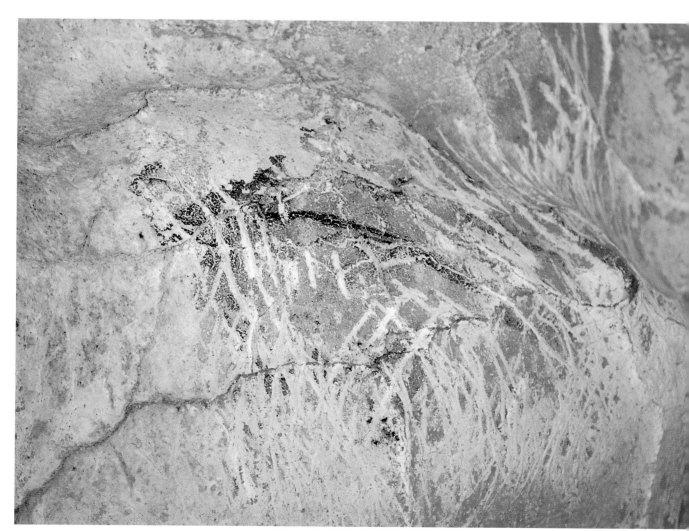

The Rhinoceroses

The image of the rhinoceros is one of the three dominant themes at Chauvet. In all, 65 have been counted, that is, about 16% of the animals depicted. This group corresponds to almost three-quarters of the representations of this animal in French decorated caves.

Their very unequal topographic distribution evolves from the entrance towards the back. After an unobtrusive and fragmentary appearance in the Chamber of the Bear Hollows, their number grows regularly from the Panel of Hand Prints onwards, with 7 individuals. It reaches its maximum in the End Chamber, where this theme is reproduced 34 times.

The majority of figures (54%) have complete outlines. The lines are not reduced to the head and neck, as for the felines. Most of the time, the limbs and the curve of the belly are missing in the incomplete animals, which means that this animal's identifying elements can be limited to the line that links the back, head and horns.

All are represented in profile, with a pronounced tendency for the left side (72%), as in the whole of the site's animal depictions (70%).

The silhouette of these pachyderms looks stocky, and yet it fits into a very stretched horizontal framework, accentuated by highly developed horns and a low, elongated head. Constructed in a ratio of one to two (the animal is twice as long as it is high), this form of depiction is similar to that of the felines, whereas for the other animals the ratio is only two to three. These characteristics imply that the most developed figures are divided between these two themes, but the most imposing subject is a rhinoceros that is 2.80 m (over 9 feet) long, engraved and drawn in black in the centre of the Panel of the Big Lions. The average recorded for the 65 rhinoceroses is 88 cm (almost 35 in.), as opposed to 70 cm (almost 28 in.) for the other mammals.

In the Upper Palaeolithic, two species of rhinoceros are known in western Europe.[17] They belong to the same sub-family that is characterized by its long face with two horns. This is the steppe (or narrow-nosed) rhinoceros (*Dicerorhinus hemitoechus*), perhaps depicted in Lascaux's Shaft scene, and the 'woolly' rhinoceros (*Coelodonta antiquitatis*), by far the more abundant. It is almost always the latter that was the subject of portable or parietal depictions, as at Chauvet, where the great detail in the drawings confirms this attribution.

Two anatomical features that are easy to depict make it possible to recognize this species: on the one hand, the head is carried low; on the other, there is more of the very thick wool under the head, neck and belly, with a mane completing this coat. These characteristics, which are clear in the parietal drawings of Rouffignac and Font-de-Gaume, are found on most of the rhinoceroses in Chauvet.

Apart from the details that relate to repeated stylistic conventions, especially the depiction of the ears as juxtaposed semicircles and of the extremities of the legs (plug-shaped, ball-shaped or pointed), just one characteristic remains enigmatic: the broad transverse stripe that covers the middle of the body, reproduced on a number of these animals. It does not correspond to anything that is known and has never been recorded on the rhinoceroses in other caves.

The woolly rhinoceros has numerous affinities with one of the five present-day species, Africa's white rhinoceros (*Ceratotherium simum*), which is a similar size, and also has two horns, a long head carried low, and heavy limbs. These analogies do not signify a close kinship, as the two species belong to two different sub-families, but rather some superficial anatomical resemblances brought about by adaptation to analogous living environments: the woolly rhino and the white rhino inhabit the same

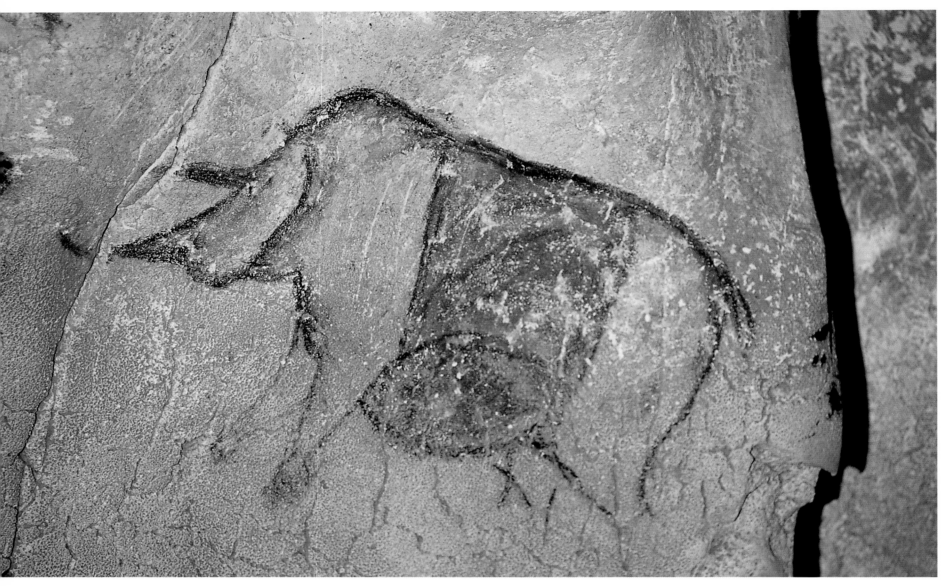

type of landscape, a steppe or savannah with differing degrees of tree cover, and they consume the same type of abrasive plants, gramineae. There are both ecological and ethological convergences: the white rhino is territorial and sedentary, and lives in groups of about ten individuals comprising a dominant male, several females and a few youngsters of both sexes. According to the results of palaeontological excavations, it seems that the woolly rhino lived in groups of the same size and structure, which explains their depictions in groups (ills. 129 and 130) and in lines, as at Chauvet or Rouffignac.

The white rhino's front (nasal) horn can exceed 1.50 m (5 feet) in length – the record is 1.66 m (nearly 5½ feet) – that is, 33 to 40% of the length of head + body – 3.75 m (over 12 feet), but able to reach 4.50 m (14½ feet). It is depicted in a wide variety of shapes – straight, S-shaped or sickle-shaped.

The females have longer and more slender horns than the males (ills. 173 and 174); they usually use them for guiding their young, which generally walk in front of their mother. A few rare fossil finds from Siberia show that the woolly rhino also possessed a front horn that varied in shape, with a length – which can exceed 1.20 m (nearly 4 feet) – that displays a clear sexual dimorphism. This fact is confirmed by the figures in Chauvet, where the nasal horn reveals that animals of both sexes are represented.

Finally, the sexual display of present-day rhinos includes brutal confrontations between partners and behaviour of this type could explain the diptych of the 'confronted rhinoceroses' on the Panel of the Horses.

Norbert Aujoulat and Claude Guérin

The Felines

Along with mammoths and rhinoceroses, the felines, of which there are 71, are among the predominant animals in the cave. Their muzzle, sometimes detailed, is in many cases simply sketched as two superimposed arcs of a circle. The bears' muzzle was drawn in the same way, but a steep break of slope (the 'stop') can be seen on their nose, whereas the lions' muzzle is rectilinear or slightly concave. The depiction of the whiskers by dots is peculiar to the felines, just as the long tail ending in a tuft. In addition, at Chauvet, when the shoulder of an animal is evoked by a sinuous vertical line on the forequarters, it is always a lion. The ears are round and often (in 19 cases) joined by a short curved line. The cave's only panther can be recognized from its spotted coat, depicted with some realism (ill. 71). Whether they be lions or panthers, they belong to extinct species.

Complete felines are rare (6 or 8.5%). Frequently, the head is depicted, with or without the forequarters, whereas the body is succinct. The lines of the back and belly, the legs, the hindquarters may or may not be present. Hence, partial felines are strongly predominant: 44 or 62%. Isolated heads form a sizeable minority (21 or 29.5%).

Some animals have their mouths open and sometimes show teeth. The scrotum can be seen on a single individual (ill. 127), but the massive size of certain lions means that they can be identified as males as well. None of them has a mane, which makes it possible to solve a problem that was posed long ago: in cave lions, the males did not have the abundant mane found on African lions.

Three-quarters of the felines face left (52 or 73.2%); the others (19 or 26.8%) face right. This choice is obvious on the left wall of the End Chamber. It could indicate a desire to show animals heading from the back towards the entrance. Two-thirds of the felines (47 or 66.2%) are black. The others are red (20 or 28.2%) or engraved (4 or 5.6%). Only 10 (14%) are both drawn and engraved.

The positioning of the felines is by no means random. The first part of the cave only contains 14 (19.7%), but those in the deep part of the cave are unequally distributed: none of them occurs among the engravings in the Hillaire Chamber, while the End Chamber contains 52 (73.2%), the others (7.1%) being in the Skull Chamber, on the Panel of the Horses and in the Megaloceros Gallery. Some choices are also obvious, in terms of location, in the techniques of depiction: 12 of the 20 red animals are in the first part, none occurs in the Hillaire and Skull Chambers, and there are only 8 in the End Chamber. The proportions are the other way round for the black animals (2 in the first part, 4 in the middle zone, 41 at the end).

Differences in terms of the sectors are also clear in the depiction of the animals and their size. The felines in the first chambers are relatively succinct and somewhat small. By contrast, resemblances abound between the middle part (niche in the Horse Sector) and the End Chamber, leading to the conclusion that they were both created in the same period.

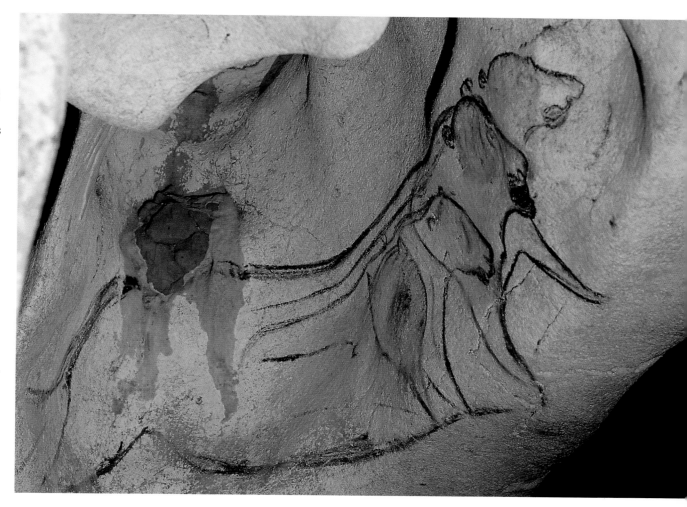

Above

Ill. 175. The group of strange lions in the End Chamber.

Left

Ill. 176. The distribution of felines.

Double page overleaf

Ill. 177. A couple of lions in the Alcove of the Lions. The upper one, a female, is crouching and showing its teeth, whereas the other one, a male, is stretching its neck.

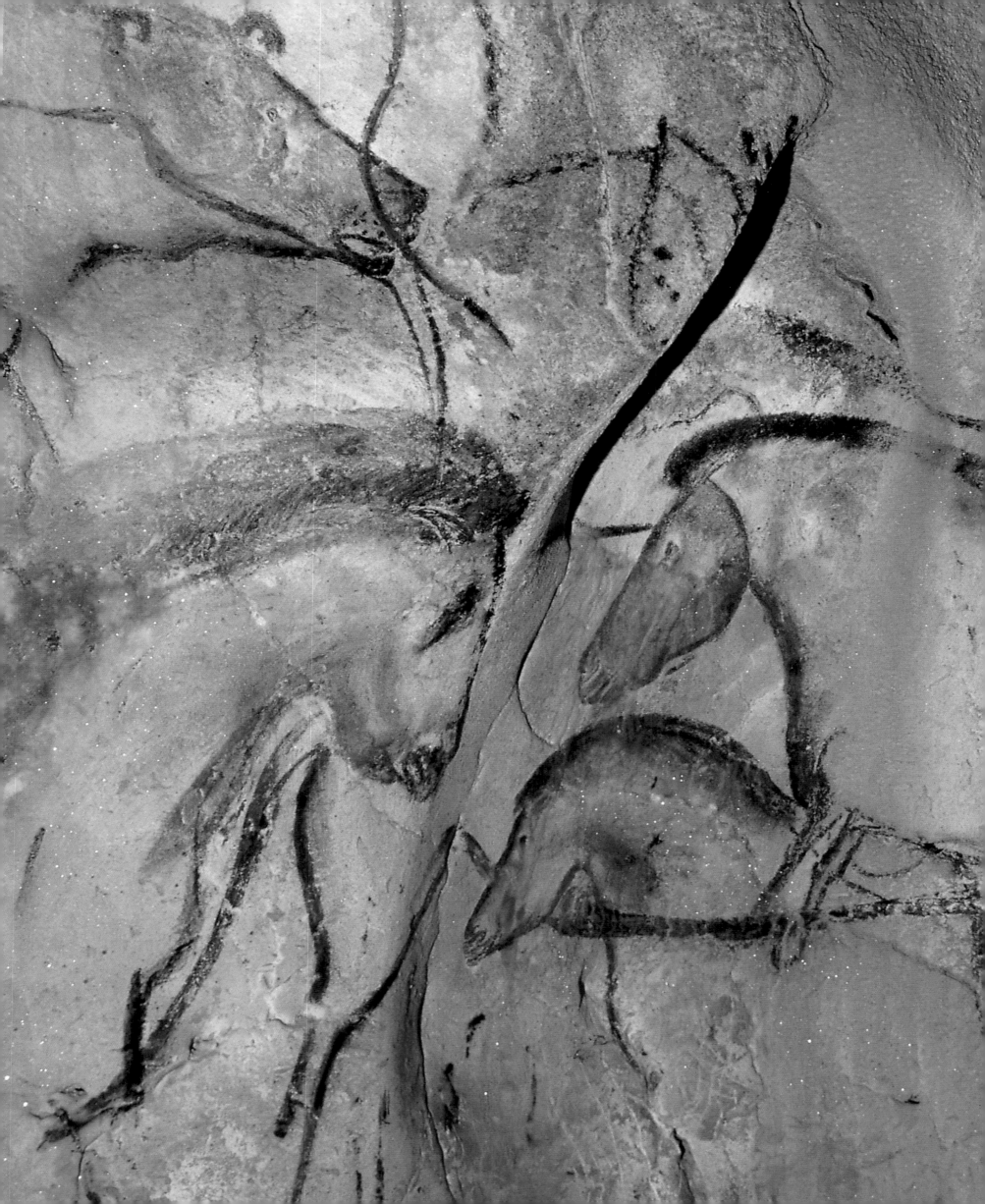

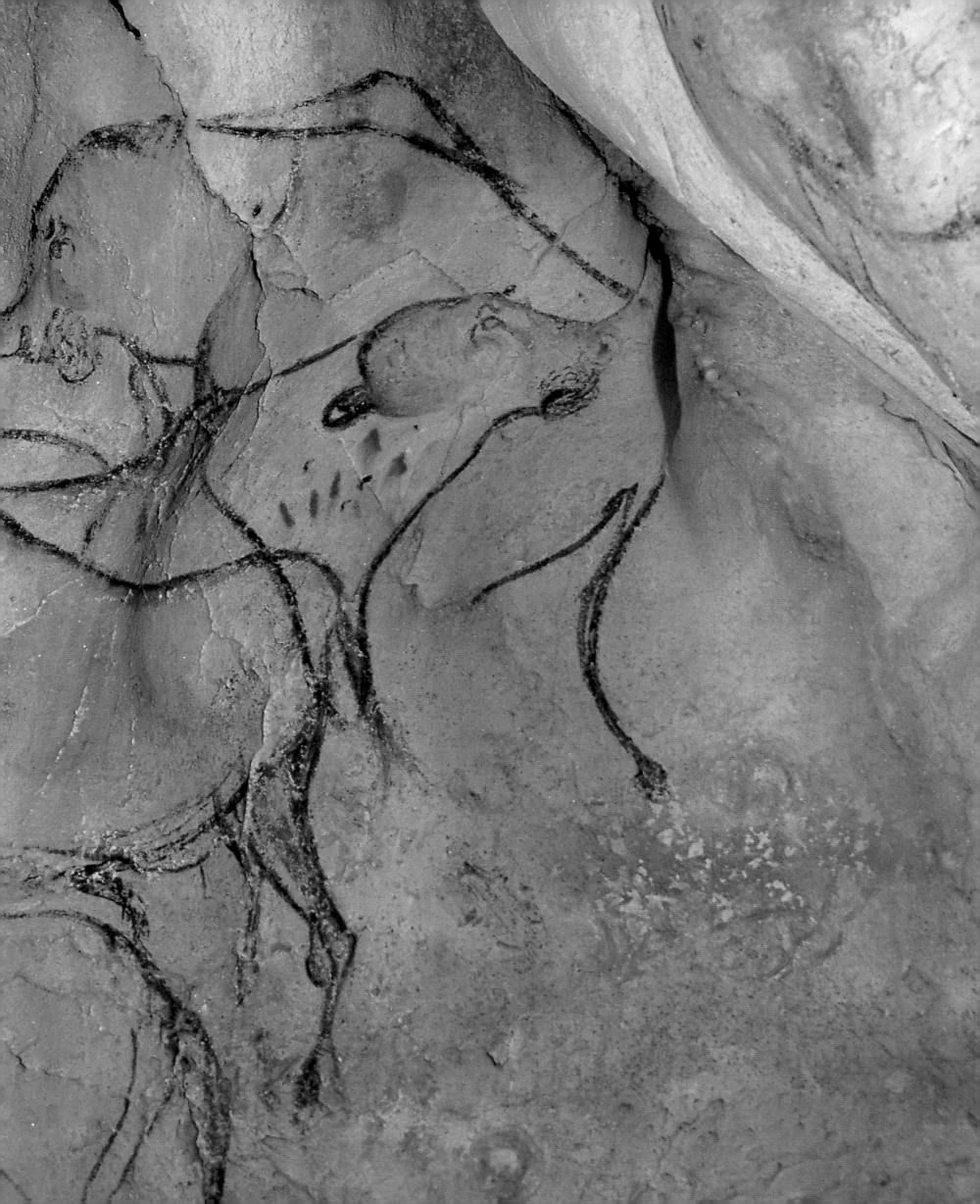

In the End Chamber, some heads are larger than lifesize (ill. 128). They are the only mammals in the cave to which this applies.

We cannot distinguish most of the felines in terms of sex or postures, even if this was not the case for their creators. Ten probable males and six females have been identified, as well as a possible lion cub.

Three scenes refer to known types of behaviour. In the Alcove of the Lions, a sitting lioness snarls, showing her teeth. Close to her, a young male faces in the opposite direction. The posture is that of a solicited female who is refusing advances and protecting herself (ill. 177). In the End Chamber, a lion and a lioness walk side by side. In contrast to the previous couple, the consenting female is rubbing against her companion before mating (ill. 127). As for the big panel to the right of the niche, in the same chamber, this is a hunting scene that combines animals of both sexes, with tense expressions (ill. 133), facing in the same direction, towards a group of bison.

Certainly, when lions are hunting big game, as here, males would join females in the chase.

Present-day lions sleep a great deal and are rarely seen in action. This fact, together with the precise details, shows that the creators of the drawings observed the animals for a long time, from quite close quarters. These Palaeolithic people did not hunt lions. Nowadays in Africa, even when the hunters do not use firearms, the lions flee humans and remain unapproachable.

The images of lions are more numerous in Chauvet Cave than in any other Palaeolithic site. They cover a broad range, from the most succinct to the most elaborate, from expressionless isolated heads to the monumental and exceptional hunting scene. Some felines are strangely deformed (disproportionate bodies, muzzle too big; ill. 175). In these cases, the stories attached to them are no longer lion stories, they are human stories.

Jean Clottes and Craig Packer

Above
Ill. 178. The distribution of mammoths.

Opposite
Ill. 179. The four-tusked mammoth in the Sacristy, superimposed on bear clawmarks.

The Mammoths

The 66 mammoths represent about 16% of the animals portrayed. There are 3 painted in red, 3 brown,[18] 18 black (sometimes with engraving on top) and 42 white or beige, engraved or scraped with a tool or by hand. Complete or incomplete, they can be detailed (eye, eye-socket, mouth, prehensile organ at the end of the trunk, tusks, ventral fleece and tail hair, three or four ball-shaped feet), especially in the End Chamber (ill. 180), where four animals have one ear.[19] Sometimes, the forequarters or the bodies are blackened with stumping or whitened through scraping. Others, rapidly drawn and crude, have one detail highlighted: curled up trunk, thick-lipped mouth, anal flap. Finally, there are sketches, simple sinuous lines that are difficult to identify when the forehead, trunk or tail are missing. In all cases, the use of relief is frequent (rump and trunk simulated by the rock, calcite growths for the wide splay of the legs, arched belly that follows a niche, neck in

a cavity and withers of the same animal on a natural bump), as is the integration with natural contours. More rarely, movement is suggested (oblique animal, trunk undulating or edged but always downward, leg outstretched, tail raised). Perspective, frontal or semi-frontal, is conveyed by the asymmetrical curving of the tusks and the differing positions of the legs.

Mammoths are not distributed in an even way: nine at the start of the cave, the rest at the back. They are present in the remote zones, and sometimes it is even the only species to be seen (Morel Chamber, Candle Gallery and Belvedere Gallery). This disparity is even more marked in terms of colours and dimensions. The smallest – 25 × 25 cm (nearly 10 × 10 in.), a red figure – is at the entrance of the Cactus Gallery (ill. 68). The most imposing[20] – 2.35 × 1.35 m (7¾ × 4½ feet) – overlaps two other big mammoths, both of which are also totally scraped, thus creating

a white surface, 4 m (about 13 feet) in length, in the Skull Chamber (ill. 98), a veritable mammoth chamber: from the centre and without powerful lighting, it is possible to see about ten of them. Moreover, a massive rock evokes the silhouette of a proboscidian.

Mammoths are abundant, and are often found in twos, threes and, exceptionally, fours.[21] They may follow each other, be in

the End Chamber, Hand Stencils). On the ceiling of the Gallery of the Crosshatching, a horse and four mammoths, which are increasingly schematic towards the top of the panel, were drawn by hand (ill. 99). This drawing evokes a large composition at La Baume-Latrone (Gard).[23] Several works in the two caves show other similarities: detailed sinuous trunk, thick-lipped mouth, divergent tusks, tapering limbs,

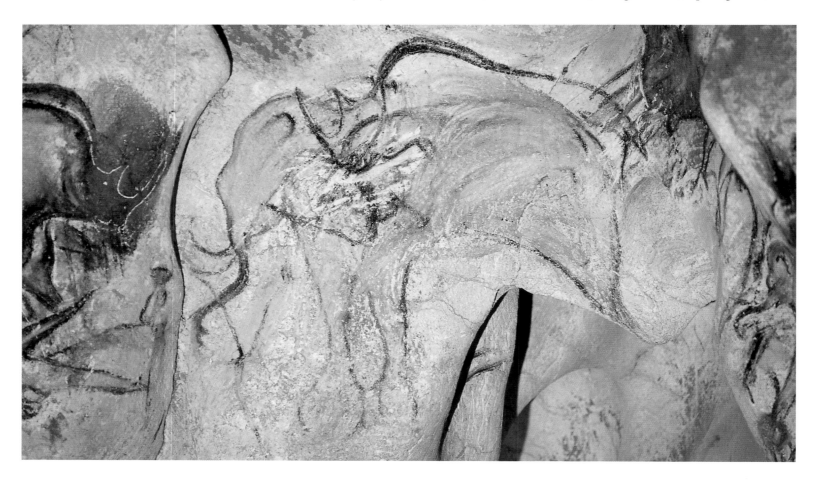

Above

Ill. 180. A mammoth above the central niche of the Lion Panel in the End Chamber. Note its big front feet, the trunk ending in 'finger and thumb', and the two tusks.

confrontation, or face each other on opposite walls. When they are tiered or superimposed, they may be arranged in such a way that, for example, a belly line is shared by two animals (ill. 145). The overlaps between figures and their state of freshness also indicate time differences that still have to be checked: on the one hand, lively and angular engravings[22] and cervico-dorsal lines are late; on the other hand, others are destroyed by scraping carried out before black drawings were made.

Finally, several times, there is clearly a close relationship with horses (niche in

withers added on to a rectilinear back. These characteristics had hitherto not appeared in the Ardèche;[24] by contrast, the arched belly, which is reputedly classic, is not common here.

The mammoth is the animal that was drawn most frequently in the Rhône Valley and as far as Burgundy. At Chauvet, as is often the case, the treatment of the figures is variable – a striving for naturalism or a tendency towards abstraction – but analogies in non-specific details confer some unity to this group.

Bernard Gély

The Horses

Forty horses have been identified using criteria such as the presence of a mane, a sinuous back line or a long tail. The head must have at least a round muzzle, a rectilinear nose or small ears. In terms of numbers, the horse is the fourth species of the cave, far behind the lion, mammoth or rhinoceros. Half of the horses are complete animals; the rest are represented by the head or forequarters. As for techniques, 13 are drawn in black, 12 simply engraved or sketched with a finger; the 9 most elaborate figures employ stump drawing (ill. 183), underlined by engraving.

The stylistic treatment of the horses is very diversified, from schematic profiles sketched with a few movements – small horses painted in yellow in the Brunel Chamber (ill. 62) or engraved in the Hillaire Chamber – to the most accomplished works – Panel of the Horses, Megaloceros Gallery. There are no graphic conventions that are widely shared, as in the case of the rhinoceroses or bison, for example. However, some analogies make it possible to compare certain horses belonging to the same panel, or even specimens located in different sectors (Alcove of the Lions and Panel of the Engraved Horse, Panel of the Horses and Megaloceros Gallery). In general, the head is often more carefully drawn, even when the animal is complete.

The horses are distributed throughout the cave, from the entrance to the back; in at least two cases (on the Panel of the Horses and in the niche at the centre of the composition in the End Chamber) the place where they have been drawn seems remarkable.

Carole Fritz and Gilles Tosello

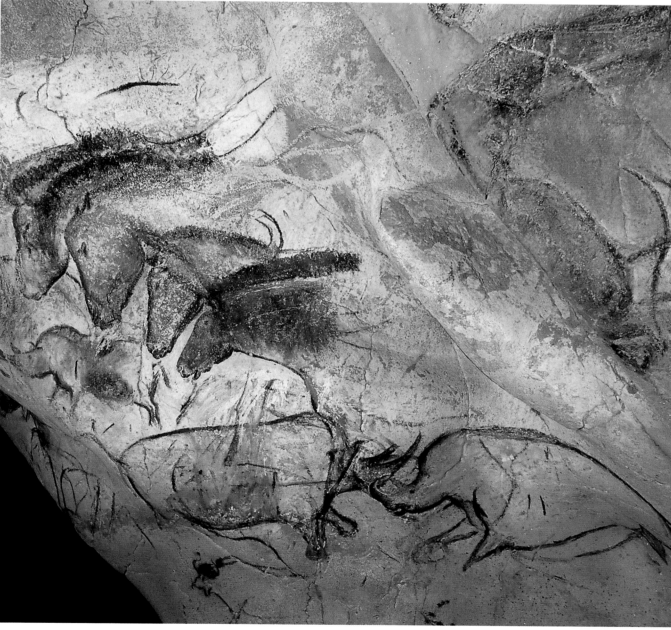

Left
Ill. **181**. The distribution of horses.

Below
Ill. **182**. The Panel of the Horses.

Double page overleaf
Ill. **183**. The horses in the Alcove of the Lions in the Horse Sector.

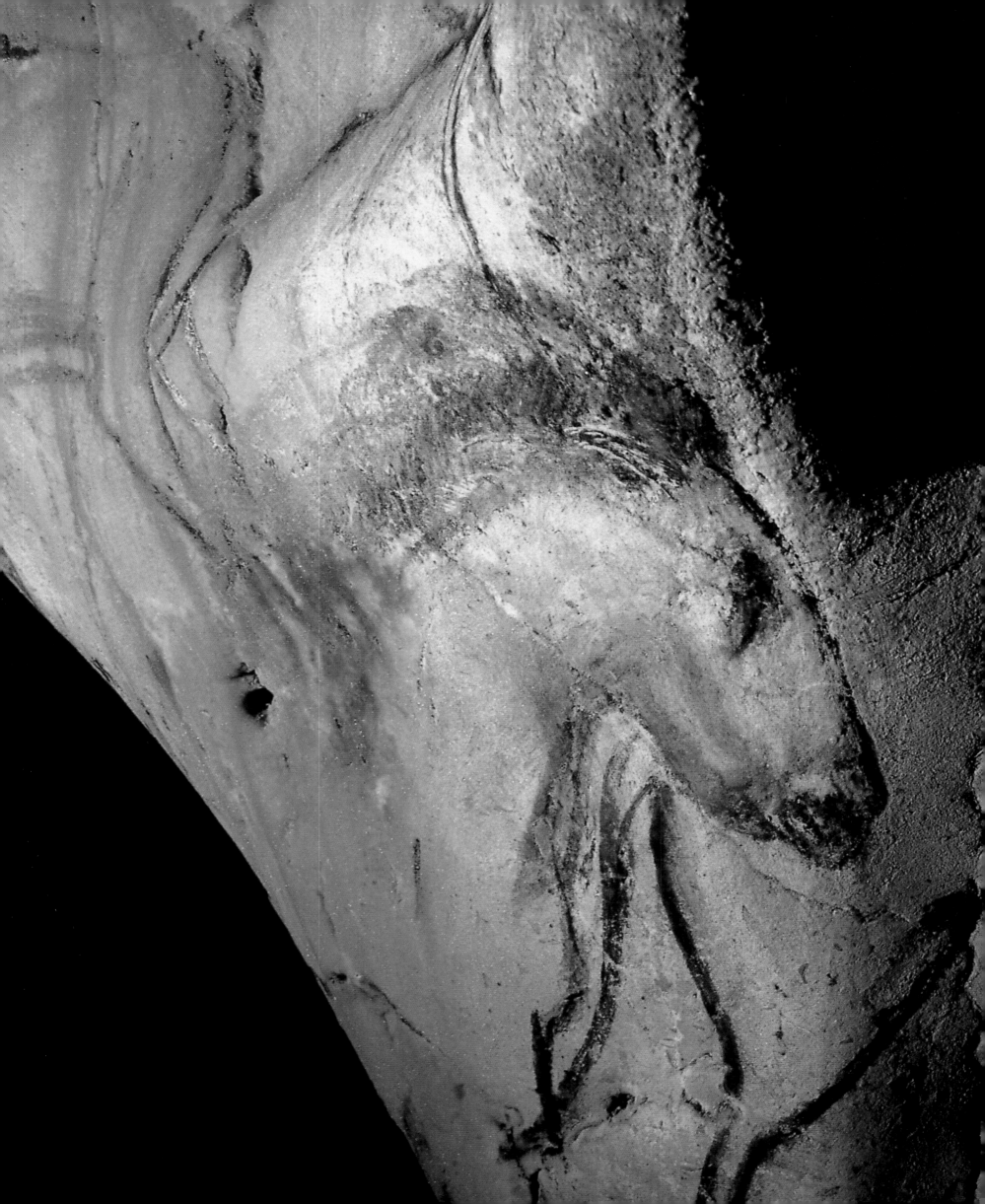

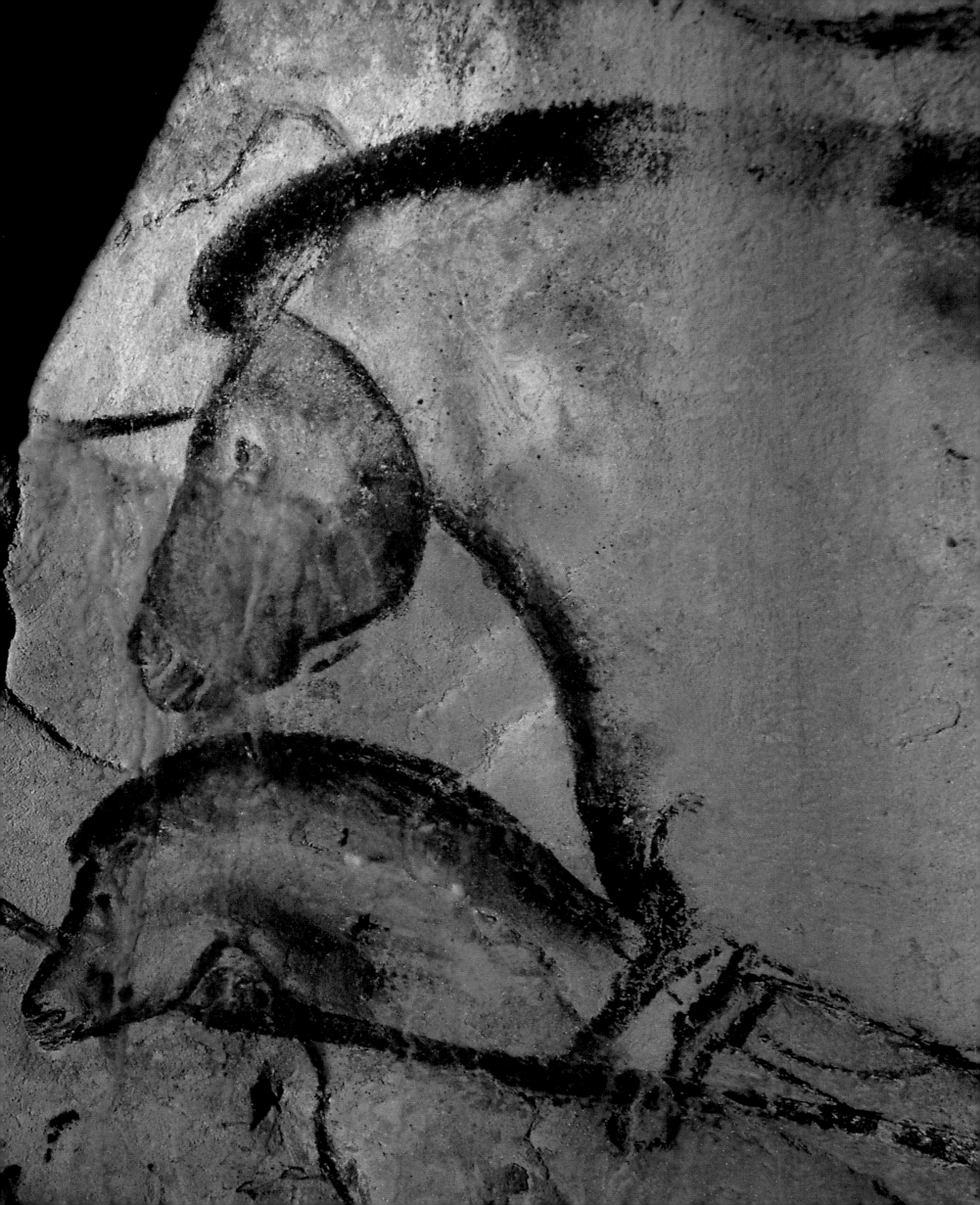

The Bovines

Above
Ill. 184. A large engraved bison in the Sacristy. It displays the same characteristics as its fellows drawn in black in the cave: seen in profile, its horns in frontal perspective, with a big tuft of hair on its head.

Right
Ill. 185. The distribution of bovines.

With 31 specimens, the bison is the fifth most frequent species. Apart from one red painting and five engravings (ill. 184), the bison are drawn in black (perhaps embellished with engraving on some animals that are too far away for us to be able to examine them in detail). Most of the time (in 23 instances), they are incomplete, reduced to the head or head and neck. The hump is not strongly marked. The representation of the bison is highly systematic, especially where the head is concerned: linear, arch- or lyre-shaped horns arranged on both sides of a voluminous chignon, pointed beard, small round eye. This image is found, give or take a few variations, in all individuals.

The most striking figures are the eight-legged bison (Alcove of the Lions) and, especially, the four heads seen from the front, arranged vertically on a ridge (ill. 132); this collection is unique in

parietal art. Another bison combines a head seen full face and a body in profile drawn in two different planes, taking advantage of a corner of the wall in the End Chamber (ill. 136). This sector alone contains 21 animals: so the bison appears to be a species that is not only rare but also limited to the deepest parts of the cave.

About 10 aurochs have been identified on the basis of determining anatomical characteristics that distinguish them from the other bovine, the bison (horns with an elongated S-shape, projecting forwards, absence of dewlap, frontal chignon and hump). They are grouped around the Large Collapse and in the Skull Chamber. Most of them (8) are found in the Horse Sector (Panel of the Horses and its reverse, Alcove of the Lions, Reindeer Panel).

While 4 aurochs are complete, the others are drawn as a head and neck (3) or simply a head (3). The techniques used are predominantly drawings in black (8); however, the 2 specimens in the Skull Chamber are engraved (ill. 96) or sketched with a finger. The 3 most elaborate figures, the aurochs on the Panel of the Horses, employ stumping (ill. 186).

The stylistic treatment of the aurochs rests on a few very well codified attributes; the sinuous horns, strongly projecting forwards, make it possible to identify even the most succinct examples; the small, round ear is placed just at the base of the horn. A few details are peculiar to some individuals: a 'short beard' on the chin of the aurochs on the Panel of the Horses; a fold of skin placed between the forelegs or immediately behind them (Reindeer Alcove and Panel). These features must have corresponded to an anatomical reality that permitted precise recognition of the species.

Carole Fritz and Gilles Tosello

The Ibex

It has been possible to count about 20 ibex on the basis of one determining factor: the presence of at least one arching horn at the top of the skull. Failing that, a thick body, short limbs and a short tail have enabled us to identify a few additional animals. The ibex are more often schematized than complete, being reduced just to their head or simply the horn followed by the start of a back line (9 times). Even on the complete individuals, details such as the eye, ear, mouth and indications of the coat are missing. Three figures are closely linked to the contours of the wall (ill. 187).

Apart from one male with impressive horns in the Megaloceros Gallery (ill. 121), the ibex were sketched rapidly and, even if there are some sketches that are full of expression, the species was not researched as thoroughly as the horse or lion were. Most ibex were drawn by incising the clay, with fingers or a stick.

The ibex is only distributed in the first half of the cave (Recess of the Bears, Panther Panel) around the Large Collapse and in the Skull Chamber; a single example is present in the Megaloceros Gallery.

Carole Fritz and Gilles Tosello

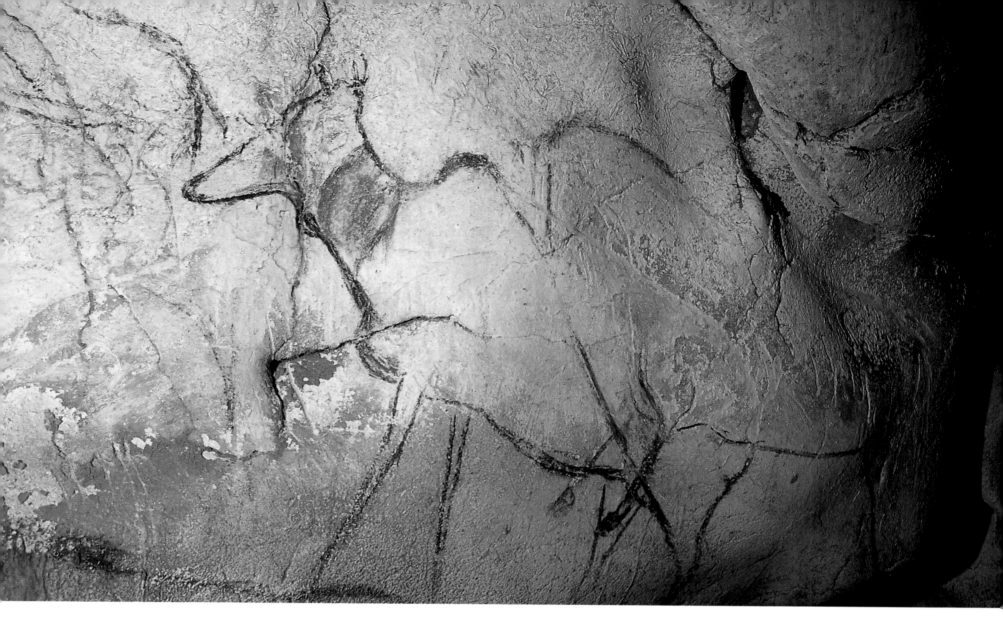

The Cervids

There are 25 cervids, which thus constitute the seventh species represented. Most of them are drawn in black, one is engraved and three are red. With the exception of those three, which, unsurprisingly, are located in the first part of the cave, they are all to be found in the second part, especially in the Hillaire and Skull Chambers, where they are even grouped in panels. The criteria for identifying them are obviously the antlers and their general appearance.

The difference between the reindeer (ill. 191) and the red deer (ill. 192) can be seen in the antlers, which are more or less rectilinear for the red deer, but curve forwards in the reindeer. The body is also different. The back line is more sloping in the red deer, more rectilinear in the reindeer. The withers and the thicker coat around the chest – even forming a dewlap in some – are the attributes of the reindeer. Conversely, for

Above

Ill. 189. A megaloceros, recognizable by its enormous withers, in the Megaloceros Gallery.

Left

Ill. 190. The distribution of cervids.

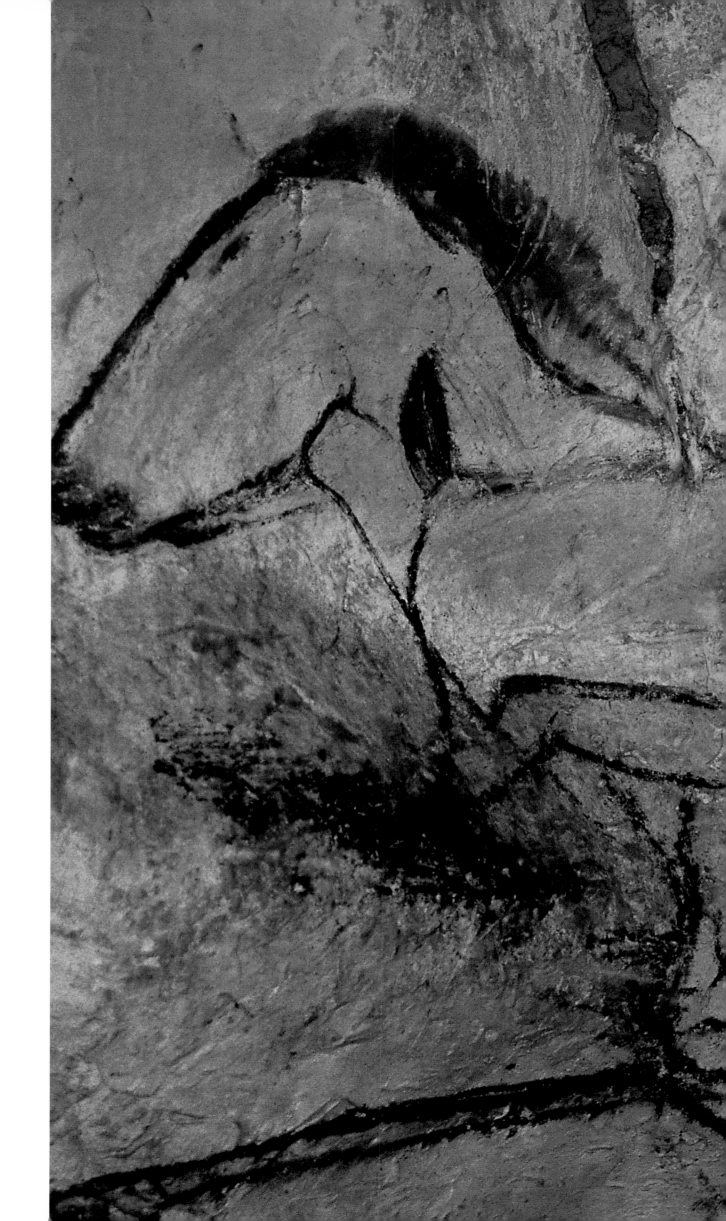

Ill. 191. Running reindeer on the
Reindeer Panel.

the red deer, the withers disappear at the base of the neck. As far as the megaloceros is concerned (ill. 189), the hump on the withers, the supple neck and the fairly small head are used as a means of identification.

A few generic species are thus identifiable. It is possible to recognize 12 reindeer, 7 megaloceroses, 2 red deer and 4 indeterminate individuals. Almost half are complete. The partial elements are most often the forequarters and the head. Only the megaloceroses (with one exception) lack antlers, whereas their spectacular development in the living animal could have been considered characteristic of the species. All the cervids have some indication of the variations in the coat. Only the reindeer on the rock pendants in the Skull Chamber were given particular attention when they were drawn, but they may have been produced in another period (see the Megaloceros Gallery). The others seem to have been drawn rapidly, by a sure hand that often tried to indicate movement. Apart from the Reindeer Panel, to the right of the Panel of the Horses, these animals are rather isolated. Almost a quarter of them were drawn in relation to those natural contours that inspire artists.

Dominique Baffier and Valérie Feruglio

The Bears

There are 15 bears. Out of concern for methodology, a few probable bear depictions have been classified with the indeterminate animals, as doubts remain about whether they belong to this species; this is the case with the 'hyena', whose spotted coat can be interpreted as a carnivore's, but which displays most of the morphological characteristics of bears (ill. 71). Primarily located in the first part of the cave, they are thus mostly red, like the majority of the figures in this sector. In the second part, two are scraped and one is painted in black, but has noticeably different features (ill. 91).

The red bears vary in size, but nevertheless have a homogeneous style (ills. 195 and 196). They are characterized by the

Above
Ill. 192. Red deer on the Reindeer Panel. All four legs are depicted, but the right pair are much paler, thus giving an effect of perspective.

Right
Ill. 193. The distribution of bears.

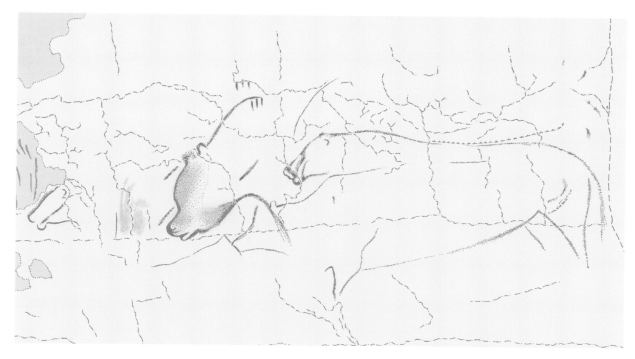

low way they carry their head, which brings out the marked shoulder. They have a receding rump and a small tail. The legs, with open extremities, are set broadly.

The outline of the head, which is generally executed with three lines, emphasizes the very pronounced stop, a characteristic of the cave bear. The first line draws the forehead and the stop and ends in a comma to indicate the nostril. The second draws the mouth, while the third depicts the chin and the cheek. The eye, in contrast to most of the cave's animals, is never represented. Only the drawing of the ears varies from one individual to another: either they are both placed on the external outline, or one of them is drawn inside the head, which is closer to actual reality. A few traces of stumping are generally located on the head, muzzle and shoulder.

The style of these depictions suggests that they were produced by the same artist. The bears are often grouped, and several times they are linked with other animal species such as the ibex, felines or cervids. It should be noted that no bears are depicted in the big compositions like the Panel of the Horses.

Dominique Baffier and Valérie Feruglio

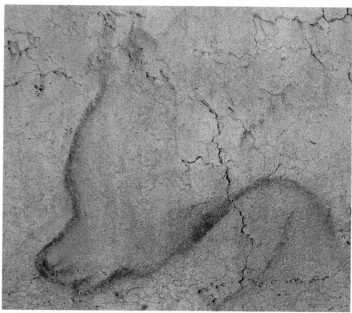

Top
Ill. 194. A tracing of the whole of the Panel of the Red Bear, at the back of the Cactus Gallery. The bear is placed between two lions; the body of the right-hand feline merges with an undetermined figure, thus forming a two-headed creature. Only the tracing makes it possible to read these paintings, which are now much eroded.

Left
Ills. 195 and 196. There is a stylistic similarity between the red bears in the Cactus Gallery (middle) and the Recess of the Bears (bottom).

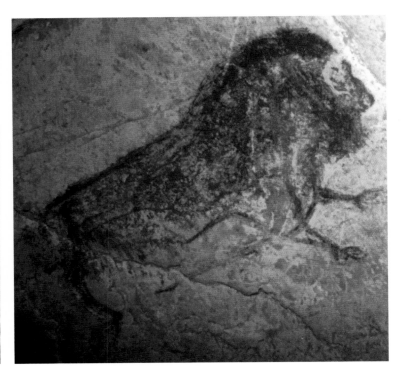

The Musk Oxen

Above left
Ill. 197. The distribution of musk oxen.

Above centre
Ill. 198. The musk ox discovered on the back of the Sorcerer Panel.

Above right
Ill. 199. The musk ox of the Skull Chamber.

The ovibos or musk ox, which today lives in the Arctic regions, is represented twice in the animal depictions of the cave: once in the Skull Chamber, on the descending rock that overhangs the entrance of the Gallery of the Crosshatching (ill. 199), the other in the End Chamber, on the far left of the Sorcerer Panel (ill. 198). These drawings are the oldest known depictions of musk ox in parietal art.

Although located 80 m (262 feet) from each other, these black musk oxen have similarities in their outline that make it possible to identify them without ambiguity. The low horn turns forwards. On the Skull Chamber drawing, it is left in white, a characteristic colour in the present-day musk ox. The break in the nose is also typical for this animal. The voluminous chignon follows on from the withers. The throat is very marked. The tail is not shown, but, in the present-day musk ox, it is only a few centimetres long and disappears totally in the fur. The way the animal's hair has been treated is more surprising. The hairs of the

beard and throat seem to be marked in the Skull Chamber drawing. The long fur, which can be seen at first glance on the chest and hindquarters of the present-day species, is not drawn. This absence may be intentional: the depiction of animal hair is rare in the cave. It is also possible that this is a seasonal feature or a characteristic of the prehistoric European species. In the same way, the presence of an undulating line crossing the body of both animals may indicate anatomical features.

As we are giving top priority to the protection of the floors, we have not been able to get close to these drawings. The drawing in the End Chamber has never been seen directly, so we do not have its exact dimensions: the animal in the Skull Chamber is no more than 50 cm (nearly 20 in.) long; the other is clearly smaller. Their location in the cave only indicates that they are peripheral to the big decorated collections.

Yanik Le Guillou

Conclusion

The depictions in Chauvet Cave can readily be classified in the three major categories that are usual in the Upper Palaeolithic: signs and indeterminate marks, humans, animals. From this viewpoint, and despite its originality, this cave's art fits well into the general schema of parietal art. The visual – if not numerical – preponderance of animals reinforces this observation.

The non-figurative lines – the signs, in the broadest sense of the term – are very numerous: there are hundreds of them, in particular the big hand dots that are so frequent in the chambers of the first part of the cave. Determining how they were executed represents a major advance. The 'insects' constitute an original feature that is peculiar to Chauvet. The other signs are generally very banal, but this does not make their meaning any clearer.

The Aurignacian is known for the depiction of isolated vulvas. Chauvet is no exception to this rule. By contrast, hand stencils had hitherto not been reported before the Gravettian. However, in this cave they are associated with panels in which the animals display exactly the same conventions as those directly dated to the period of 32,000–30,000 BP. Nothing suggests that they are more recent. It is therefore necessary to suppose, at least as a provisional hypothesis, that they first appeared in the Aurignacian. One major discovery, made quite recently by Yanik Le Guillou, is of a woman's body seen from the front, reduced to the pubic triangle and the legs, associated with a strange composite creature, a bison-man, on the same rock pendant opposite the Panel of the Big Lions. It is improbable that these two figures are juxtaposed by chance. There is a feeling that a complex story, probably a myth, was depicted in this special place.

The 420 or so animals in the cave were certainly not drawn at random. The unusual species – long-eared owl, musk ox, panther – only appear occasionally. Even though the dominant themes (felines, mammoths and rhinoceroses) are found all over the cave, some themes are concentrated on certain panels – horses, ibex (ill. 200), cervids, rhinoceroses, lions, bison – and there are some animals missing, such as bovines in the first part of the cave. The cavern was thought about and used with specific aims in mind. Among its original features, the relative abundance of scenes (lions hunting, herds of rhinoceroses and bison, couples of lions) should be noted.

The depiction of the same animals by means of different techniques, the recurrence of the same themes in different parts of the cave, the generalized conventions used in representing each species – all of these factors argue once again that this art is homogeneous, not only conceptually but also probably chronologically. It is possible, if necessary, to accept the idea that the same themes lasted for thousands of years, but certainly not that this was the case for such minor conventions as the drawing of the rhinoceros ears or the bison heads. The art of Chauvet as a whole was not built up over the millennia. Even if it was produced by several artists and in a number of well-spaced visits, it bears witness to an unquestionable unity.

Jean Clottes

Above

Ill. 200. A group of ibex in the niche on the other side of the Panel of the Horses. The edge of the wall has been marked with torch wipes.

7

Ill. 201. The Panel of the Dominoes,
with groups of dots and a few isolated animal
figures, could have had much more decoration.

OTHER POINTS OF VIEW

To ask those who are not specialists in Palaeolithic art for their point of view meets a double concern. On the one hand, Chauvet Cave, like Lascaux or other masterpieces, reaches a far wider audience than the relatively small circle of archaeologists involved with it. We cannot monopolize its study. On the other hand, as was the case for the ethologists looking into the behaviour of the depicted animals, different outlooks, experiences other than those of prehistorians, are likely to bring fresh perspectives, a different understanding of the phenomena that confront us. Because of the lack of space, we have not been able to present as many of these personal statements as we would have wished. That will come later.

7

OTHER POINTS OF VIEW

Chauvet: A New Chapter in the History of Art

It seems to be generally accepted as a basic notion (in formal description) and, probably, as an anthropological given (allied to a question of interpretation), that parietal paintings are closely integrated with the configuration of the caves, something certain paintings and signs particularly underline. The earliest stage, so to speak, of placing any signs in a cave is to mark space like a meaningful whole, to differentiate its parts and set them out. The empty spaces, the zones with dense numbers of figures and the dramatization of some panels, thus play a part in the overall perception of the cave. It is probable that, ideally, one should take this into account in the analysis of each group of paintings or graphic works: the first thing to note, the most modest, is that the space itself is filled with significance through the deployment of graphic work, and that, logically therefore, one should have the means of considering the works in a cave in terms of their own characteristics and relationships; none of them has exactly the same value (the same effect of presence, the same affirmative force, the same connective function).

The example of Chauvet Cave, in what for the moment seems to be a particularly well-emphasized linear organization, should make it possible to understand the general outline of a 'syntax' comprising major

differences between the figures, or notable changes in rhythm from one chamber or one panel to the next. This remark should be compatible with two attitudes or two objectives: that of a formal analysis that defines its own content (the idea of a symbolic activity configuring collections of works in function of constant rules: a structure), or that represented by an anthropological choice, if considering the cave and paintings as the place primarily elected for magical types of action. In both cases, it is necessary that an option concerning forms, their connections, their differentiations, and the option concerning content (referent, convening or magical invention of a reality) should take into account how both the space and the paintings, including their details of line or technique, are organized.

The very particular organization of Chauvet Cave (two successive big collections of red-line and then black-line paintings, separated by a very dense area of signs and figures) provides, in a way, an example of how figures can be classified (but the lists of figures or animals tend to blur those distinctions): the collections, be they painted, drawn or engraved, gather together, combine or compose figures of the same type (of the same 'style' or the same treatment): hence, the rhinoceroses belong to several figurative types: and the art historian or painting analyst, of course, is first interested in classifying types, not figure referents. The remarkable linear organization (that is to say, the successive groupings of figures) in this cave is easily readable, and perhaps presents a very particular case in Palaeolithic art: it seems to me that reading the parietal layout shows a kind of linear composition, both in the whole of the cave and in the way its panels are composed.

The last point that I feel needs to be emphasized, in this brief sketch, is the way in which figures on the big panels are grouped. Clearly, these panels (Panel of the Horses, Reindeer Panel, Lion Panel) present utterly unprecedented characteristics. The diagrams that are usually recorded in the whole of the Palaeolithic repertoire include dominant animals, often confronted in a heraldic position, to which animals in a complementary position are added. This diagram, or this figurative structure, is generally valid, but cannot be found in the cave of Vallon-Pont-d'Arc.

The extraordinary dramatization presented by the two big panels (Panel of the Horses, Lion Panel) features qualities that have to be described particularly carefully. These panels are clearly very elaborate compositions in which forms are assembled according to similar types (reindeer and related outlines) and according to certain 'characteristics' (horses).

The most interesting case is the Lion Panel. A group that is not only very complex but also easily and immediately legible, this panel is organized to achieve an effect: the gallop of a kind of imaginary herd, lions, bison, rhinoceroses, mammoths. The realistic effect is remarkably coherent and very dramatic (especially in the 'reserve' of a small horse in the niche that divides the panel: this figure is there for scenography, not for the composition).

The most remarkable characteristic of this panel is the way all the figures are facing in one direction (except for one, located near the floor) and the unity in the artistic and technical means used to produce this effect. A completely unprecedented case in prehistoric art (and for a long time, in the 'historic' arts), this long panorama of figures over a dozen metres (40 feet) long, suggesting movement, power and speed (it is a fantastic herd that seems to burst into this gallery), shows great technical prowess and astounding powers of invention: the figures are grouped by category or type, each group almost has a specific treatment, and the figures are identified here in accordance with a scale peculiar to this grouping; some figures are, at the technical level, treated with a concern for geometry (the 'rose' of lions, to the left of the panel, is made by joining lines between the figures; a few profiles use the remnants of earlier drawings as lines of construction and so offer a succession of angles). The general logic of this very beautiful panel is absolutely consistent with producing an effect: its technique is exactly like a montage of different sized parts of the body that, in a way, varies the power, speed and character of the animals depicted with a vivid suggestion of movement.

Without doubt, what is most incredible is the possibility of taking a detailed look at the different elements that make up this montage: the figures are in fact motionless; it is their lines and the art of their composition that produce movement. These remarks obviously come before an in-depth analysis of the paintings. Despite their brevity, I shall at least point out the following: Chauvet Cave, through its programme of analysis or of simple formal description, cannot fail to call into question many of the ideas about Palaeolithic art, particularly the use of catalogues of figures detached from their contexts; they can easily lead to the invention of ideal structures, in which it is assumed that figures can be reduced to a collection of quantifiable graphic traits.

The other astounding conclusion is that the technical and artistic mastery displayed by the artists in this cave (the art of using natural contours as outlines, the mastery of stumping, the invention of several kinds of logic in composing collections of figures) open up, from the perspective of our work, a new chapter in the history of art.

Jean-Louis Schefer

An Anthropological View

It is tempting to look at the contemporary traditional cultures in the Arctic for information that can link together the scattered materials collected in Chauvet Cave, particularly as there are numerous analogies between the ways of life of the populations in the Far North and of the Aurignacians in Vallon-Pont-d'Arc. The similarity in environment between Ice Age France and the present-day Arctic or sub-Arctic regions (climate and fauna of a cold country, tundra landscape) and resemblances between the way of life of the populations in question (small groups of mobile individuals, living essentially by hunting, supplemented by fishing and gathering) are certainly arguments in favour of making such comparisons. So everything points to the conclusion that there may have been, in the hunting communities of the Palaeolithic Ardèche, as among the Inuit or the North Siberians, a perfect integration of daily preoccupations, religious thought and artistic expression.

Although the reservations expressed by André Leroi-Gourhan concerning a methodology based on comparisons, and establishing often seductive (but always risky) comparisons between contemporary ethnographic observations and prehistoric remains, constitute a useful warning,[1] and although one has to agree with him that 'in tackling documents from just one perspective out of any context, one runs the risk of the most bizarre misunderstandings'[2] – for all that, can one endorse his mistrust or his rejection of ethnology in the domain of prehistory? Can an anthropological view not open up the field of 'scientific imagination' by encouraging analysts to detach themselves from their own cultural legacy and to face up to ideas that are completely different from their own? Finally, if one agrees with Leroi-Gourhan that 'prehistoric people only left us truncated messages',[3] what kind of knowledge can help us reconstruct the whole message, when archaeology only produces fragments of it?

Certainly, there is something of an apparent contradiction in wanting to reconcile the data from prehistoric archaeology with the information from anthropology, as the methodologies and subjects of these two disciplines are so diametrically opposed. Whereas, in the case of the traditional societies of the Arctic, the materials studied are essentially based on oral testimony and observed behaviour, with a fairly poor pictorial tradition, Chauvet, conversely, only offers mute pictures and clues that have to be 'made to talk' and interpreted. Nevertheless, knowledge of contemporary northern peoples can without doubt make a contribution in interpreting cave art, by at least shedding some light on symbolic representations and the perception of nature.

A Dualistic Conception of the Universe?
It is a characteristic of every culture, and perhaps every consciousness, that it discriminates between phenomena, seeking to put some order, no matter how succinct, into reality. Every depiction, because it is never a simple reproduction, is imprinted with a meaning that the artist, whether deliberately or not, inserts into the creation. The rock art of Chauvet Cave cannot go against the principle that an artistic production is, above all, a reading of the world, that it obeys an intellectual or cultural code that should be elucidated and reconstructed. On the basis of just the depictions in this cave, is it possible to work out a system of interpreting the universe that was peculiar to the Aurignacian culture? Can one detect in it an ordering principle that governs all of the figures and symbols?

A System of Opposites in Depiction…
Faced with the cave art, the modern-day spectator would immediately notice that the works naturally fall into two categories or groups, which are distinguished by repeated effects of interruption or opposition.

The clearest difference is in colours. Red, which is omnipresent in the 'first part' of the cave, contrasts with the use of black in the deepest chambers and side passages. With very few exceptions, the use of ochre or charcoal is very selective. On top of this essential dichotomy, there are a number of differences in the pictorial techniques used: engraving/painting, simple outline/infill animals are always depicted in profile, except for several bison heads and the head of a long-eared owl, seen full face), in the posture of the animals (static or dynamic).... Finally, it should be noted that *two systems* of depictions are found together: one of them is figurative, extremely realistic, revealing the artist's skill in observing nature; the second system, which comprises not forms but

with dots or use of stumping, flat/three-dimensional, when using the natural contour of the wall. Other contrasts also occur in the direction the animals are facing: horizontal or vertical (and, in that case, ascending or descending), left or right (the signs, is symbolic and its meaning is still unknown.

The walls of Chauvet Cave thus seem to reveal an Aurignacian art that is profoundly marked by the theme of duality. When we observe the distribution of the animal

Ill. 202. In the Skull Chamber, a bear skull lying on the floor has a few torch marks on it.

species according to the opposing types of depiction outlined above, we realize that the animals portrayed by these hunter-gatherers can be divided into two large groups, which clearly do not correspond to any classification that might seem logical to us. Aurignacian taxonomy, as it appears to us, does not follow any opposition between predators and prey, between dangerous and harmless animals, large and small, or between species of land, sky and water. Conversely, one can envisage that there is a difference between gregarious species (mammoths, lions, horses, aurochs, bison, reindeer…) and solitary species (bear, panther, megaloceros…). Few mistakes seem to have been made regarding the social or non-social behaviour of the species, and the depictions show not only the artists' very acute sense of observation but also a well-developed knowledge of ethology.

Apart from these contrasts, which could be called formal, it is tempting to divide the cave's very layout, its superstructure, into two. On the one hand, the hand prints, the signs and the use of ochre are much more common in what is currently identified as the 'first part' of the cave, that is, the area closest to the supposed entrance at the time when it was visited by humans. On the other hand, animal depictions and the use of wood charcoal in paintings appear predominantly in the deepest part of the cave, separated from the first sector by a low and narrow passage. Almost 85% of the identified animal figures are thus located in the 'second part' of the cave, while black is used in 97% of the paintings in this same area (versus 3% in the 'first part').[4] This strong dichotomy could correspond to a kind of initiatory route inside the cave, with traces of different rites that took place during the journey, or it could indicate that different individuals were given access to the cave in different places: women, children, non-initiates perhaps entered the first part of the cave, whereas only veritable 'initiates' could go deeper.

…which perhaps Expresses a Conception of the Universe

Distinct techniques of depiction, space divided into two, indicating a religious

hierarchy – if these interpretations are confirmed by future discoveries, all this makes it possible to put forward the hypothesis of a dual structure of the universe among the Aurignacians. This idea seems to be corroborated by the great fresco of the Panel of the Horses, which appears to be part of a *composition* rather than a simple juxtaposition of figures. On the left, there is a dense herd of painted herbivores (horses and aurochs), all facing left; on the right, on a more extensive surface, the simply sketched animals scattered about, heading both right and left, indiscriminately. The break between these two groups is made more evident by the confrontation of two rhinoceroses (a scene which, according to Jean Clottes, is unique in Palaeolithic art).[5] Does this not reveal the conception of a nature that is driven and governed by two antagonistic forces that engage living beings in confrontation, both between species (scenes of lions hunting herbivores) and within the same species (rhinoceros duel)?

The idea of a universal binary principle in the cosmos, governing all opposing phenomena – light/dark, life/death, male/female – is notably central in the Inuit's understanding of the world. This dualistic view is also to be found in their metaphysical beliefs and, consequently, in their system of depictions, where, for example, the great figures of the Universe are sexed and opposite/complementary (in their cosmogony, the Sun, a female element, and the Moon, a masculine element, are ascribed – like the stars, the winds, the rain – a gender, and interact as a couple). Among animals, their tradition sees a marked distinction between terrestrial and marine species (a distinction that goes back to their mythical origins, with no consideration for their appearance: animals with hair or feathers, mammals or fishes). Finally, their beliefs give two possible destinations after death, which they locate at the two poles of the Universe: celestial and submarine.[6]

Certainly, such a way of thinking is favoured, in the Far North, by a natural environment with an extremely marked contrast between the seasons, with two periods of total daylight and permanent night, but it could also be characteristic of a society that lived from hunting, in which times of plenty and of penury followed each other, sometimes abruptly. Perhaps, by virtue of a comparable environment and way of life, the Palaeolithic hunters of the Ardèche conceived a similar cosmogony, structured by the motif of duality and attached as much importance to the figures themselves as to the general configuration of the sacred space.

The Fusion of the Human and Animal Worlds

Although the cave evokes a structured universe through the theme of duality, this binary conception in no way rules out a continuity – or openness – between the human and animal worlds. This, at least, is what the example of the northern cultures teaches us, whereas our western culture has introduced a fundamental dichotomy between these two orders.

Humans: 'Absentees' Suggested by the Animals

Strangely – and this applies as much to Chauvet as to most of the other Palaeolithic decorated caves – human beings did not reproduce their own image in full on the walls, but through the simple act of representation they defined their relationship with the object drawn. What kind of relations between the Aurignacians and their environment do the Chauvet frescoes reveal? It seems that the most basic links can be dismissed.

In the first place, the simple relationship of predator and prey: the selection of the fourteen animal species depicted [lions, panther, mammoths, rhinoceroses, horses, bison, aurochs, ibex, reindeer, megaloceroses, red deer, bears, musk oxen and an owl] rules this out completely, because the paintings of Chauvet Cave particularly highlight some of the biggest and most powerful representatives of the fauna of the period, whose flesh was not eaten; they are almost exclusively mammals (often carnivores), except for the rare depiction of birds and perhaps insects, and the whole group clearly does not constitute an inventory of the animals they hunted.[7]

Nor do the cave's frescoes reveal an exorcism of the fears of Aurignacian people in the face of adverse Nature. Certainly, most of the animals depicted all over the walls are the most fearsome and dangerous species known to the people of that period: felines, mammoths, woolly rhinoceroses, bison, bears, musk oxen and aurochs make up over sixty per cent of the animals that have been listed and identified with certainty. Nevertheless, these animals are never depicted in a position that threatens the people who 'gave them life' through the intermediary of their art. Rather, the figures suggest harmonious relationships between humans (spectators or actors) and these big mammals, which must have been respected, admired, even venerated, for their power, their strength, their imposing bearing or their speed, and which were perhaps depicted in order to appropriate their qualities. This hypothesis gives rise to the idea that the relationship between humans and a certain category of animals may govern the group's spiritual as much as its material life.

In the end our intuition tells us that there was a symbolic type of relationship between animals and humans. The image – positive or negative – of the human hand is found associated with a variety of animal figures, whether it is placed close to them (black-painted mammoth or horse, small yellow horses, red rhinoceroses and felines) or it contributes to the actual depiction of the animal. This is the case with the ninety-two palm impressions, dots of ochre, which as a group make up the silhouette of a large herbivore.[8] In this instance, it seems, we have moved well beyond the often-mentioned hypothesis of a simple desire of grasping or appropriation that is supposedly the meaning of placing the human hand on the animal figure. On the contrary, making a zoomorphic depiction by using images of the human attribute par excellence, the hand, suggests a merged perception of humans and the animal kingdom.

This proposition seems to be supported by several animal images that appear to be 'anthropomorphized'. Several feline muzzles in the End Chamber are strongly evocative of human profiles (ills. 127 and 203). In the artists' system of representation, could these felines, painted with humanoid traits and expressions, and seeming to pursue their prey, be in a way the symbolic doubles of the men, hunters like them? Still in the End Chamber, opposite the Lion Panel, the composite creature, associated with a woman's body (ills. 162 and 163), evokes in the same way the ambivalent nature of some animals, or even a possible transmutation between the categories of living beings: humans and animals.

The Bear as Mediator between Humans and the Cosmos

In what appears to be a network of connections between humans and animals, the bear seems to be entrusted with an eminent role. The special place that it obviously holds in the depictions of Chauvet Cave recalls its status as an occupant of the site. Traces of it are omnipresent: prints, clawmarks, hollows, polishing marks and bones left in great numbers. So it is hardly surprising that bears are depicted numerous times (about fifteen recorded up to now), particularly in the 'first part' of the cave. Walking through this series of galleries and niches decorated with bears must have served as a prelude to the climax represented by the big chamber known as the Skull Chamber. In this second part, where skeletons and traces of the big plantigrade abound, a bear skull was intentionally placed on a natural stand (ills. 204 and 205). The periphery of this 'pedestal' is littered, over a radius of 7 m (23 feet), with about forty other bear skulls (mostly accompanied by the rest of the skeleton).[9] One of these skulls bears a charcoal mark: an intentional sign or a simple trace of wiping a torch (ill. 202). This very confined place, where numerous bears died, could have been the inspiration that caused the cave's human visitors to choose this area for the celebration of a bear 'cult'.

Bears and humans apparently took it in turns to occupy the underground space.[10] Like humans, the bears left their traces engraved in the rock. Should one deduce from this that, out of a spirit of competition or imitation, the Aurignacians also wanted to make their own mark on the walls, by applying palms, hands and finger tips,[11] sometimes at the same heights as the highest bear clawmarks? In any case, humans cannot fail to have been deeply influenced by this presence, imposing and familiar at the same time, of an animal that resembled them in terms of its gait, being able to stand on its hind feet, and leaving on the ground, like them, imprints of palms that ended in five digits, and finally also an omnivore, like humans.

However, there no doubt existed another facet in the relationship between humans and bears. This theory seems particularly plausible if one refers to the Arctic cultures, both ancient and modern, in which the bear is perceived as an intermediary between men and animals. For the Eskimo or Inuit, its mythical role is analogous to the part played by the shaman, both of them being considered as mediators between the human community and the spirit world. According to the ethnologist Boris Chichlo, the existence of links between the myth of the bear and shamanism already appears in the Neolithic rock art of Yakut.[12] Moreover, in several vernacular languages of Siberia, such as Chukchi, Yukaghir, Even and Evenk, the bear is designated as a relative (ancestor) of human beings; most often taboo, its name is replaced by a substitute nickname: 'the father', 'the grandfather' or even 'the old man', which shows the respect given to it and its symbolic place in society.[13] The bear's peculiar status makes it the subject of rituals (among the Inuit of eastern Greenland, for example, the head of a polar bear killed in the hunt used to be exposed for several days in the communal house, in a place of honour, where it received offerings) or even of a special cult, as in certain regions of North America or Siberia.[14]

In the case of Chauvet Cave, the hypothesis of a metaphysical link between humans and bears raises a fundamental question: was the animal deified, or was it perceived, as the host of the cave, as an intermediary between the tangible world and a supernatural world of spirits living in the cave?

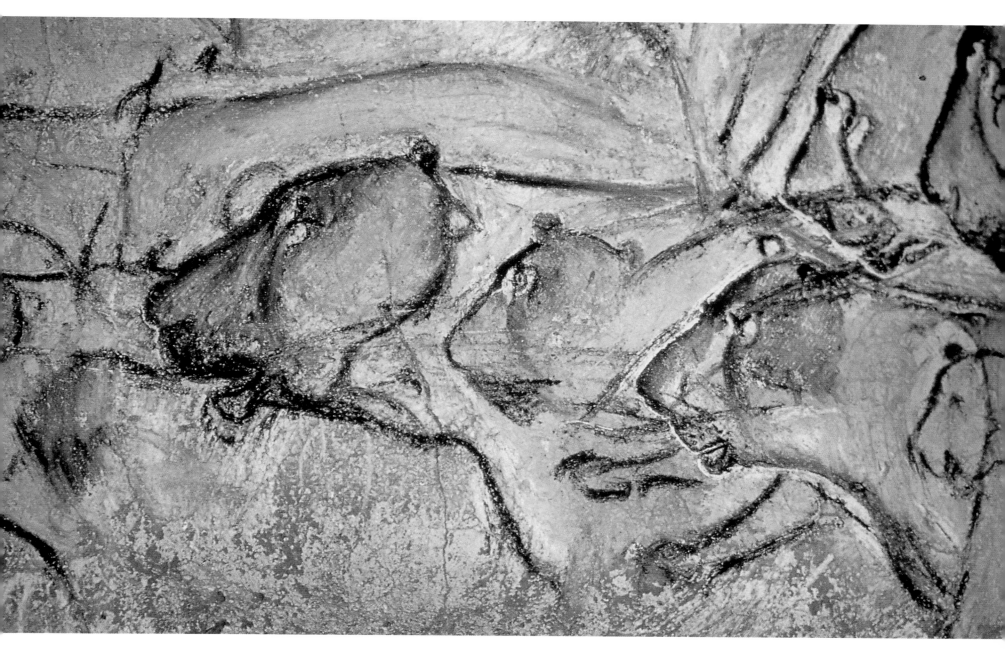

Ill. 203. The Lion Panel showing the big hunting lions in the End Chamber.

The Cave and Its Site: Religious Function of a Natural Anomaly

The cave's very location, with its (now collapsed) big entrance dominating the canyon of the Ardèche gorges, holds the attention of present-day visitors, as it most certainly must have struck humans in prehistoric times. From the cave's entrance, one has a vast view, overlooking the loop of the river's backwater – the Cirque d'Estre – which is located just below. It is easy to imagine that this ideal position constituted a remarkable observation post for groups of hunters trying to track animals that had come to graze or drink or making seasonal use of this narrow passage along the steep slopes of the hillside. The path leading to the cave, partly hollowed out of the cliff by water, as well as the existence of the spectacular arch of the Pont d'Arc, close to the cave, must have bestowed a bewitching or even sacred character on the whole place.

The site combines at least two remarkable characteristics: it is a site suited to hunting and a place bearing the stamp of the unusual, in close proximity to the magnificent natural arch, which, in the Aurignacian period, still formed a veritable bridge between the two banks of the Ardèche. Perhaps, in the minds of the people that visited it, the cave even combined extraordinary manifestations of all three elements: the water passing through the rock, the earth being penetrated deeply, and the air being conquered by this same earth.

As for the decorated cave itself, a dark and fearsome subterranean world, probably a place inhabited by spirits in the eyes of the humans who ventured into it with their limited means of lighting, can it not be considered as a kind of womb-lair that generated the animal fauna, with its galleries, its niches, its fissures and its rock pendants, from which the engraved and painted animals seem to emerge thanks to the use of its contours? One is certainly left wondering why certain walls of the cave, which were completely accessible and flat, and apparently suitable as a support for figures, remained untouched, while others, which, to our eyes, seem far less adequate, were chosen for presenting the animal world or for placing symbolic signs.

The idea that the 'bowels of the earth' symbolized fecundity is reinforced by the fact that the number of animal depictions increases as one penetrates further into the deepest parts of the cave. The End Chamber alone contains no less than 148 depictions or 35 per cent of all the animals identified so far. Does the Lion Panel not give the impression of a great profusion, a veritable flood of animals, surging from right to left?

At first glance, Inuit culture, which has no experience of this physical subterranean world, scarcely seems able to shed light for us on this subject. However, it should be remembered that, traditionally, hollows in cliffs or crevices in rocks were feared by ordinary people, who carefully avoided them for fear of meeting dangerous spirits or the wandering dead there. Conversely, some individuals, especially shamans during their initiation, actively sought out these dark and secluded places to work evil magic. These shamans acquired the experience of solitude and the mastery of fear. For the apprentice shaman, confrontations with terrifying beings, which manhandled him to symbolic death (hence the mythical bear devoured him, then regurgitated the skeleton, which later came back to life), before becoming his allies, was the obligatory path to be followed in order to achieve the accomplishment of his destiny as a mediator, interceding between people and the forces of the Universe.[15]

Traditionally, for the Inuit, the Earth was the creator of the animals that inhabited it, whereas the marine mammals remained under the supervision of the 'Woman of the Sea', who had the power of calling them back to her when the mood took her. It was then up to the shaman, after a long and treacherous voyage, to pay her a visit at the bottom of the ocean in order to entreat her to send the animals she was holding back to the humans who were threatened with famine. In the same way, it is not impossible that the Aurignacians entered the cave to ask the Earth to meet their needs by providing them with the game that it keeps or liberates from its depths.

The knowledge derived from studying several populations of Arctic hunters helps us to understand the very particular and very strong links that human beings have with animals in an environment similar to that of the Aurignacians. The northern cultures establish such a close relationship between the living beings of this world – all equally endowed with a 'soul' – that their oral traditions often maintain that, in times immemorial, people and animals spoke the same language and understood each other. Forced, nevertheless, to sacrifice game in order to survive, the hunter must obtain the prey's absolution, and carry out various rituals to appease its wrath, dissuade it from fleeing men close by, and exhort it to let itself be taken again. In addition to the practices that precede the hunt and the thanksgiving that follows it, the figurative or symbolic depiction of the hunted and venerated animals that decorate the hunter's weapons and clothing are intended to seduce the prey. When nothing comes of its pursuit, despite all these steps, and there is a threat of food shortage, people turn to the shaman, the mediator between the natural world (human and animal) and the great forces of the Universe.

With regard to the cave-sanctuaries that were not much frequented, the French archaeologist André Leroi-Gourhan himself admitted: 'Personally, I have often wondered if the fact of knowing that this organized world existed in the depths of the earth was not the most effective of the representations, and if a competent man or men (not to say initiates) were not able to visit it, in body or in mind. It is just a small step from there to imagining a shamanic journey, but one should abstain from crossing that line in order to avoid having so much information, borrowed from the most varied cultures, springing up any old how.'[16] Although we cannot assert that Chauvet Cave was the scene of real 'shamanic practices', as we have not so far found any traces of rituals that could have accompanied the production of the depictions, we nevertheless think that it may have been a sanctuary, inside which those who lived essentially from hunting came to celebrate a site that was particularly rich in game or to communicate with the animal kingdom and perhaps the supernatural world.

Mircea Eliade remarks quite correctly that 'between nomadic hunters and sedentary farmers there are similarities in behaviour that seems to us to be infinitely more important than their differences: *both of them live in a sacred Cosmos*, and take part in a cosmic holiness, which is manifested as much in the animal world as in the plant world'.[17] Chauvet Cave seems to correspond in ideal fashion to this definition of sacred space, according to which 'we are dealing with a series of religious concepts and cosmological images that are integrated in a system called the "World System" of traditional societies: a) a sacred place constitutes a break in the homogeneity of space; b) this break is symbolized by an "opening", by means of which it is possible to pass from one cosmic region to another (from Heaven to Earth and vice versa: from Earth to the Underworld); c) communication with Heaven is expressed indiscriminately by a certain number of images that all refer to the *Axis Mundi*: pillar…ladder…mountain, tree, liana'.[18] Associated with the natural arch, Chauvet Cave seems to correspond well to this 'sacred place' or 'Centre of the World' described by Mircea Eliade, favourable to communication between 'the three cosmic levels: Earth, Heaven, Underworld'.

Joëlle Robert-Lamblin

Above and opposite

Ills. 204 and 205. A bear skull placed on
purpose on a stone that had fallen from the
ceiling in the Skull Chamber.

8

CONCLUSION

Since the publication of the first book, *Chauvet Cave: The Discovery of the World's Oldest Paintings* (1996), the research carried out has considerably increased our knowledge. We have more than doubled the number of animals in the inventory, discovered a new species (the musk ox) and a few particularly important images on the Sorcerer Panel, rectified errors,[1] and acquired information that has changed our approach to some animals (the long-eared owl) or some signs (the hand dots). The techniques used for the drawings have begun to show how complex they are. The detailed topography of the cave has given us a better understanding of how Palaeolithic people used the spaces that confronted them. We have a clearer idea of both the construction of the major decorated panels and the frequent use made of fissures and irregularities in the wall.

The images were certainly not distributed at random. In the flickering light of the torches, animal forms seemed to spring out of the rock, its hollows or its reliefs. These forms were made material by drawing in some places, but not in others, because precise choices were made, as in the Megaloceros Gallery or in the spectacular End Chamber. We have seen that one of the principal interests of a vast cave like Chauvet was this very possibility of being able to discern more clearly the choices made by those who visited it so many millennia ago. The undecorated walls and zones therefore have as much importance as the others. The observations provide evidence of a state of mind and a certain conception of the subterranean world. They are *clues*. From the moment when,

with their help, we begin to understand the thought processes of Palaeolithic people in the caves better, numbers and percentages become of secondary importance, strictly speaking. Nothing forced the artists continually to draw animals emerging from holes in the wall. They did so because of numerous other factors (transcribed myths, particular ceremonies, local conditions). The essential point is that they drew animals enough times for their attitude towards the wall and the cave itself to become clear to us. It is this kind of evidence that enables us not to provide an 'explanation' of the paintings and engravings, but to propose an 'explanatory framework', which is something very different.[2]

All these findings bring these people closer to us. We have been able to lift a few pieces of the veil. We now know that they explored the slightest recesses of the cave, and that they paid more attention to certain parts than to others. The immense Chamber of the Bear Hollows, in the half-light of the entrance, was not embellished with any drawings, in contrast with the galleries and chambers that were plunged in total darkness, which were not exploited in a uniform way. The Brunel Chamber could have been decorated far more than it was, just like the walls of the Gallery of the Crosshatching, the left wall of the Hillaire Chamber, those of the Candle Gallery, or the whole of the first part of the Megaloceros Gallery, with its little chambers or lateral passages. This only emphasizes all the more the profusely decorated zones, the Red Panels Gallery just before the Candle Gallery, the engravings in the first part of the Hillaire

Opposite

Ill. 206. This small bison was not completed on purpose, as if it were emerging from a fissure.

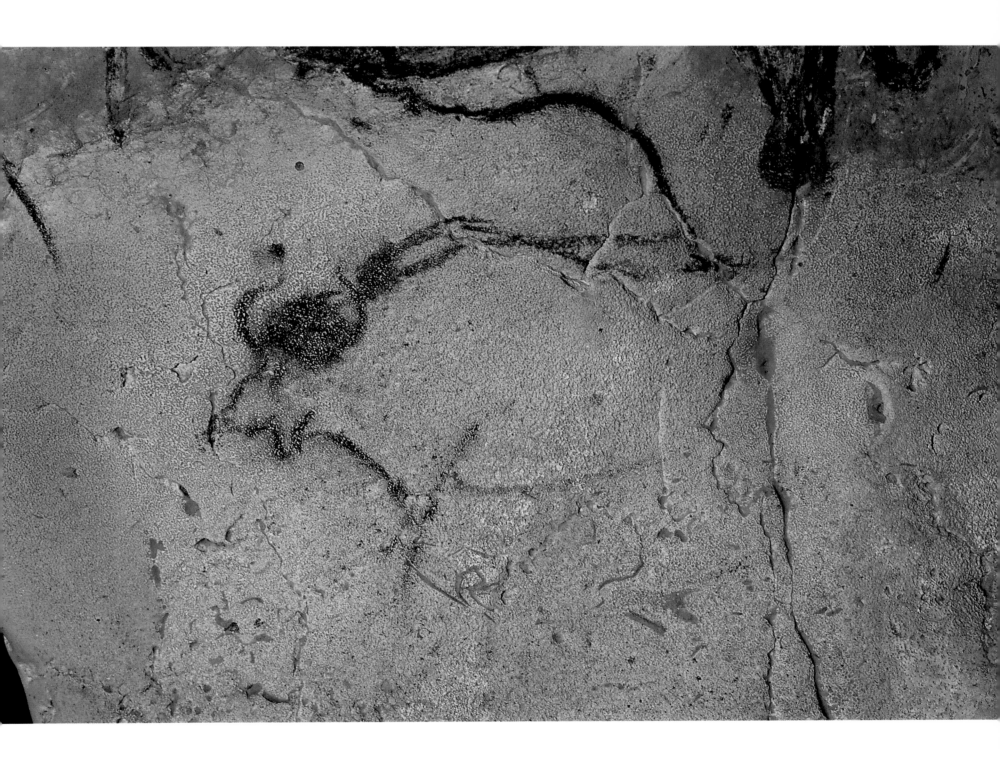

Chamber, the Panel of the Horses and the entrance to the Megaloceros Gallery, the Skull Chamber and the End Chamber (especially the left wall). In these areas they concentrated their drawings and, probably, the ceremonies and practices to which they bear witness.

We have been able to confirm that those who visited the cave did not live in it. Fires were lit, here and there, especially at the back of the Megaloceros Gallery. The fires may have had various purposes, but certainly were not intended for cooking food, as there are no remains that point to such usage. The excavation of cooking-hearths in habitations always reveals hundreds or thousands of burnt bone splinters, the remains of consumed animals. That was not the case at Chauvet. Some fires may have been used for lighting or for marking out a particular place (such as the one found on the block on which a bear skull was placed). Close to the End Chamber, in the last part of the Megaloceros Gallery, the numerous fires were certainly meant to produce the charcoal for the drawings on the nearby big panels. It is possible that the concentration of carbon dioxide that has been noticed in the End Chamber explains the fact that the fires were made higher up. Some activities remain a mystery. Why did prehistoric humans pile up slabs and blocks in front of the Panel of Hand Prints or in front of the engravings near the Large Collapse? What was a child aged about ten doing in the Gallery of the Crosshatching?

Animals, especially cave bears, visited the cave before and after humans. We now have a better knowledge of their activities, the traces left on the walls (innumerable clawmarks, polished areas of rock in places where they were obliged to pass) and on the floors (hollows, bones). Other species (wolves, ibex, brown bears, birds) joined them. The bear skull placed on a big stone had caught our imagination. We now know that more than forty other skulls can be found close to it, that another was marked with black lines, that two bear bones, vertical in the floor, were deliberately stuck there. This kind of action – sticking bones into the ground or into cracks of the walls – has been encountered over a period of at least

14,000 years, from the Gravettian (27,000 BP) to the final Magdalenian (around 13,000 BP), especially in the Pyrenees. Its presence in the Ardèche in such an ancient context shows that this practice was common for those who visited the decorated caves, throughout the period and in several regions. In this way the idea of a community of beliefs and attitudes during the whole of the Upper Palaeolithic is reinforced.[3]

The inventory of the animals depicted in Chauvet Cave has also given prominence to the development of the themes represented on the walls of caves. What changes is not the range of animals (apart from the long-eared owl and the panther, as all the other subjects are known elsewhere), but the respective proportions of the animals. The first inventory,[4] covering 263 animal figures, had established that the percentage of non-hunted dangerous animals (felines, mammoths, rhinoceroses, bears) was 54% of the identified animals. It has now turned out, with 345 identified animals, that their percentage reaches over 81%, which reinforces our observations even more. It was necessary to compare these findings with those carried out at other Aurignacian sites to determine whether this discovery was a local peculiarity or a widespread phenomenon.

Apart from the paintings of Chauvet, we know of half a dozen Aurignacian sites in the Dordogne and remarkable portable art represented by seventeen well-dated German statuettes, in the Swabian Jura. This is sufficient to note the importance, in this culture, of dangerous animals such as the mammoth, the rhinoceros, the lion and the bear. Also in the Périgord, the Aurignacians used these themes with much greater frequency than is found in the more recent art of the same region. These comparisons are emphasized further by the presence of the engraved or painted vulvas, which recall the abundance of this theme in the Aurignacian of the South-West. The parallels with the Grande Grotte of Arcy-sur-Cure (Yonne), although its art is probably more recent, with the portable art of the Swabian Jura[5] and with La Baume-Latrone (Gard) are even closer, even if the number of subjects in these sites is lower than in Chauvet Cave and lower than is required for a statistical study. The proportions of these animals vary from place to place, but their repeated association cannot be the result of chance, as these species were subsequently in the minority.[6]

This reversal of themes in relation to what is known elsewhere poses a problem. Even if lions, rhinoceroses and mammoths were more abundant in the Aurignacian fauna of the Ardèche than they were several thousand years later, which remains to be proved, it has long been accepted that the depicted animals were not necessarily representative of the biotype in which the artists lived, and did not imitate it closely; otherwise it would be necessary to imagine that in the Magdalenian the Dordogne was crammed with mammoths around Rouffignac, where they are so numerous.

Beyond this finding, which constitutes a drastic break with the theories of Leroi-Gourhan and with accepted ideas, there are lots of unknowns. The first, and probably the most important, concerns meaning. Why was there a preference for depicting dangerous animals?[7] The most plausible hypothesis is that a change or an evolution occurred in the fundamental myths which the art cannot fail to express, even when it is executed – wherever that may be – within the framework of shamanic practices and beliefs.[8]

Two major problems are linked, both of which concern chronology. Do the differences observed between the two principal parts of the cave result from the use of each part at very different times? Are the dates obtained by the radiocarbon method reliable? This question was posed[9] after the first dates to be published caused such surprise by going against the hitherto accepted theories concerning stylistic criteria and the evolution of art.

We have seen that the first part of the cave was not used in the same way as the second. There are much fewer drawings in it. Engraving and black pigment were employed far less here, whereas red representations predominate. Bears are numerous in this part, but neither reindeer nor bison nor aurochs are depicted. These drawings appear far less lively than

in the deep chambers. Moreover, in the End Chamber, a few red feline figures are earlier than the black animals that are painted over them. These findings were made as soon as the cave was discovered, and the perspectives that they opened up were then envisaged, including the possibility of an earlier date for the red drawings. This hypothesis was rejected after discussion, even before the radiocarbon dates were known.[10]

Despite this, it was recently taken up again and presented as an established fact by Christian Züchner, on the basis of stylistic comparisons with selected parietal works in other caves of France and Spain.[11] His remarks are founded on one major postulate: the deciding factor of stylistic criteria. However, although these criteria are often enough to give a general idea of the period under consideration, they are far from allowing an infallible diagnosis to be made. In order for this to be the case, one would have to accept that we know the essentials of what there is to know about Palaeolithic art – the first use of a particular theme or technique, its exact duration, its precise distribution in an area – and also acknowledge that coincidences need to be ruled out. It is on the basis of such unformulated presuppositions that every original discovery is invariably challenged and comes under suspicion.[12] Yet each major discovery brings new ideas and causes us to readjust our thinking.[13] That was the case with Chauvet Cave. So it is impossible to follow Züchner when he considers that a particular theme did not exist before a particular period. In some cases that may be true, but one always needs to add 'in the present state of our knowledge' or 'until we are better informed', and bear in mind our very great ignorance.

By contrast, the similarities between the animals drawn in the first and in the second part of the cave are an established fact, whether they are themes or techniques. The same animals (bears, felines, rhinoceroses, mammoths, megaloceroses) are found throughout the cave, whereas, with the exception of the mammoths, these themes are not common in parietal art. What is more, we have seen that they were depicted with the same techniques (for example, the use of stumping) and with the same conventions for details (for example, the ears and the mysterious stripe across the belly of the rhinoceroses). These findings point towards a homogeneous whole.

That does not mean that all the works of art in the cave were produced at the same time and, all the more, that they were done by the same person or people. It is impossible for us to date red drawings and engravings completely. There is nothing to rule out a time-lag between various decorated panels. However, it is doubtful if this time-difference – if it exists – is measured in millennia. If that were the case, it would mean that not only had the animals depicted not varied, which is, after all, conceivable, but also that, at the moment when the animals had materialized, the artists had employed the same conventions in drawing, for details as minor as the ears for example, as their remote predecessors. It seems more likely that the various chambers were used for specialized practices, perhaps even by people at different levels of initiation, as can be observed in so many religions.

The very early radiocarbon dates caused a shock in the scientific community. Most people accepted them because of their coherence; some, after accepting them, are returning to a position of 'wait and see';[14] others – very few – have rejected them,[15] because they break with received ideas and the accepted stylistic evolution. For Züchner, the black series is Magdalenian and the red series Gravettian.

At present, Chauvet Cave is the parietal site where the largest number of radio-carbon dates has been obtained, from black drawings, from torch marks and from the floors. None of them is attributable to the Magdalenian,[16] and we have seen that the dates fall into two groups, one centred around 27,000–26,000 BP and the other around 32,000–30,000 BP. As always, when there is a large series of dates, two or three are unlikely, because of the inferior quality of the sample. The dates obtained make sense, as a torch mark superimposed on a veil of calcite that covers ancient paintings gave a date of 26,000 and identical torch marks have produced similar results. This invalidates the bizarre arguments that fossil wood was employed for the fires or that ancient charcoal was re-used, many millennia later, to make drawings. For if one were to suppose that the animals in the sample had, by some remote chance, all been drawn with fossil wood – which already seems difficult to believe – the torches should also have been made from fossil wood, but a little more recent than those for the animals. This type of hypothesis cannot be taken seriously.

Finally, the oldest dates can be compared with the discoveries of portable art in the Swabian Jura, where ivory statuettes, found in Aurignacian layers, represent subjects identical to those of Chauvet: mammoths, felines, bison, bears, a horse, a rhinoceros, a composite being. This remarkable portable art had caused surprise because of its accomplished techniques and its fine quality. The discovery and dating of the parietal art in Chauvet Cave shatters its isolation. The art of the earliest times – at least figurative art, whether two- or three-dimensional – can indeed be attributed to the Aurignacians, our direct ancestors.

Jean Clottes

Above
Ill. 207. Some cervids on the Reindeer Panel
were deliberately effaced for reasons that
remain a mystery.

NOTES

Notes for Chapter 1

1. Clottes *et al.*, 1995a and 1995b.
2. The text cited here is an extract from our initial proposal. Some unavoidable cuts have been made, but nothing has been added.
3. We have not called upon all of these specialists yet. Their involvement will depend on how the investigations progress and in which direction the work goes.
4. For more details, see Clottes, 2000f (Chapter 10, 'Une journée dans la grotte Chauvet'). It should be stressed – as this undoubtedly has an influence on our living conditions and the quality of our work – that our base camp in the département, at Salavas, near Vallon-Pont-d'Arc, is perfectly well adapted to our needs, and that its manager, Christian Faure, has always ensured, with competence and good humour, that the practical problems we have encountered are solved rapidly and efficiently.
5. This collective work implies many different approaches and points of view. Each person presents his or her own view in the area that he or she has handled, with total freedom and under his or her own responsibility. There are obviously various differences of opinion, whether they are expressed in this book or not.
6. For technical reasons, it has not been possible for *all* the specialists in the team to contribute to this book, which simply constitutes a stage in our research. In a few years another volume will, without a doubt, mark another stage. It is also obvious that we have not been able to go into technical details here. This book is aimed at not only specialists in rock art but also the general public. In order to compensate for what may seem to be a gap, it has been decided to create a collection of monographs entitled *Les Cahiers de la grotte Chauvet*, in which particular volumes will, over the years, publish in full the research carried out on various subjects.
7. This plan has emerged from two topographic databases: the surveys by Y. Le Guillou and F. Maksud: Entrance Chamber, Morel, Brunel and Rouzaud Chambers, Gallery of the Crosshatching, Sacristy, Belvedere Gallery; and the surveys by the Perazio Cabinet (ordered by the Ministry of Culture): Cactus Gallery, Red Panels Gallery, Candle Gallery, Hillaire and Skull Chambers. Other information comes from both these databases: the Chamber of the Bear Hollows, Megaloceros Gallery, End Chamber.

Notes for Chapter 2

1. Collective work, 1984; Gély, 2000a, p. 10.
2. Combier, 1967, p. 222.
3. This type of object is known in the Gravettian in Provence. Moreover, floor F10 has been dated to 29,400 ± 800 BP. Lhomme, 1976, p. 6.
4. On the basis of about ten radiocarbon dates.
5. The 14C dates obtained in the Ardèche, about ten of them, are tricky to use in view of their wide statistical margins and results that are considered to be odd.
6. The archaeological floor at the foot of the paintings has been dated to 21,650 ± 800 BP.
7. In Les Deux-Avens, the layer that yielded the bones decorated with hinds, a reindeer, salmon, birds, chevrons and palmette motifs has been dated to 12,350 ± 200 BP. As for the fragment of carved bone depicting a mammoth, from the Grotte du Figuier, and the engraved bones from La Baume d'Oulen, they come from early excavations and have therefore not been dated with any precision – though they are probably between the Solutrean and the Magdalenian.
8. Bosinski and Schiller, 1998, p. 104.

Notes for Chapter 3

1. Before being dated, the samples underwent a chemical treatment (acid-base-acid), and then a thermal treatment in the case of the pigments, aimed at eliminating all contamination by foreign carbon (Clottes *et al.*, 1995a and 1995b, Valladas *et al.*, 1999); then they were prepared for measurement, using the protocol peculiar to each laboratory. The dates presented here are those obtained on the charcoal fractions that underwent this pretreatment, with the exception of the horse depiction, for which the age obtained from the humic fraction from the basic treatment has also been indicated, as it seems more reliable to us.
2. Individual variations in this domain are far from exceptional; our hypothesis is purely speculative and liable to be revised in the light of new data in the future.
3. Pales, 1976; Félice, 1959.
4. Terrestrial carnivorous mammals, with free digits.
5. It can be assumed that, when the animal crossed, there was water here. The canid jumped from rock to rock, then floundered in the mud before reaching the opposite side.
6. Extremities of the limbs (feet, hands).
7. Boessneck, 1987.

8. Morell, 1997.
9. Ichnology is the study of fossil prints and tracks.
10. Clottes *et al.*, 1995b.
11. Jean-Jacques Delannoy *et al.* in Chapter 2 of this book, pp. 22–23.
12. See Hélène Valladas *et al.* in Chapter 3, p. 32.
13. See Michel-Alain Garcia in Chapter 3 of this book, pp. 34–43.
14. Chauvet *et al.*, 1995, p. 49.
15. Identified by S. Thiébault in 1994 and June 1999 (Clottes in Chauvet *et al.*, 1995, p. 88).
16. Clottes in Chauvet *et al.*, 1995.
17. See Dominique Baffier and Valérie Feruglio in Chapter 5 of this book.
18. Observation made by Jean Clottes in 1999.
19. See Hélène Valladas *et al.* in Chapter 3 of this book, p. 32.
20. Identification by S. Thiébault in June 1999, on 16 samples, 6 of which were dated in this sector.
21. See Norbert Aujoulat and Bernard Gély in Chapter 4 of this book, pp. 88–93.
22. Ibid.
23. Albrecht, Hahn and Torke, 1972.
24. Peyrony, 1935; Knecht, 1991.
25. Garcia, 1999a.

Notes for Chapter 4

1. See Michel-Alain Garcia on the prints in Chapter 3 of this book, pp. 34–43.
2. See Carole Fritz and Gilles Tosello on 'The Cactus Gallery' in Chapter 4 of this book, pp. 74–76.
3. Hence the present route is misleading. The principle of a linear decoration constructed from the Brunel Chamber towards the end of the cave would be equally hypothetical.
4. Philippe Morel, a Swiss palaeontologist, was a member of our first team right from the beginning. He had studied this chamber with me. After his death in a mountain accident, I wanted it to bear his name.
5. Baffier and Feruglio, 1998.
6. For example, one can cite the 'Recess of the Tectiforms' in El Castillo and La Pasiega (Spain); the 'Indicator Panel' in Niaux; the 'Side Passage of the Claviforms' in the Tuc d'Audoubert.
7. After his sudden death, I wanted to give the name of François Rouzaud, a prehistorian and speleologist, to one of the few chambers that had not yet been named.
8. These techniques are difficult to differentiate when it is not possible to go close to the works.

9. Ceilings that are too low were not used, except for a little schematic mammoth. Moreover, two lines are clearly out of the artist's reach, between 3.5 and 4.5 m (11 and 14¾ feet) above the floor, so he or she must have climbed on blocks in this place.

10. Another rhinoceros, this one black and of the same dimensions, also springs from an alcove located diametrically opposite in the chamber, close to the entrance of the Megaloceros Gallery. These two animals also show other similarities.

11. At the foot of the panel, erosion has removed the wall's clay coating and its weathered surface, so only the base of the engravings and clawmarks remain. A small torch wipe marks this surface, and could thus be later than the phase of decoration, like the one dated on the Panel of the Horses.

12. Placing horses in a central position is known on other panels in the cave, on the Panel of the Horses, the Lion Panel, and, to a certain extent, the Owl Panel, as well as in the Gallery of the Crosshatching.

13. A 'jumping' mammoth on the ceiling of a niche is drawn in a very similar posture in the black frieze of Pech-Merle, Lot (Lorblanchet, 1981).

14. This hairiness, centred on the head, recalls certain mammoths of Pech-Merle, which are considered much later than the Aurignacian.

15. This could include – though not exclusively – the small yellow horses of the Brunel Chamber, the renewal of a horse head on the left wall of the Sacristy, and a horse head at the bottom of the Reindeer Panel.

16. See Chapter 2 of this book on the dates, pp. 28–29.

17. Fritz and Tosello, 2000.

18. Unless one imagines that several artists co-operated, which seems difficult in view of the coherent composition and the sequence of the different stages. Naturally, the possibility of a collective work produced by individuals with very similar techniques and levels of skill, formed in the 'same school', cannot be entirely discarded. What is most important in our view is the idea of the work conceived as a whole.

19. In the previous book, this figure was wrongly interpreted as an incomplete horse head (Chauvet et al., 1995, p. 91).

20. Barrière in GRAPP, 1993, p. 158.

21. For the details of the superimposed animals on this panel and the various stages in its production, see Clottes, 1999b.

22. See Dominique Baffier and Valérie Feruglio on the Brunel Chamber in Chapter 4 of this book, pp. 64–72.

23. See Yanik Le Guillou on the depictions of humans in Chapter 6 of this book, pp. 167–71.

Notes for Chapter 5

1. One obvious clue to the presence of plant material in the black lines has been provided by the possibility of carrying out 14C dating on several figures, including the confronted rhinoceroses.

Notes for Chapter 6

1. Clottes in Chauvet et al., 1995; Clottes, 1997.

2. This is a convention, because one cannot differentiate stencils, as the palm or back of the hand could equally well be turned to the wall.

3. The term 'sign' is employed to describe geometric figures with a symbolic character, which may be represented alone or associated with animals.

4. Dots have already been described in this chapter – by Dominique Baffier and Valérie Feruglio, pp. 164–65.

5. I consider that there are two large groups of human depictions that correspond to two different relationships between the creator and his work: between the creator and the support of this work; and between the creator and his own body as the tool of mediation. The first concerns the painted or engraved depictions; the second involves the hand prints and the hand stencils, and any imprint caused by a hand being placed on the wall on purpose; at one extreme, they may only be signs, where the hand, as a simple tool, was never meant to be a realistic human depiction. So these two groups, from the artist's viewpoint, correspond to two different approaches. In a thematic approach, an adequate sub-classification can help to bypass this problem by establishing links between a category of anthropomorphs and a category of sign, but the same does not apply to any structural approach.

6. A drawing on the right wall of the End Chamber, described by the discoverers as a human silhouette, is in fact a bison head seen from the front. A rhinoceros on the Panel of the Horses was published by Sophie Tymula (1995) as a composite being, half-man and half-animal: this interpretation was caused by the erroneous reading of a heavily distorted photograph.

7. These stereotypes persisted throughout the Upper Palaeolithic, to judge by the similarities between the pubis of Chauvet Cave and those, for example, from the sites of La Ferrassie, Pergouset, Cazelle or Micolón.

8. This 'Venus' type is characterized by the statuettes found particularly in Central and Eastern Europe. The best-known example is the Venus of Willendorf from Austria. The Venus of Chauvet was discovered very recently by using a digital camera fixed to a ball-and-socket joint, itself fixed to a telescopic pole. It was in this way that Yanik Le Guillou was able

to explore the whole reverse side of the Sorcerer Panel, as well as numerous inaccessible walls in various parts of the cave.

9. It is this depiction that, through a different reading, has been mentioned several times under the name of 'Sorcerer'.

10. This layout is characteristic of prehistoric depictions of humans such as the 'Horned God' that dominates the Sanctuary in the cave of Les Trois-Frères in Ariège or the man in the cave of Sous-Grand-Lac in the Dordogne.

11. As a hypothesis, if the rocky ridge is taken to represent the back line of the composite being, a number of black motifs – an erect animal tail and a human testicle located on the right side of the ridge, as well as a left testicle and a human leg on the left side of the ridge – could be linked to it. If that is the case, the stomach would be absent, and the penis could be depicted directly on the ridge, by a black line. The human genitalia and the animal tail would thus be laid out in a very similar way to the position they occupy in the depiction of the 'Horned God' in the cave of Les Trois-Frères.

12. See Yanik Le Guillou on 'Beyond the End of the End Chamber' in Chapter 4 of this book, pp. 144–48.

13. See Jean Clottes on 'The End Chamber' in Chapter 4 of this book, pp. 128–48.

14. See Yanik Le Guillou on 'Beyond the End of the End Chamber' in Chapter 4 of this book, pp. 144–48.

15. For more details, see Clottes, 1989, and Clottes in GRAPP, 1993.

16. When this was the case, we opted for the most methodologically prudent solution, that is, an albeit provisional classification among the 'indeterminates'. This is what we did for the figure called the 'Hyena' on the Panther Panel and for the big scraped figure on the edge of the Large Collapse, although, in both cases, some of us are convinced they are bears.

17. Guérin, 1981.

18. This is clay from the wall, spread in pure form by hand, or mixed by stumping with wood charcoal.

19. One of them, tuskless and smooth, was described as a youngster. The great variability of the depictions, the rarity, both of the tusks being depicted (two-thirds of the animals have no tusks) and of the hairy coat (only two or three cases) do not corroborate this finding. Moreover, there is no obvious criterion for sexing the figures, nor any scene of amorous sparring.

20. It is considered lifesize, but mammoths reached a length of 2.7 m (8¾ feet) and a height of 3.2 m (10½ feet). This illusion, which was sought by the artist, is reinforced by the height of the picture,

80 cm (31 in.) from the floor, which is spotted with residue from the scraping of the wall.

21. It is the artist's reach that is taken into account above all.

22. The engraved tusks on the mammoth in the Sacristy, which already has two black ones, may be a late addition.

23. Traced by a hand coated with clay; there is a big feline, possibly a horse and six or seven very stylized mammoths.

24. About thirty mammoths are known in the caves of Chabot (10 to 12), Les Deux-Ouvertures (10 to 12), Oulen (7 or 8), Le Figuier (1 or 2 and 1 fragment of a portable art object), Huchard (1 or 2) and Ebbou (1).

Notes for Chapter 7

1. Leroi-Gourhan, 1995, p. 4.
2. Ibid., p. 150.
3. Ibid., p. 3.
4. Clottes, Gély and Le Guillou, 1999a, p. 24.
5. Chauvet *et. al.*, 1995.
6. Victor and Robert-Lamblin, 1993, p. 336.
7. Moreover, this poses the question of the non-represented animals: wolves, foxes, wolverines, hares, birds (apart from the long-eared owl depicted in a striking engraving), small rodents, fish…. What role did they play in the Aurignacians' view of the world? Did the Aurignacians conceive of a hierarchy of the animal world?
8. Baffier and Feruglio, 1998, p. 3.
9. According to the information provided by Philippe Morel in May 1999.

10. There is no mark on the bear skeletons to indicate that people took advantage of the animal's weak state during its hibernation to hunt it; so one cannot infer that the cave was a Mecca for bear hunting. By contrast, one cannot rule out the possibility that they looked for the animal coming out of the cave, at the time of year when it emerged from its sleep.

11. Garcia, 1999a, pp. 26–27.
12. Chichlo, 1981, p. 39.
13. Robert-Lamblin, 2000.
14. Larsen, 1969–70.
15. Victor and Robert-Lamblin, 1993, p. 230.
16. Leroi-Gourhan, 1977, p. 23.
17. Eliade, 1998, p. 22.
18. Ibid., p. 38.

Notes for Chapter 8

1. For example, the 'Crosshatching', which gave its name to a gallery, does not exist, any more than the 'bird' does on one of the rock pendants close to the owl.
2. On this topic see Clottes and Lewis-Williams, 1996 and 2001.
3. On this topic see Bégouën and Clottes, 1981, Clottes and Lewis-Williams, 1996 and 2001.
4. Clottes, 1998.
5. J. Hahn stressed the originality of the themes in the German statuettes. This originality was such that he even envisaged – erroneously, as we now know – that southern Germany might have lived in cultural isolation during the Aurignacian (Hahn in Albrecht *et al.*, 1989, p. 35). He was the first to notice that the species depicted were the biggest, the most powerful and the most dangerous.

6. Detailed comparisons with the sites and decorated shelters mentioned were developed in Clottes, 1998.
7. For convenience we have called them 'dangerous' animals, although we are fully aware of the subjective nature of this evaluation; after all, an aurochs or a bison could also be very dangerous.
8. On this topic see Clottes and Lewis-Williams, 1996 and 2001.
9. Züchner, 1995, 1996 and 1999.
10. Clottes, 1995d, pp. 110–11.
11. Hence the title of his article, 'Chauvet Cave, Dated Archaeologically'; see Züchner, 1999, pp. 170–85.
12. This was the case for Altamira, Rouffignac and, more recently, Cosquer; see Clottes and Courtin, 1995, pp. 23–26.
13. See the discovery during the past ten years of a very important open-air Palaeolithic art in the Iberian peninsula.
14. Lorblanchet and Bahn, 1999, p. 120.
15. Züchner, 1995, 1996 and 1999.
16. We do not know with any certainty when the cave's entrance was blocked. If it were after the Magdalenian, it would be possible that some people visited it. The presence of a claviform-type sign close to the entrance could be evidence for this, but that depends, of course, on whether this is really a claviform, and that this geometric sign did not last much longer than is currently thought (see Clottes, Gély, Le Guillou, 1999b). It would not mean that they produced other drawings in the cave, because there is no evidence for this.

FURTHER READING

Albrecht, G., Bosinski, G., Feustel, R., Hahn, J., Klima, B., and Müller-Beck, H., 1989, *Los comienzos del Arte en Europa central*, Museo Arqueológico Nacional, Madrid, 123 pp.

Albrecht, G., Hahn, J., and Torke, W.-G., 1972, *Merkmalanalyse von Geschossspitzen des mittleren Jungpleistozäns in Mittel- und Osteuropa*, Verlag W. Kohlhammer, Stuttgart

Alcalde del Rio, H., Breuil, H., and Sierra, L., 1912, *Les Cavernes de la région cantabrique (Espagne)*, Institut de paléontologie humaine, Peintures et gravures murales des cavernes paléolithiques, Monaco, 265pp.

André, D., and Chabaud, M., 2000, 'Le plus grand mammouth totémique de la préhistoire? Le Pont-d'Arc et son possible rapport avec l'ornementation de la grotte Chauvet (Vallon-Pont-d'Arc, Ardèche)', *Bulletin préhistorique du Sud-Ouest*, publication de l'Association Préhistoire quercinoise et du Sud-Ouest, no. 7/2000–1, pp. 19–39

Baffier, D., and Feruglio, V., 1998, 'Premières observations sur deux nappes de ponctuations de la grotte Chauvet (Vallon-Pont-d'Arc, Ardèche, France)', *International Newsletter on Rock Art*, 21, pp. 1–4

Bégouën, R., and Clottes, J., 1981, 'Apports mobiliers dans les cavernes du Volp (Enlène, Les Trois-Frères, Le Tuc d'Audoubert)', *Altamira Symposium*, pp. 157–88

Boessneck, J., 1987, 'La domestication et ses conséquences', *Revue médicale, Vétérinaire*, 138, pp. 163–76

Bosinski, G., and Schiller, P., 1998, 'Représentations féminines dans la grotte du Planchard (Vallon-Pont-d'Arc, Ardèche) et les figures féminines de type Gönnersdorf dans l'art pariétal', *Bulletin de la Société préhistorique Ariège-Pyrénées*, LIII, pp. 99–140

Breuil, H., Obermaier, H., and Alcalde del Rio, H., 1913, *La Pasiega à Puente-Viesgo (Santander) (Espagne)*, Institut de paléontologie humaine, Peintures et gravures murales des cavernes paléolithiques, Monaco, 64pp.

Chauvet, J.-M., Brunel-Deschamps, E., and Hillaire, C., 1995, *La Grotte Chauvet à Vallon-Pont-d'Arc*, with an Epilogue by Jean Clottes, Seuil, Paris. Translated by Paul G. Bahn, 1996, as *Chauvet Cave: The Discovery of the World's Oldest Paintings*, with a Foreword by Paul G. Bahn and an Epilogue by Jean Clottes, Thames & Hudson, London, and Harry N. Abrams, Inc., New York

Chichlo, B., 1981, 'L'Ours-chamane', *Etudes mongoles et sibériennes*, 12, pp. 35–112

Clottes, J., 1989, 'The Identification of Human and Animal Figures in European Palaeolithic Art', *Animals into Art*, ed. H. Morphy, *One World Archaeology*, 7, pp. 21–56

Clottes, J., 1995a, 'Changements thématiques dans l'art du paléolithique supérieur', *Bulletin de la Société préhistorique Ariège-Pyrénées*, L, pp. 13–34

Clottes, J., 1995b, 'La Grotte Chauvet à Combe-d'Arc, Ardèche (France)', *International Newsletter on Rock Art*, 10, p. 1

Clottes, J., 1995c, 'Rhinos and Lions and Bears (oh, My!)', *Natural History*, 5, pp. 30–35

Clottes, J., 1995d, *Les Cavernes de Niaux. Art préhistorique en Ariège*, Seuil, Paris, 1995, 178 pp.

Clottes, J., 1996a, 'Les dates de la grotte Chauvet sont-elles invraisemblables?', *International Newsletter on Rock Art*, 13, pp. 27–29

Clottes, J., 1996b, 'Découvertes récentes d'art pariétal paléolithique en France', *La Vie des sciences*, vol. 13, no. 1, pp. 39–52

Clottes, J., 1996c, 'L'originalité de la grotte Chauvet-Pont-d'Arc, à Vallon-Pont-d'Arc (Ardèche)', *Comptes rendus de l'Académie des inscriptions et belles-lettres*, pp. 561–66

Clottes, J., 1996d, 'Recent Studies on Paleolithic Art', *Cambridge Archaeological Journal*, vol. 6, no. 2, pp. 179–89

Clottes, J., 1996e, 'Thematic Changes in Upper Palaeolithic Art: A View from the Grotte Chauvet', *Antiquity*, 70, pp. 276–88

Clottes, J., 1997, 'Observations nouvelles sur les peintures de la grotte Chauvet', *Bulletin de la Société préhistorique Ariège-Pyrénées*, LII, pp. 17–32

Clottes, J., 1998, 'The "Three C's": Fresh Avenues toward European Paleolithic Art', *The Archaeology of Rock Art*, ed. C. Chippindale and P. Taçon, Cambridge University Press, pp. 112–29

Clottes, J., 1999a, 'The Chauvet Cave Dates' in A. F. Harding (ed.), *Experiment and Design. Archaeological Studies in Honour of John Coles*, pp. 13–19

Clottes, J., 1999b, 'The Latest on the Chauvet Cave Paintings', *Glyferoch arkeologiska rum – en vänbok till Jarl Nordbladh*, ed. A. Gustaffson and H. Karlsson, pp. 609–23

Clottes, J., 2000a, 'Chauvet Today', *General Anthropology*, vol. 6, no. 2, pp. 1–7

Clottes, J., 2000b, 'Dernières nouvelles de l'équipe scientifique de la grotte Chauvet', *Envol*, 498, pp. 10–11

Clottes, J., 2000c, 'La Grotte Chauvet interdite à jamais au public?', *Envol*, 500, p. 17

Clottes, J., 2000d, 'Interpretar un panel decorado: los rinocerontes de la cueva Chauvet', *BARA, Boletín de Arte Rupestre de Aragón*, 3, pp. 43–50

Clottes, J., 2000e, 'Travaux 1999 de l'équipe scientifique de la grotte Chauvet', *Ardèche Archéologie*, 17, pp. 1–4

Clottes, J., 2000f, *Grandes Girafes et fourmis vertes. Petites histoires de préhistoire*, La Maison des Roches, Paris

Clottes, J., 2000g, 'Vallon-Pont-d'Arc. Grotte Chauvet-Pont-d'Arc', *Bilan Scientifique 1998*, Service régional de l'archéologie, DRAC Rhône-Alpes, 2000, pp. 55–57

Clottes, J., Chauvet, J.-M., Brunel-Deschamps, E., Hillaire, C., Daugas, J.-P., Arnold, M., Cachier, H., Evin, J., Fortin, P., Oberlin, C., Tisnérat, N., and Valladas, H., 1995a, 'Dates radiocarbone pour la grotte Chauvet-Pont-d'Arc', *International Newsletter on Rock Art*, 11, pp. 1–2

Clottes, J., Chauvet, J.-M., Brunel-Deschamps, E., Hillaire, C., Daugas, J.-P., Arnold, M., Cachier, H., Evin, J., Fortin, P., Oberlin, C., Tisnérat, N., and Valladas, H., 1995b, 'Les Peintures paléolithiques de la grotte Chauvet-Pont d'Arc (Ardèche, France): datations directes et indirectes par la méthode du radiocarbone', *Comptes rendus de l'Académie des sciences de Paris*, vol. 320, series IIa, pp. 1133–40

Clottes, J., and Courtin, J., 1995, *La Grotte Cosquer. Peintures et gravures de la caverne engloutie*, Seuil, Paris. Translated by Marilyn Garner, 1996, as *The Cave Beneath the Sea: Paleolithic Images at Cosquer*, Harry N. Abrams, Inc., New York and London

Clottes, J., Gély, B., and Le Guillou, Y., 1999a, 'Dénombrements en 1998 des représentations animales de la grotte Chauvet (Vallon-Pont-d'Arc, France)', *International Newsletter on Rock Art*, 23, pp. 18–25

Clottes, J., Gély, B., and Le Guillou, Y., 1999b, 'Compléments iconographiques à la grotte Chauvet', *International Newsletter on Rock Art*, 24, pp. 4–8

Clottes, J., and Lewis-Williams, D., 1996, *Les Chamanes de la préhistoire. Transe et magie dans les grottes ornées*, Seuil, Paris. Translated by Sophie Hawkes, 1998, as *The Shamans of Prehistory: Trance and Magic in the Painted Caves*, Harry N. Abrams, Inc., New York and London

Clottes, J., and Lewis-Williams, D., 2001, *Les Chamanes de la préhistoire. Texte intégral, Polémique et Réponses*, La Maison des Roches, Paris

Collective work, 1984, 'La Région Rhône-Alpes' in *L'Art des cavernes. Atlas des grottes ornées paléolithiques françaises*, Imprimerie nationale – Ministère de la Culture, Paris, pp. 589–633

Combier, J., 1967, *Le Paléolithique de l'Ardèche dans son contexte paléoclimatique*, Editions Delmas, Bordeaux, 462pp.

Delannoy, J.-J., Debard, E., Ferrier, C., Kervazo, B., and Perrette, Y., 2000, 'Contribution de la cartographie morphologique souterraine dans l'étude spéléogénique de la grotte Chauvet: Premiers éléments spéléogéniques et implications paléogéographiques, préhistoriques et paléontologiques' in Debard, E. (ed.), *Moyenne vallée du Rhône et Vivarais (Drôme et Ardèche): Loess de Saint-Vallier, karst du Bas-Vivarais, volcanisme quaternaire du Vivarais*, Université Claude-Bernard Lyon 1, UFR des Sciences de la terre, Lyons, pp. 78–95. (Guide booklet of the annual excursion of AFEQ, August 2000)

Eliade, M., 1998, *Le Sacré et le profane*, 'Folio Essais', Gallimard, Paris, 1st edition 1957. Translated by Willard R. Trask, 1959, as *The Sacred and the Profane: the Nature of Religion*, Harcourt Brace, New York

Fagan, Brian M. (ed.), 2001, *The Seventy Great Mysteries of the Ancient World: Unlocking the Secrets of Past Civilizations*, Thames & Hudson, London and New York

Félice, S. de, 1959, 'Etude anthropologique du pied et de sa croissance comparée à la stature chez 947 enfants de 3 à 8 ans', *Bulletin et Mémoires de la Société d'anthropologie de Paris*, X, 10th series, no. 1, pp. 207–39

Fritz, C., and Tosello, G., 2000, 'Observations techniques sur le panneau des Chevaux de la grotte Chauvet (Ardèche): l'exemple des rhinocéros affrontés', *International Newsletter on Rock Art*, 26, pp. 23–30

Garcia, M.-A., 1999a, 'Grotte Chauvet: éléments nouveaux du contexte archéologique', *International Newsletter on Rock Art*, 23, pp. 25–29

Garcia, M.-A., 1999b, 'La piste de pas humains de la grotte Chauvet à Vallon-Pont-d'Arc', *International Newsletter on Rock Art*, 24, pp. 1–4

Gély, B., 2000a, *Les Grottes ornées de l'Ardèche*, Editions du Dauphiné Libéré, Veurey (Isère), coll. 'Les Patrimoines', 52pp

Gély, B., 2000b, 'Vallon-Pont-d'Arc. Grotte Chauvet-Pont-d'Arc', *Bilan scientifique 1998*, Service régional de l'archéologie, DRAC Rhône-Alpes, 2000, pp. 57–58

GRAPP, 1993, *L'Art pariétal paléolithique. Techniques et méthodes d'étude*, Editions du Comité des travaux historiques et scientifiques, Paris, 427pp.

Guérin, C., 1981, 'Les Rhinocéros (*Mammalia, Perissodactyla*) du miocène terminal au pléistocène supérieur en Europe occidentale: Comparaison avec les espèces actuelles', *Documents du Laboratoire de géologie de Lyon*, 79, 3, 1185pp.

Knecht, H., 1991, *Technological Innovation and Design During the Early Upper Paleolithic: A Study of Organic Projectile Technologies*, Ph.D. thesis, Department of Anthropology, New York University

Larsen, H., 1969–70, 'Some Examples of Bear Cult among the Eskimo and Other Northern Peoples', *Folk, Dansk Etnografisk Tidsskrift*, vols. 11–12, pp. 27–42

Leroi-Gourhan, A., 1965, *Préhistoire de l'art occidental*, Mazenod, Paris. Translated by Norbert Guterman, 1968, as *The Art of Prehistoric Man in Western Europe*, Thames & Hudson, London

Leroi-Gourhan, A., 1977, 'Le préhistorien et le chamane', *L'Ethnographie*, Voyages chamaniques un, *Revue de la société d'ethnographie*, 74–75, pp. 19–25

Leroi-Gourhan, A., 1995, *Les Religions de la préhistoire*, Quadrige/PUF, Paris, 1st edition 1964

Lewis-Williams, D., 2002, *The Mind in the Cave*, Thames & Hudson, London and New York

Lhomme, G., 1976, 'Un nouveau gisement paléolithique en Ardèche', *Etudes préhistoriques*, 13, pp. 1–8

Lorblanchet, M., 1981, 'Les dessins noirs du Pech-Merle' in *Congrès préhistorique de France*, XXIst session Montauban-Cahors, September 1979. *La Préhistoire du Quercy dans le contexte de Midi-Pyrénées*, vol. 1, pp. 178–207

Lorblanchet, M., and Bahn, P. G., 1999, 'Diez años despues de la Era post-estilística: donde estamos ahora?', *Edades, Revista de Historia*, 6, pp. 115–21

Morell, V., 1997, 'Evolutionary Biology. The Origin of Dogs: Running with the Wolves', *Science Magazine*, vol. 276, pp. 1647–48

Packer, C., and Clottes, J., 2000, 'When Lions Ruled France', *Natural History*, vol. 109, no. 9, pp. 52–57

Pales, L., with M. de Saint-Pereuse and M.-A. Garcia, 1976, *Les Empreintes de pieds humains dans les cavernes*, Archives de l'Institut de paléontologie humaine, Paris, Mémoire 36, 166pp.

Peyrony, D., 1935, 'Le gisement Castanet, Vallon de Castelmerle, commune de Sergeac (Dordogne). Aurignacien I et II', *Bulletin de la Société préhistorique française*, 42, pp. 418–43

Robert-Lamblin, J., 2000, *Notes de terrain inédites d'une mission en Sibérie nord-orientale*

Schefer, J.-L., 1997, 'L'Art paléolithique. Préliminaires critiques', *Les Cahiers du Musée national d'art moderne*, pp. 5–33

Thomas, Herbert, 1995, *The First Humans: The Search for Our Origins*, Thames & Hudson, London, and, as *Human Origins: The Search for Our Beginnings*, Harry N. Abrams, New York

Tymula, S., 1995, 'Figures composites de l'art paléolithique européen', *Paléo*, 7, pp. 211–48

Valladas, H., Cachier, H., Arnold, M., Bernaldo De Quiros, F., Clottes, J., and Uzquiano, P., 1992, 'Direct Radiocarbon Dates for Prehistoric Paintings at the Altamira, El Castillo and Niaux Caves', *Nature*, 357, 7 May, pp. 68–70

Valladas, H., Tisnérat, N., Cachier, H., and Arnold, M., 1999, 'Datation directe des peintures préhistoriques par la méthode du carbone 14 en spectrométrie de masse par accélérateur', Supplement 1999 of the *Revue d'archéometrie*, pp. 39–44

Vialou, Denis, 1998, *Our Prehistoric Past: Art and Civilization*, Thames & Hudson, London, and, as *Prehistoric Art and Civilization*, Harry N. Abrams, New York

Victor, P.-E., and Robert-Lamblin, J., 1993, *La Civilisation du phoque. Vol. 2. Légendes, rites, croyances des Eskimo d'Ammassalik*, Raymond Chabaud, Bayonne

Züchner, C., 1995, 'Grotte Chauvet (Ardèche, Frankreich) – oder – Muss die Kunstgeschichte wirklich neu geschrieben werden?', *Quartär*, 45/46, pp. 221–26

Züchner, C., 1996, 'La grotte Chauvet. Radiocarbone contre archéologie', *International Newsletter on Rock Art*, 13, pp. 25–27

Züchner, C., 1999, 'La cueva Chauvet, datada arqueológicamente', *Edades, Revista de Historia*, 6, pp. 167–85

GLOSSARY

algology The branch of botany concerned with algae

anthracologist A scientist who specializes in identifying and studying charcoal

Aurignacian An Upper Palaeolithic culture from 37,000 to 27,000 years ago characterized by the use of bone tools and blade flint technology

autopodia Extremities of the limbs (hands, feet)

BP Before the present

burin A stone tool common in the Upper Palaeolithic. Usually made of flint, it had a bevelled edge that was in particular used to carve and engrave bone

canid Any animal from the family Canidae, which includes dogs, foxes and wolves

Carbon 14 method A method of dating ancient organic materials by studying the radioactivity left in a sample. All organic matter contains carbon and a very small amount of Carbon 14 (14C or C14), which begins to decay very slowly after the organism dies

claviform A geometric sign, generally red, comprising a vertical line with a slight outgrowth on one side of its upper part. Generally attributed to the Magdalenian

coprolite Fossilized animal or human faeces

dimorphism In an animal species, the occurrence of two distinct types of individual

ethology The study of behaviour displayed by animals in their normal environment

fissiped Terrestrial carnivorous mammals with toes that are separated from one another, as in cats, dogs, etc.

gours Small, round or polygonal basins that form on cave floors through the build up of natural little walls by water deposit of calcium carbonates

Gravettian An Upper Palaeolithic culture that followed the Aurignacian and came before the Solutrean, between 28,000 and 22,000 years ago. It is characterized by the Gravette point and was named after the site of La Gravette in the Dordogne region of France

Holocene or **Postglacial** The current geological period, beginning about 10,000 years ago, after the Pleistocene

ichnology The study of fossil prints and tracks

iconometry Measurements of artistic images

interstadial A short warm period between two colder periods in a glaciation

karstic The typical scenery of a limestone region

Magdalenian The last Upper Palaeolithic culture in Europe from about 17,000 to 10,500 years ago

Messinian A stage of the Tertiary, corresponding to the end of the Miocene

Miocene The fourth era of the Tertiary, which came after the Oligocene and before the Pliocene

mondmilch A natural coating, a carbonate precipitate, on cave walls

morphometry The process of measuring the outside shape and dimensions of landforms or living organisms

palynologist A scientist who studies living and fossil pollen grains and plant spores

parietal Art, including drawings, engravings, carvings or paintings, produced on the rocky walls of prehistoric caves

phreatic Relating to ground water below the water table

Pleistocene Beginning about 2 million years ago and lasting to 10,000 BP, it was characterized by major climatic contrasts, particularly the advance of ice sheets

Pliocene The last period of the Tertiary era lasting for ten million years. During this time many modern mammals first appeared

Quaternary The latest and shortest of the four geological eras. Colder than the Tertiary, it started about 1.8 million years ago. Humans appeared during this time

retouch The art of detaching small flakes from a stone to make a tool

Salpetrian Contemporary to the Solutrean in Provence, south-east France, where it was defined by its tools at the site of La Salpêtrière

Solutrean An Upper Palaeolithic culture found mainly in France and Spain from about 23,000 to 18,000 years ago, a period of particularly severe conditions

speleology The exploration and study of deep caves

stop In cave bears, a marked break of slope that separates the brow from the muzzle

stumping Spreading the pigment with the hand or with a piece of cloth or hide in order to achieve shading or relief on the image

talweg The line that descends most steeply from any point on land

tine The sharp terminal branches of a deer's antler

unguis A claw, hoof or nail or the part of the digit giving rise to it

ungulate Any group of mammals that have hooves

Urgonian A particular limestone facies of the Lower Cretaceous period

vermiculation Any decoration that has wormlike marks or carving

Würm glaciation The last Quaternary glaciation in Europe, ending around 10,000 BP

PHOTO CREDITS

The photographs, maps, tracings, drawings and montages come from the following sources:

N. Aujoulat: 4, 47, 50, 71, 72, 75–79, 81, 85, 86, 88, 113, 142, 145, 153
N. Aujoulat and V. Feruglio: 52, 114, 119, 126
N. Aujoulat and P. Morel: 92
D. Baffier and V. Feruglio: 60, 64, 115, 117, 118, 120, 144, 151, 152, 156, 157, 165, 196, 201
S. Caillault: 13–18
J. Clottes: 1, 5–8, 33, 48, 49, 51, 54, 56, 58, 59, 61–63, 65, 84, 87, 90, 94–97, 101, 116, 121, 122, 124, 125, 127–40, 146, 166, 169, 171, 173–75, 177, 179, 180, 184, 187, 189, 192, 200, 202–207
J.-J. Delannoy and Y. Perrette: 12, 19
V. Feruglio: 11, 22 (production), 26 (montage)
C. Fritz: 3, 32 (production)
C. Fritz and G. Tosello: 67, 68, 73, 74, 102–106, 108–111, 141, 143, 147–50, 154, 158–60, 182, 183, 186, 194, 195, 209
M.-A. Garcia: 23, 27–31, 34, 44, 91
M.-A. Garcia and P. Fosse: 24
M.-A. Garcia and P. Morel: 26 (photographs)
M.-A. Garcia and F. Rouzaud: 32 (recording)
B. Gély: 22 (map)
J.-M. Geneste: 35, 36, 38, 39
J.-M. Geneste and J.-P. Lhomme: 37, 40
M. Girard: 20, 21
Y. Le Guillou: 53, 55, 57, 66, 70, 80, 82, 83, 93, 99, 100, 112, 123, 155, 161–64, 167, 168, 170, 172, 176, 178, 181, 185, 188, 190, 193, 197–99
Y. Le Guillou and F. Maksud: 10
R. Mark and E. Billo: 2, 122 (montage)
P. Morel: 9, 41–43, 45–46, 98, 191
G. Tosello: 69, 89, 107
H. Valladas and N. Tisnérat: 25

ACKNOWLEDGMENTS

Without the willingness, support and funding of the Ministry of Culture (Direction du Patrimoine, sous-direction de l'archéologie, Direction régionale des affaires culturelles, Services régionaux de l'archéologie et des monuments historiques), this exceptional research project could not have been carried out. The département of the Ardèche provides us with invaluable and much appreciated help. The departmental Leisure Centre, under the efficient directorship of Christian Faure, is an indispensable base camp for us. Mr H. Helly kindly gave us authorization to cross his property. We work in close collaboration with the Musée de préhistoire d'Orgnac, as well as with the municipalities of Salavas and Vallon-Pont-d'Arc and local cultural societies. The Ardèche people have always shown an unfailing interest in this cave and our work. Thanks to Mr Y. Coppens and the Collège de France (Chair of Palaeoanthropology and Prehistory), part of the team has had the use of premises in Paris. The EDF Foundation has helped us by placing powerful data-processing software at our disposal. Mr J.-J. Gaeschter, of Sympatap, kindly provided us with equipment for protecting the floors. Finally, this book owes an enormous debt to Françoise Peyrot and Valérie Gautier, of the publishers Le Seuil, with whom we worked closely.

We would like to extend our warmest thanks to all.

Paul Bahn would like to thank the following friends for assistance of various kinds during the translation of this book: Jim Enloe, Carole Fritz, Pat Helvenston, Alice Kehoe, Adrian Lister, Alex Marshack, Graham Mullan, Paul Pettitt, Geneviève Pinçon, Gilles Tosello and Linda Wilson.

THE AUTHORS

ARNOLD, Maurice, CNRS, dating
* AUJOULAT, Norbert, CNP, Ministry of Culture,
    parietal art
* BAFFIER, Dominique, CNRS Ministry of Culture,
    parietal art, curator of Chauvet Cave
* CLOTTES, Jean, director of scientific study
* DEBARD, Evelyne, University, geology
* DELANNOY, Jean-Jacques, University, karstology
EVIN, Jacques, CNRS, dating
FERRIER, Catherine, University, geology
* FERUGLIO, Valérie, graphic artist, parietal art
* FOSSE, Philippe, CNRS, palaeontology
* FRITZ, Carole, CNRS, parietal art
* GARCIA, Michel-Alain, CNRS, ichnology
* GELY, Bernard, Ministry of Culture, archaeological
    context and parietal art
* GENESTE, Jean-Michel, Ministry of Culture,
    archaeological study in the cave

GIRARD, Michel, CNRS, palynology
GUERIN, Claude, CNRS, palaeontology (rhinoceros)
* KERVAZO, Bertrand, Ministry of Culture, geology
* LE GUILLOU, Yanik, Ministry of Culture, topography
    and parietal art
* MAKSUD, Frédéric, topography and speleology
† MOREL, Philippe, palaeontology
OBERLIN, Christine, CNRS, dating
PACKER, Craig, University, ethology (lions)
PERRETTE, Yves, University, karstology
* PHILIPPE, Michel, Museum, palaeontology
ROBERT-LAMBLIN, Joëlle, CNRS, anthropology
† ROUZAUD, François, Ministry of Culture, topography
    and speleology
SCHEFER, Jean-Louis, history of art
TISNERAT, Nadine, CNRS, dating
* TOSELLO, Gilles, graphic artist, parietal art
VALLADAS, Hélène, CNRS, dating

Above

Ill. 208. Some of the authors of this book. Only those marked
with an asterisk* appear in the photograph, while those with
a cross † have since died.

INDEX

Numbers in *italic* refer to illustration numbers.

Ill. 209. The little mammoth at the entrance of the Cactus Gallery.